RECONSTRUCTION
THE ENDING
OF THE CIVIL WAR

Avery Craven

HOLT, RINEHART AND WINSTON, INC.

NEW YORK   CHICAGO   SAN FRANCISCO
ATLANTA   DALLAS   MONTREAL   TORONTO   LONDON

To Grace Greenwood Craven
without whom nothing would
have been possible

"We have got rid of nothing by the war but slavery and the faith in the possibility of secession by which the South was pervaded. We have not got rid of the imperfection of the moral perceptions—of the hard, coarse love of gain—of the cast pride and of race prejudice which made slavery possible at the South, and which down to the year 1860 secured it the sympathy and connivance of the North. Moreover, the victory was not—mark this—won by a majority of the Northern People."
—*The Nation,* January 30, 1868

PREFACE

Several years ago I wrote a study entitled *The Coming of the Civil War*. Convinced that the war did not end at Appomattox, I decided to write a companion work on *The Ending of the Civil War*, treating of so-called Reconstruction. The purpose in writing the first volume was to show how issues got into such shape that they could not be solved by the democratic process of rational discussion and compromise. This required selection of materials and emphasis on those factors that explained the final outcome. It was never an attempt to state the causes of the Civil War or to say whether it was either needless or necessary.

The same is true of the present volume. It is not a detailed study of the last phase of the war. It attempts only to show how and why problems became such that they could not be openly and completely solved but were again pushed aside and the effort at solution left to a future generation. The object is not to allocate blame or to say that one factor above all others produced final results. I have not rejected old points of view just because they are old or adopted new points of view just because they are new. I have viewed Reconstruction as I viewed the *coming* of the war: as something to be understood and that will teach a people whatever history, as such, can teach.

To me the Civil War from its "coming" to its "ending" is a clear-cut revelation of a basic problem in a democratic society: that of permitting a maximum of *freedom* and at the same time preserving a necessary degree of *equality*. These two enemies encased in a single system portend unending strife; for if men are free, they seldom remain equal, and equality must be enforced at

the expense of freedom. So when the Civil War involved the freedom of a race and victory brought the problem of equality for the
Negro, democracy was again on trial. To me this is the fundamental meaning of Reconstruction.

That is why I prefer to view slavery as a vicious obsolete labor
system that had no place in American life, rather than as evidence
of southern depravity; the story of "labor reform" should include
the bitter criticism of "wage slavery" in northern textile mills and
not be confined to "the antislavery vanguard." It has also seemed
reasonable to suppose that if a southern sectionalism existed, so
did a northern sectionalism; that if "big business" on southern
plantations produced an "aristocracy," it must have done the same
in northern industry. If there are pro-southern historians, it is
reasonable to suppose that there might be pro-northern historians.
I cannot see how one would exist and not the other. Where a national view is not taken, history degenerates into polemics.

I have been conscious at all times that underneath the surface-
events lay the steady advance of a new age in which steam in
engines was cutting space in half and creating a new national
interdependence; that the old stabilizing factors of family, church,
and law were being weakened and that a new urban, financial-in-
dustrial order was taking over. Reform under such conditions was,
of course, assuming a new character.

I have treated so-called Reconstruction as the final phase of the
American Civil War. If the sin of slaveholding had been the symbol of a nation's betrayal of a dream of possible social perfection,
then justice for the Negro freedmen was an imperative obligation
to be met before the war was truly over.

I have in the main avoided the use of footnotes to cite authorities
and have used them largely for information needed to give emphasis. I have not thought it necessary to demonstrate the fact
that I am acquainted with the manuscript and printed sources.
I have attempted to reread the older works and to acquaint myself
with the revisionist efforts of present days. I have refused to allocate blame and guilt either to individuals or groups. I have tried
to see men and situations in their own time and place as a scholar,
not as a southerner or a northerner. I have just wanted to know
why Reconstruction failed and was abandoned.

My obligations are heavy. Especial thanks must go to Pro-
fessors Stanley Kutler and Richard N. Current—colleagues at the
University of Wisconsin—and to one of my students, Bernard
Weisberger, whose mind is never at rest. To Gladys Hamilton I
owe much for help of all kinds. My eternal gratitude to Kenneth
L. Culver for his part in making this volume what it is.

Dune Acres, Indiana   A. C.
September 1968

CONTENTS

CHAPTER

1

THE SETTING

I

The American Civil War did not end at Appomattox. Lee's surrender only marked the abandonment of organized armed resistance in a struggle that had been going on between two groups of Americans for a generation or more. The immediate task, however, had been successfully accomplished. The southern armies melted away and the Confederate States of America came to the end of its brief existence. The experiment in secession had failed. The northern military machine and the northern economy had at last proved their superiority over the agriculturally dominated South. The question as to whether this was a consolidated union or a confederation of sovereign states had been permanently answered.

Had the war been fought only to preserve the Union, as

both Lincoln and Congress had insisted, then the resumption of national life might have been painful but relatively peaceful. That it was not to be so was clearly evident from the beginning—clearly evident for the simple reason that far more than union was always involved. To some, the destruction of slavery as the symbol of all social evils was as much a justification for war as was the saving of the Union, for a union that harbored slaves was hardly worth saving. Emancipation in 1862 was only the first step in a great moral revolution that would restore equality to all men and bring America back to its original dream of possible social perfection. When the fighting ended and slavery was abolished, there remained a race problem to be faced and solved. Until the Negro's place in American life was fixed, the war was not over. In its brutal way slavery had met that problem. Now the victorious North in Republican hands must assume responsibility. The task was not merely one of securing a satisfactory peace but one of consolidating a revolution.

II

The American Civil War did not come suddenly; nor was it the product of a single cause. It resulted from an accumulation of problems which had not been frankly faced and solved, and which had at length found expression in sectional differences between the North and the South symbolized by the institution of Negro slavery. In that form differences could not be rationally discussed or compromised. They had to do with morals, with civilizations in conflict. Men fight and die for such things. They are not easily surrendered.

Only when the long-overdue emancipation of Negro slaves became a war measure did the nation officially accept the equality and unalienable rights proclaimed in the Declaration of Independence. Only when war made it necessary did men discover in the Constitution the powers not only to achieve victory but to permit the emergence of efficient nationalism. Only when the South was rendered helpless did industrial capitalism, already dominant elsewhere, have a chance to emerge in fullness. The nation in war was simply trying to catch up with unfinished business. Reconstruction would have to take up where the fighting left off.

This would be difficult, for the vexing questions of the status of the defeated southern states and the place of the freed Negro in American life would have to be faced in a nation where respect for old traditional constitutional forms was still strong, and where a race prejudice that associated inferiority with color was still dominant. It might, therefore, be that such matters would still outweigh the right of millions of Americans to first-class citizenship.

Reconstruction would take its course under these difficult conditions. Those who would close the gap between American professions and American practices would in the end have to be content with constitutional amendments capable of varied interpretations and even the abandonment of much reform that war had made possible.

III

To understand such an approach to Reconstruction, it is necessary to look briefly at the steps that led to the coming of the Civil War itself. A convenient place to begin is 1815. That year ushered in a hundred years of peace for the Atlantic Basin, which for three centuries had been intermittently distracted by war. The American people, both as colonists and in early national days, had been embroiled in those struggles either as participants or as neutrals. Their faces had been kept eastward. Now for the first time they could turn about and seriously begin the great domestic task of occupying their vast, rich continent and transforming the larger part of it from wilderness simplicity to social and economic complexity.

They would be aided in this task by the fact that a new

age in the history of mankind was now well under way. Francis Bacon had noted long ago that man equipped with only the energy of his own body could do little. Progress was the result of man's ability to discover nature's abundant energy and to create the tools by which it could be put to work for his benefit. A new energy and a new technology meant a new age. In this case it was compressed steam in engines for communication and industry. Nothing comparable in power and technical competence had ever before been placed in the hands of man. Americans thus began their work equipped for material success as no other people anywhere had ever been.

Moreover, they began in a patriotic mood. While they had not been exactly victorious in the late war with England, there were still reasons for national pride. The very fact that on occasion America's sailors had held their own against the recognized "mistress of the seas" and that at New Orleans their citizen-soldiers had all but annihilated an army that had just defeated Napoleon did wonders for the nation's morale. As Albert Gallatin said, it "renewed the national feelings and character which the Revolution had given." Sectionalism, always a part of American life, reached a new low as shamefaced New Englanders made their way home from the protesting Hartford Convention.

In 1814 Francis Scott Key, stirred by a flag that still waved, wrote a song that was to become the national anthem. In 1818 Congress decided to replace the old flag with its thirteen stars, with one in which each state had its own star. We now had a national emblem. Noah Webster, meanwhile, was contributing "his mite to patriotic exertions" by seizing the present moment to reject old British standards and establish a new "national language."

Niles' Weekly Register, in turn, noted that the American people were increasingly assuming a national character, and Ralph Waldo Emerson would soon be urging them to stand on their own feet and think their own thoughts. The day of our dependence on other lands, he insisted, was at an end.

IV

The accomplishments in the next thirty years, the life span of a single generation, can be considered only in terms of revolution. There was something excitingly new even in the old story of growth and expansion. Population exploded from 7,239,881 in 1810 to 31,443,321 in 1860—a population greater than that of the British Isles and rapidly closing the gap on France and the German states. The native-born formed the major part of this increase but between 1840 and 1860 some 4,300,000 immigrants arrived in America. Only once again did the percentage of immigrants to the population already here, equal that reached six times in this period.

Expansion kept pace with growth. By 1860 settlers had crossed the Mississippi into Kansas, Nebraska, Arkansas, and Texas, and had reached the Pacific in California and Oregon, with scattered groups in between where soils, precious metals, or freedom lured. So rapid was the growth of population that despite the acquisition of vast new territory following the Mexican War, only temporary decreases in the average density occurred. Urban population, which made up only about 4 percent in 1820, stood at 16.1 percent by 1860. New York City, including Brooklyn, had passed the million mark, while Baltimore, Boston, Chicago, New Orleans, Philadelphia, and St. Louis all ranged above 100,000.

Basic in it all was the application of steam to transportation on water and on land. Steamboats were now plying their way up and down the rivers, along the lakes, and out across the oceans. Some 30,000 miles of railroads connected the important eastern seaboard cities with the interior, and projects for transcontinental lines were already well advanced. A new national economic and social interdependence was emerging, and another land-mass nation was rising to dispute the dominance of those that had long ruled by control of the seas.

Through these developments space had been cut in half, and internal commerce was now clearly more important than foreign trade. Both business and finances had meanwhile undergone the transformations necessary to meet the new demands. A new group of entrepreneurs and capitalists had emerged. The wide occupation of land, of course, implied unparalleled agricultural expansion and change. This one generation broke a hundred million acres to the plow and produced ten million bales of cotton, a billion bushels of wheat, and nearly two billion bushels of corn. Livestock rose in equal proportion. Improved methods, especially in the older parts of the nation, both adjusted crops to new urban markets and checked, to some degree, the rapid depletion of soils. Northern wheat farmers, especially, profited from the inventions and improvements which Cyrus Hall McCormick, John Deere, and Jerome I. Case made in farm machinery, but southern cotton growers still depended primarily on the Negro slave's muscle power. Family farms and slave-worked plantations were social as well as economic facts.

Meanwhile, in the northeastern corner of the nation, industrial developments had set some two and a half million spindles to work and provided factory jobs for 122,000 men, women, and children. Capital employed in industry rose from $250 million in 1840 to over a billion in 1860. The value of industrial products in 1860 stood at over $1,885,861,000. Eastern merchants, meanwhile, had built ships that could sail from Boston or New York to California around the Horn in a hundred days, and could sometimes attain speed, day after day, equal to that reached by modern racing crafts. Their clipper ships were the greatest combination of utility and beauty the young nation had produced and well deserved such names as the *Flying Cloud,* the *Surprise,* the *Sword Fish,* and the *Sovereign of the Seas.*

Never perhaps in the history of any people in any land had there been such far-reaching changes in such a brief period of time. Never had there been such wide displacement of people and such a strain on values and institutions. Bray Hammond, speaking only of the first years in these developments, writes:

> Men who had spent their childhood in a thin line of seaboard colonies, close even in their little cities to the edge of the westward continental wilderness . . . lived to ride on railways and steamships, to use the products of steam-driven machinery, to dwell in metropolitan centers and to feel within the grasp of their sons more potential and accessible wealth than had ever before excited the enterprise of man.[1]

Alexis de Tocqueville added a social note:

> Their ancestors had given them a love of "equality and freedom" but God himself had given "the means of remaining equal and free" by placing them upon a boundless continent unmatched in its possibilities by any other "at any period in history."

V

Such rapid changes and displacements had their price. Both the westward movement and the rise of urban industrialism weakened the old stabilizing forces in American life. The family lost something as its young people scattered to the West or to the new factory town. For the same reason the old established churches lost much control, and even more of influence, as new competing sects arose with strange new doctrines. The law suffered everywhere as society returned to more primitive levels and professional training became more difficult. In the economic realm the vast opportunities that opened on all sides encouraged speculation, risk-taking, and overexpansion, which played havoc with old "respectable" ways of doing business. The nation would pay in periodic panics and depressions. A greedy, grasping, materialistic quality characterized the age; Americans were constantly tempted to do "un-American," or at least "un-Jeffersonian," things.

[1] Bray Hammond, *Banks and Politics in America from the Revolution to the Civil War* (Princeton, N.J., 1957), pp. 326–329.

The worker in this America, whether free or slave, carried a heavier load and found good reason for complaint against exploitation. Men with tender consciences would denounce both wage slavery and Negro slavery as things that had no place in a Christian, democratic society. Yet there was so much to be done and not enough hands to do it.

More important for our purposes was the fact that a people in motion were turning the nation into a bundle of distinct sections. Social and economic patterns, already sharply differing with one another in the older eastern states, were now carried into new geographical environments, there in turn to undergo further changes. Conflict of interests between the old and the new were inevitable, and as new societies developed in regions where physical conditions and resources varied greatly from East to West and from North to South, the strain on a common central government grew increasingly heavy.

The most common demands for legislation that arose in this era of growth and expansion had to do with land policies, internal improvement programs, finances, tariff schedules, and, in the end, slavery in the territories. Fortunately, in the early years each section was interested more in some one of these matters than in the others. Bargaining and compromise were therefore generally possible, as the American politician learned his trade. Reciprocal combinations could be made and a degree of interest served even if the total demand could not be met.

The democratic process, however, began to falter as the Northeast with its industry, its cities, and its financial developments caught step with the modern age that steam and technology were creating, and as its emigrants, its railroads, and its markets steadily drew the old Northwest into its orbit. Equally important, as a divisive factor, was the growing opposition to slavery as a great national disgrace. Then something like a northern section bent on "progress" and "freedom" began to emerge. Its emphasis, based on interests, was toward a stronger and more active central government. It demanded the kind of legislation

that aided industry, banking, and trade. A new feeling of
nation-wide interdependence went with the growing requirements in raw materials and wider markets. This
could easily be translated into a regard for the Union and
a more liberal interpretation of the Constitution. Economic nationalism had become a fact. Political consolidation should follow. Its spokesmen, such as Daniel Webster
and William H. Seward, could easily find constitutional
justification for northern demands. A William Lloyd
Garrison could express its revulsion to Negro slavery.

The development of a corresponding southern sectionalism out of an even more diverse set of geographical and
social units, was based on a rural, agricultural as opposed
to the urban, industrial foundation. Geographically and
socially, there had been from the beginning several very
differing Souths. They stretched from the old colonial
peoples who faced the Atlantic and who differed widely
from one another, to the recently acquired nation of Texas
on the Gulf. In between were America's only uniquely
mountain folk, a great new swaggering cotton kingdom,
and that strange tangle of peoples and ways that was the
Louisiana Sugar Bowl.

In spite of physical diversity, staple crops gave some
unity, and all (except the Sugar Bowl and the hemp and
stock areas) generally favored free trade. Then, because
of the danger to Negro slavery, most southerners opposed
consolidation of the national government and a liberal
interpretation of the Constitution. Their institutions, they
thought, were safer under local and state control. John
Taylor of Caroline and John C. Calhoun could demonstrate
beyond a doubt that the Constitution was on the southern
side.

VI

To deal with the difficult problems on the national level
which growth, expansion, and diversification produced
and to balance sectional demands, American political
genius had evolved the two-party system and turned it

over to that matchless American product, the American politician. The political parties would select such issues as could be safely presented to the people and which could be adopted or rejected without serious danger to continued national progress. A minimum of interference with growth and prosperity could be achieved, and men with ideals and morals could give their loyal support to parties, which paid only lip service to such things.

The practical job of securing legislation and making the democratic process work was left to the politician. Generally honest but realistic, he avoided abstractions, bargained for advantage, specialized in double talk, and never allowed an issue to get stated in such terms as to make compromise impossible. It was better to secure a slice where a whole loaf was unobtainable. Party success was a worthy end. Where solutions by rational discussion, tolerance of differences, or compromise proved impossible, time could be bought at the best price possible and the future would take care of itself.

Most of the time up to the 1840s, this worked rather well, but there was always one great difficulty. Americans had entered these boisterous years with certain basic questions unanswered and with certain impossible commitments to keep. They had not decided whether they had created a consolidated union or a confederacy of sovereign states. They had proclaimed the Constitution to be the law of the land, but had insisted that there was a higher law which justified civil disobedience. Some said that the equality announced in the Declaration of Independence should be taken seriously as self-evident truth. Others said it was neither self-evident nor true, and hence should be ignored.

Equally troublesome was the fact that Americans still clung to the idea that the United States was a kind of "city on the hill"—a Christian-democratic experiment, a dream of possible perfection, which placed the United States under moral obligations to all mankind. Americans must accept all the material values necessary for the conquest of a great raw continent, but at the same time they must maintain equality and insure justice to all men.

It is thus perfectly clear that the politician, whose method was one of avoiding troublesome issues or of resorting to compromise, was only buying time and postponing the solution of fundamental constitutional and moral problems. That made the reformer as much a national figure as the politician. It was somebody's business to point out the inevitable gap between actions and commitments. If politics was a profession in the United States, so was reforming. As Wendell Phillips stated: "The republic which sinks to sleep, trusting to Constitution and machinery, to politicians and statesmen, for the safety of its liberties, never will have any." It was the reformers' business to prevent the postponing, compromising politician from having too much success. There was a time in a Christian-democratic society when men should frankly face and come to final terms with realities.

It seemed for a time in 1850 that such a point had been reached. The slavery issue, tangled with territorial expansion, had brought from John C. Calhoun the blunt, uncompromising declaration of the strictly federal character of our government and the right of the slave-holding southern states to equality in the territories. The North, he said, must cease to discuss the slavery question and must enforce the fugitive slave law. If this slavery question were not now settled, "it is uncertain whether it ever can hereafter be." He added: "Every portion of the North" entertained "views and feelings more or less hostile to it," while the South regarded the existing relation between white and Negro races "as one which cannot be destroyed without subjecting the two races to the greatest calamity. . . ." Slavery as practiced in the South was a positive good.

William H. Seward had answered with equal assurance that the "States were not parties to the Constitution as States" but had "surrendered their equality as States, and submitted themselves to the sway of the numerical majority without qualifications or checks." As to slavery, it belonged to the Dark Ages; as to the South's constitutional rights, there was a higher law, the law of human decency. To which Charles Sumner added that the Constitution should always be interpreted in terms of the Declaration of Independence.

Evidently many people in both North and South were weary of compromise and halfway measures. Wide northern support for the Wilmot Proviso, which would bar slavery from any territory acquired from Mexico, and equally wide southern support for the calling of the Nashville Convention, which was to be the southern answer to the Wilmot Proviso, were evidence enough. Southern-rights groups, convinced that their "peculiar institution" was no longer safe in the Union, were ready for secession. Some abolition groups in the North would yield the Union rather than see slavery extended.

Others, however, were unwilling to admit the failure of the democratic process. Older leaders who had helped the nation over rough spots in other days were willing to try again. With Henry Clay in the lead, they pushed aside the troublesome fundamental, abstract issues and worked out a bundle of compromises designed to solve all pressing problems—even that involving the return of fugitive slaves. Few were completely satisfied, but fewer were ready to face the alternatives. The death of John C. Calhoun in March, followed by that of President Zachary Taylor in July, removed the chief obstacles in the path of compromise, and the members of Congress turned homeward proclaiming "finality" to all sectional differences.

VII

How completely the politicians had misjudged the depth of public feeling and the demand for fundamental reform was soon apparent. In the decade that followed, realities played little part. So thoroughly had the struggle between nationalism and states' rights, between freedom and slavery, taken hold of men's minds that regardless of the realities involved, reactions instinctively took the form of a struggle between these basic differences. Regardless of how much northern men talked "finality," they revealed their true feelings by refusing to obey the new fugitive law, a part of the late compromise. They accepted the purely fictitious Uncle Tom as revealing a true picture of slavery and took pride in the aid given escaping slaves by the illegal "underground railroad." They rejected Stephen A. Douglas' realistic statement that his Kansas-Nebraska Bill meant free territories, and embraced the totally false charges of the "Appeal of the Independent Democrats," which said that the territories were now open to slavery. They saw the Dred Scott decision as a threat to expand slavery, even though slavery had had no chance in either Kansas or California. Wise and good northern men, meanwhile, hailed the insane John Brown as a saint and his gallows as sacred as the Cross; southerners saw him as an expression of fanatical northern purposes. The frightening thing about it all was the wide gap between realities and reactions.

Southerners, meanwhile, evolved the tragic fiction of a superior civilization based on human slavery. In 1860–1861, eleven southern states seceded from the Union because of a threat to slavery within their borders—a threat which then did not exist. At a time when northern mills took a larger percentage of their cotton; when Virginia gardens depended on New York and Philadelphia markets for the sale of their produce; when the cotton planters of the Lower South looked to the farmers of the Upper Mississippi Valley for their supplies—their horses and mules, their rope, their bagging and their whiskey—when most of the South looked north for their banking, their shoes, and clothing; in all, when economic nationalism was a reality and steam had just begun to perform its miracles, southerners turned their backs on reality and staked their all on localism and slavery.

VIII

The inevitable conformation—economic, social, political, and moral—came with the 1860 breakup of the Democratic party and the consequent triumph of the Republicans. The acceptance of the modern industrial world, the solidarity of the Union, the obligation to accept the Declaration of Independence, and the condemnation of slavery were all there. True, the slavery question was only halfway met by opposition to expansion, but as Charles Sumner said: "They have proclaimed slavery to be wrong. . . . It is difficult to sense how they can longer sustain themselves on that grounds. . . . They must become Abolitionists."

For practical political purposes in a dividing nation, the Republicans had to appear as conservative as possible. They had broadened their appeal and avoided radical leadership. They had triumphed in 1860 by shrewd American political maneuvering. Yet from both choice and necessity the Republican party was still a party dedicated to reform. It had not dared to leave the Declaration of Independence out of its platform.

Thus was the stage set for Reconstruction as the last phase of the Civil War. Peace after bloody fighting between two civilizations for the right to shape a nation's future course involved far more than merely putting the house back in order. Interests and values and emotions had to be taken into account. The war had been fought for the preservation of the Union and the wiping out of slavery; but now the Negro, something different, was in the fore of the picture. Many therefore understood that the restored nation must of necessity be a different and better kind of a nation. More than just four years had passed.

CHAPTER

2

SECESSION
AND CIVIL WAR

I

Civil War began in the United States when the southern batteries opened fire on Fort Sumter in Charleston harbor and the guns of the fort returned the fire. It became a declared war when Lincoln called for troops to put down what he termed a rebellion.

Back of these events, and responsible for them, lay the election of 1860 and the secession of seven southern states. And still further back lay the whole tangled complex of economic, social, political, and moral factors that had gradually divided the nation into a North and a South—differences that had been compressed, canalized, and factored down into a conflict, symbolized by the institution of Negro slavery.

II

The first problems to be faced, therefore, are why the election of Abraham Lincoln should have caused the secession movement on the part of these southern states and why the Lincoln government refused to accept their right to secede if they so desired. On seceding, most of the southern states attempted to justify their action and to defend their right to act. South Carolina was first with a rather elaborate assertion regarding the federal-compact character of the American government, which permitted withdrawal when one party to the compact did not live up to its obligations. It called attention to the fact that the stipulation to return fugitive slaves had been written into the Constitution and that this compact could not have been made without it. Yet northern states had openly refused to live up to this obligation and had passed laws that nullified the acts of Congress or "rendered useless any attempt to exercise them." Some states had even refused to surrender those who had incited servile insurrections; all had denounced the southern domestic institution of slavery as "sinful" and had now "united in the election of a man to the high office of President of the United States whose opinions and purposes were hostile to slavery." Public opinion in the North had thus "invested a great political error with the sanction of a more erroneous religious belief."

Other seceding states, varying their statements to fit local conditions, followed this same general pattern. Some stressed the fact that the South was now a permanent minority "in the hands of a majority reckless of Constitutional obligations," but even they usually ended up with the danger which this situation imposed on slavery. Some cited the denial of expansion into territories won by common blood, but they too saw in this the threat to an institution which Mississippi said was so identified with its whole way of life that only secession remained.

What stands out in all that was said is that slavery—its security, its expansion, and even its moral standing—were

now endangered to a degree that made remaining in the
Union no longer safe. Lincoln's election made ruin not
only possible but probable. It was a case of submission or
secession.

III

Historians generally agree that Abraham Lincoln was
a moderate old "Henry Clay Whig," who on various occasions had gone out of his way to assure the southern people that he would in no measure interfere with their
existing institutions. He had stated bluntly that were he
given all power, he would not know what to do about
slavery. Alexander H. Stephens, soon to be Vice President
of the Confederate States, had said that Lincoln was just
as good, safe, and sound a man as was President James
Buchanan, and that he would administer the government
just as safely and honestly in every particular. Furthermore, the Republican party had only opposed the further
extention of slavery; and while some had talked of putting it on the road to extinction, that was too vague and
uncertain to constitute a threat.

Historians have further agreed that with both Congress and the courts opposed to him and his principles,
Lincoln in office would have been powerless to do harm.
Even the abolitionists had opposed Lincoln and the Republican party as offering them little. In other words, as
Arthur Cole has remarked, "The most thoroughgoing
champions of southern rights seldom even hinted that
they saw specific dangers looming over the horizon. The
South was moved by abstractions, not realities."

Some southerners saw the weakness in their position.
William A. Graham of North Carolina insisted that the
President was but the servant of the people and had only
the powers to do good.

> If these powers are perverted to our injury and oppression,
> [he said] resistance will be made with united hearts . . . but
> who can prepare a declaration of independence, appealing to
> a candid world for its approbation and sympathy, upon the

ground that we have been outvoted in an election in which we took the chance of success, and a candidate has been elected, who, however obnoxious, we did not deem unworthy to compete with for votes?

A neighbor from Georgia gave the answer to these critics:

It is a mistake to suppose that it is the mere election of Lincoln, without regard to anything else, that has driven the States of the South into their present resistance, and their present determination to seek that safety and security out of the Union which they have been unable to obtain within it. . . . The election of Lincoln is merely the confirmation of a purpose which the South had hoped would be abandoned by the opponents of slavery in the North. It is a declaration that they mean to carry out their aggressive and destructive policy, weakening the institution at every point where it can be assailed either by legislation or by violence, until in the brutal language of Charles Sumner, "it dies like a poisoned rat in its hole."

IV

To understand why the southern states seceded in 1860–1861, one must look briefly at the northern Americans whom the southerners found so dangerous to their institutions—so dangerous as to make secession necessary.

Criticism of slavery in the United States had been present from the beginning. Quakers especially, in both the North and the South, had opposed its existence and its spread. The doctrine of natural rights emphasized in the American Revolution had increased the opposition, ended slavery in New England, and brought sharp criticism from both Washington and Jefferson. In fact, most southern spokesmen in the early national period viewed slavery as an evil and prophesied its early extinction. Their sentiments found expression in the Colonization Society, which sought both to end slavery and solve the race question by removing the freedmen to Africa. The process was to be a gradual one.

A real antislavery crusade, however, began in the

1830s. It grew out of a strange new surge of social reform that swept across the nation and caused "the church or religious party" (as Emerson called it) to fall from "the church nominal" and to reappear in a whole series of reform movements and projects for the salvation of the world. Such a din of opinion and debate, such a keen scrutiny of institutions and domestic life, America had never known before. Nothing escaped. Crusades were directed to temperance, to peace, to diet and dress, to the stricter observance of the Sabbath, to the virtues of rural life, to the improvement of prisons and asylums, and some, in the end, to the abolition of Negro slavery. All aimed at that social perfection promised and possible in these United States but not yet realized. Something had gone wrong. America had not made the most of what some characterized as mankind's second chance.

What produced this intense and varied expression of dissatisfaction with things as they were, and this sudden determination to set everything right, is difficult to say. It centered largely, but not exclusively, in the old New England and the greater New England that stretched westward across upper New York and along the Great Lakes. One cannot, of course, ignore the fact that men in this region had always been conscious of other people's shortcomings and of their willingness to set them right. They had always been much occupied with the matter of sin, and religious awakenings had long been an important part of their story.

At this particular time, developments in the material world must certainly have played some part in convincing them that the old order had failed and something new must be tried. On every hand was the industrial town, the factory worker, the new rich, the abandoned farm, and the young people going west. Meanwhile Orestes Brownson was talking of the "wage slaves," worse off than the Negroes on southern plantations, and Theodore Parker was warning the "powerful men" that if they would not "write justice with black ink on white paper, ignorant and violent men" would "write it on the soil in letters of blood." The times were out of joint. The old stabilizing forces—family, church, and law—were breaking down as population spread westward or toward the new industrial centers.

The reaction that followed has been called a religious revolution involving "a profound and rapid change in American theology and church policy and a subterranean shift in American thought." It found expression first when the old religious establishment in the Northeast, threatened with dispossession, began flooding the new West and the new urban centers with religious tracts, Bibles, Sunday schools, home missionaries, and teachers in a frantic effort to implant the old traditional Christian virtues. This group would make sure that in the rapid expansion and changing character of American life morals and right thinking were not lost. Religion must come to the support of sound politics and right conduct.

The religious awakening brought more than a defensive movement. It produced a profound theological change in which the old doctrine of determinism gave way to the belief in free will and human choice. In the preaching of Charles Grandison Finney, salvation was free to all who chose to confess and renounce their sins. This equated sin with personal selfishness, and social wrong with the collective sins of unregenerate men. Hence, personal salvation and social perfection were matters of choice. The recognition of sin, repentance, and immediate renunciation were the steps required for redeeming the world. All problems were moral problems to be solved by individual regeneration. Where churches and political parties, by tolerating sin, failed to achieve immediate perfection, they were to be cast aside. Only conscience should be followed. Some reformers, believing that American life had been thoroughly corrupted by material motives, renounced all existing institutions and formed their own little utopias where, as a critic said, everything was in common but common sense. Some refused to vote or to recognize an earthly authority. A bit of anarchy and communism thus entered the search for social perfection.

This approach changed the whole course and character of reform. Since social evils were only the collective sins of sinful men, compromise with evil institutions was at an end and immediate action was demanded. Religion and reform had become one, and the millennium was in sight. Hence, "to the extent that slavery became a concrete symbol of sin, and support of the antislavery cause a sign of Christian virtue, participation in the reform became a supplement or even an alternative to traditional religion." Immediate emancipation was the social expression of repentance.

It was the abolition movement in this form that the South faced in the years after 1840. Until that time slavery had largely been treated as one among several ills that the reforming impulse sought to eliminate. Now, however, tangled with expansion and a sectional "power struggle," slavery rapidly absorbed, or pushed aside, the other evils and became the nation's greatest sin. The slaveholder became the most unregenerate of sinners. Immediate repentance and abandonment of slavery on religious and democratic grounds was demanded.

To the southerner, in spite of occasional pangs of guilt, slavery was both property and a vital part of his social order. As a labor system it might have serious faults, but it did not constitute a sin to be repented and immediately abandoned, regardless of the chaotic economic and social consequences.

In making such demands, said James D. B. De Bow, George Fitzhugh, George Frederick Holmes, and James H. Hammond, the abolitionist was inviting anarchy and showing himself to be the enemy of law and order. The theory under which he operated in his demands on slavery, if carried to its logical consequences, would superinduce an attack on all property North and South. He was a dangerous radical, the enemy of all established institutions.[1] Only southern society remained safe and sane.

[1] George Frederick Holmes wrote, "It strikes at the very essence and existence of all community among men, it lays bare

Not content with denouncing the abolitionist, the southern defender went a step further. He saw cities of the
North as breeders of crime, vice, and social conflict; its
free labor system was a cruel, impersonal exploitation
devoid of all responsibility; its boasted economic system
was marked by periodic depressions and bitter strife between capital and labor; and its social order was one of
restless confused isms.

In contrast, the southerner pictured a wholesome rural
south, orthodox in religion, untroubled by wild social
theories, devoid of capital-labor disputes, and with those
at the top accepting their responsibility for the care and
well-being of those below. Here was the perfect society
which the reformers themselves were seeking in their
little utopias at Fruitlands, Brook Farm, or Hopeville.

To preserve such an order from destruction by those
who would replace it with chaos and strife, southerners
asserted that they had at last been forced to exercise their
constitutional right to withdraw from the Union and to
exercise their universally recognized right to self-govern-
ment. Here was fear, guilt, anger, and pride all blended
into one—leaving no place for caution or reason! Here
was a demand that few northern men could grant, and an
evidence of supreme sectionalism that ran counter to the
economic and social forces that made nationalism a
northern necessity. Men who had wholeheartedly accepted the steam engine could not tolerate disunion. For
both moral and political reasons, the North felt bound to
reject slavery as well as secession. "And the war came."

V

If the southern states had seceded to escape the reforms
Lincoln's election threatened, no possible hope remained
when their armies melted away and the Confederacy
collapsed. Lincoln's call in 1861 for troops to put down a

---

and roots up all the foundations of law and government. It is the
very evangel of insubordination, sedition, and anarchy."

rebellion had fixed the character of the Confederacy throughout its existence. Born in conflict, it spent its every hour waging battle against superior forces, and it came to an end when it could no longer fight. It lived briefly but violently. Its heroes were soldiers and its greatest accomplishments were the armies created by Robert E. Lee, Albert S. Johnston, T. J. (Stonewall) Jackson, and Nathan B. Forrest. No one has ever been able to explain them. Military experts the world over pronounced the Confederate soldier the finest fighting man the world had ever seen; yet he was a poor soldier, restless under discipline, sullen under command, ever eager to quit and go home when the battle was over. Yet he and his fellows somehow evolved an indescribable *esprit* and a unique attachment to their commanders that turned them into what a northerner called "that incomparable infantry." For nearly four years they held their own against what became the best-fed, best-clothed, best-equipped, and best-disciplined armies the earth had ever seen. Like the Confederacy itself, its soldiers gave their all, only to be "first exhausted and then defeated," then to return southward to a devastated homeland to await whatever fate Lincoln and the Republicans might impose.

VI

Even before the fighting ended Lincoln had begun to think about the future. In February 1865, he "matured a scheme" for securing peace which he presented to his cabinet. He would issue to the southern states bonds equal in value to the cost of 200 days of the war—some $400 million—which they could use to "extinguish slavery" or for other purposes. The cabinet members were not impressed. Then in April he suggested the calling of the old Virginia legislature and allow it to re-establish the state's government. He was of the opinion that permitting the "prominent and influential men of that state to undo their own work would turn them and their neighbors into good Union men."

Again he met with no response; but as the army took over wide areas in the southern states, he went his own way, as he had done with emancipation, and began experimenting with steps toward the establishing of local governments, which he knew must come sooner or later. Lincoln was evidently attempting to provide the Republican party with a sane, conservative plan for restoring the Union. He was not including social revolution or punishment in his proposals. The trouble was that Lincoln had never been an abolitionist, nor had he clearly understood "sin and sinners." Moreover, under the strain of war Congress and the reformers had been willing to accept a kind of executive dictatorship. But now that peace seemed near, they were again inclined to assert themselves. As Senator William P. Fessenden of Maine said, much that had been tolerated in war days formed no precedents for the future. From now on, Congress must be recognized. If Lincoln did not know that the war had a social purpose, there were others who did. Wendell Phillips spoke for them:

> The doctrine of States' Rights which meant a dungeon for white men to make victims of black men is exploded forever. This is the new dispensation. This is the New Testament. 1860 is the blank leaf between the old and new. . . . We have conquered not the geographical but the ideal South; its thumb-screws and slavery, its no-schools, its white men born, booted and spurred, and its black men born saddled and bridled for them to ride, the South which imprisons teachers, which denies Bibles, which raises up half its population in concubinage, which denies the right of marriage between men and women—[that] South we have conquered, and we have a right to trample it under the heels of our boots. That is the meaning of the war.

In the same vein, *The Independent* insisted that "the crowning problem of all was: "What of the Negro?" and answered that the remedy was simple. Given two things and "the question solves itself—the easiest of all problems: Land and the Ballot—land that he may support his family; the ballot, that he may support his state. . . ."

It sounded simple, but it was far from what Lincoln

had in mind. To the very end of his life, he talked of compensation for the slaveholder and of the deportation of the Negro to some "congenial climate" outside the United States. Nor did *The Independent's* remedy take into account the fact that a black skin and an assumption of inferiority went together in the thinking of most Americans of that day and long afterward. Color was a visible line that separated one group of Americans from others and carried with it a damaging implication. Even though the Civil War had been fought in part to end slavery, that did not mean to most Americans, North or South, that all men had suddenly become equals. The race question as it emerged with northern victory would soon prove to be as significant a fact in America's future as slavery had been in prewar days. The war, in that sense, would not end until Americans had learned that the color of a man's skin did not measure his intelligence. Until the doctrine of "the diversity and inequality of races was discredited," the social revolution would not be completed.

VII

Because of his color, the Negro had been denied a place in the armed forces at the beginning of the war. His contribution had been confined to that of teamster, cook, laborer on fortifications, and so forth. But with Union military reverses in the summer of 1862, the door was opened and Negro regiments were formed. By 1864, nearly 200,000 Negro soldiers were serving in 140 regiments. About 37,000 gave their lives for their country; seventeen Negro soldiers and four sailors were awarded the Congressional Medal of Honor.

True, the Negro served under white officers and at first received inferior pay, but he wore a uniform of blue, and that made him "uniform" with all soldiers. This was important. As one officer observed, the plantation Negro, stripped of his ill-fitting rags, scoured with soap and water, dressed in a new suit of army blue, a gun placed in his hands, was completely metamorphosed, not only in appearance but in character as well. "Yesterday a filthy, repulsive 'nigger,' today a neatly-attired man; yesterday a slave, today a freeman; yesterday a civilian, today a soldier." So when the black man's uniform bore the brass letters "U.S." and his buttons an eagle, no power on earth, said Frederick Douglass, "could deny the fact that he had earned the right to citizenship in the United States."

One day the Negro would doff his uniform. Would he then become again just a black man set aside by color? And what about the thousands of refugees already placed on "abandoned lands" with vague promises of ownership? Would those northern teachers who had set up schools all over the South come home and abandon their scholars? Or would the social revolution continue? Was the war over, or had it just entered a second phase? The answers lay in Republican hands.

CHAPTER

3

THE REPUBLICAN PARTY, 1854-1865

I

Since it was the election of a Republican president that led to secession and the refusal of a Republican administration to recognize the right of secession that led to war; and since the war was conducted and brought to final victory and total defeat under Republican rule, Reconstruction cannot be understood without a thorough understanding of Republican party interests, values, and purposes. These and these alone could and would largely shape the course of Reconstruction.

II

The Republican party as a national body had sprung suddenly into being in 1854 with the passage of Stephen A. Douglas' Kansas-Nebraska Bill. Yet the party had been

27

long in the making. Its roots ran back at least to the Liberty party of 1840 and on through the Free-Soil party of 1848. Final emergence, however, came as a kind of violent explosion, an indignant protest against something long endured. From the very beginning there was a kind of crusading quality about the party, a way of saying "thus far and no farther." It brought ideals back into national politics. Its members talked about right and wrong.

The transformation of the Republican party from a kind of local outburst into the carrier of a section's political needs was the result of a chaotic political situation in which large numbers in the North found themselves either without a political roof over their heads or else with one that leaked badly. In the years after 1840 neither the Whigs nor the Democrats had been able to maintain solidarity long enough to win a second term in office. With the passing of their great leader, Jacksonian Democrats began leaving the party in numbers; with Martin Van Buren's defeat in 1840 and his rejection in 1844, they deserted almost as a body. Democratic success after that, under meaningless leadership and southern control, was due only to the weakness of the opposition. It was Stephen A. Douglas' desperate effort to revitalize the party under northern control that brought the final breakup in 1860.

The Whigs fared even worse. Their successes, with William H. Harrison in 1840 and Zachary Taylor in 1848, were achieved only by ignoring their real leaders and nominating mere figureheads on meaningless platforms. With the deaths of Henry Clay and Daniel Webster in the early 1850s, the party gradually disintegrated as a national organization.

The Liberty and Free-Soil parties which had sprung up in the meantime were but the temporary expression of widespread disgust and dissatisfaction with the failure of the major parties to face the slavery issue. The American, or Know-Nothing party which followed was little more than a frantic effort to turn attention from real issues to lesser irritations. It quickly proved too un-American to fill the gap.

III

Out of this tangled situation the Republican party had emerged. The immediate purpose was to oppose what Salmon P. Chase, Charles Sumner, and their followers said was a move on the part of Stephen A. Douglas to spread the institution of Negro slavery over the Kansas and Nebraska territories. The ultimate accomplishment, however, was to gather those dissatisfied northern Democrats, those orphaned Whigs, and those pious Free-Soilers into a new sectional party to carry all the interests, all the resentments, all the values, and all the purposes of more than a million northern men who were determined to push aside a backward, sinful south, destroy the hated Stephen A. Douglas, and take over the administration of both local and national governments.

The Republican party was a strange combination of divergent elements and conflicting values brought together temporarily by a common impulse. "It is not true," said one Democrat, "that we have joined the opponents of Democracy, and it is still more notoriously untrue that we have done anything to injure the Democratic party." "I am, and ever have been, a Democrat of the Jackson and Benton School," said Frank Blair of Missouri, "and I do not intend to abandon that faith or to surrender that proud title." He had just temporarily united with others to oppose an immediate threat, nothing more. As one Republican explained, "It was just common sense and patriotism to welcome all from whatever party or sect, country or color, whose views in this particular were congenial—who had hearts that vibrated with want and woe, cruelty and oppression, under which millions in our boasted land of democracy, suffered and groaned."

The important things about this movement were the

ideas of its temporary character and its one purpose. In the beginning, no intention seemingly existed of forming a permanent national party. It was simply an effort to check a specific threat which would cease with the certainty that slavery would not enter the territory of Kansas.

As a matter of fact that certainty already existed. Neither the purpose nor the possibility of spreading slavery to the territory being organized was ever in Douglas' mind. He stated repeatedly that not a slave state would ever be found there, and most southerners agreed with him. Even those who favored the repeal of the Missouri Compromise saw it only as a recognition of equality in principle, not a gain in slave territory. So, as an Illinois man said, "I do not think that any sane man on earth thinks that all the presidents and all the coherents and all the Congresses, and all the Supreme Courts and all the slaveholders on earth, with all the Constitutions which could be drawn, can ever make Kansas a slave state." And he was right. After all the fuss and bitterness, there were only two slaves in Kansas in 1860.

Allan Nevins, in his *Ordeal of the Union*, writes, "Indeed it may be said that the battle for Kansas was fought and won years before any settler put foot on her soil. . . . It was won when the population of the Ohio Valley and the mid-country generally . . . accepted the principle that slavery injures a pioneer race of small farmers growing mixed crops." [1]

James Malin, the distinguished Kansas historian, put it even stronger. "There was no real danger of Kansas ever becoming a slave state, and the whole Kansas Crusade of antislavery-abolitionism was a trumped-up affair in which the country was victimized by propaganda, and history has been dominated ever since by that falsehood." [2]

---

[1] Allan Nevins, *Ordeal of the Union: A House Dividing, 1852–1857* (New York, 1947), vol. 2, p. 382.

[2] James Malin, *The Nebraska Question* (Ann Arbor, Mich., 1953), p. 321.

In spite of all this, the organization of a party for the purpose of meeting a threat that did not exist resulted in a new and powerful political faction that won the presidency in its second campaign and went on to dominate the political scene for the next seventy years as completely as had the Democrats in the years before the war.

The point is that the concrete realities in the situation were not important. They merely provided the occasion for bringing a struggle long developing out into the open. A new political party to carry the interests and values of the North had become absolutely necessary. All that was needed was an excuse, however flimsy, to bring it into being.

North and South in the United States had been drawing apart in interests and values ever since the 1840s. In spite of shrinking space under a communication's revolution and a greater interdependence as finance, industrial capitalism emerged, the sections drew apart emotionally and intellectually. It is difficult to say just when any large number of Americans accepted the idea that North and South constituted two distinct and hostile sections. Some recent historians, with the Civil War in mind, have insisted that basic differences appeared even in the Constitutional Convention. Others write of an inevitable conflict between a free, progressive North rapidly entering the modern world of cities and industry and a backward, slaveholding agricultural South lagging far behind.

Differences there were, but likenesses as well. Southern cotton played an important part in the industrial revolution and the Southern planter was essentially a big business man with business values. His plantation resembled a factory far more than it did a western farm. Slavery itself was primarily a labor system, often compared favorably with the one employed in New England textile mills. The difference was that the Negro bore the burdens both of labor and of slavery.

Furthermore, it must be remembered that most of the early domestic clashes were local in character, not sectional. Open resistance to the War of 1812 developed only in eastern commercial centers. South Carolina in its efforts to nullify the tariff stood almost alone. Opposition to the annexation of Texas and to the Mexican War centered primarily in New England; bitterness over the Oregon boundary compromise was confined largely to the Ohio River Valley, and that over the checking of internal improvements and homesteads, to the Old Northwest. Not until the slavery issue began to splinter the political parties and the churches in the mid-1840s did the break become sharply sectional. When a common meeting ground for the discussion and settlement of differences no longer existed, an irrepressible conflict developed. Slavery, in the form of a moral sectional issue, confirmed the existence of a North and a South.

IV

Opposition to slavery as a social and moral evil had existed among various groups from its first introduction into the colonies. It did not, however, take on crusading proportions until American reformers in the 1830s and 1840s embarked on a crusade to rid the nation of all evil. Antislavery was at first only one goal along with peace, temperance, women's rights, and prison reform, but slavery's greater injustice and its sectional character soon moved it to the front. Entrance to politics was slow in spite of the fact that the Missouri Compromise struggle had revealed antislavery's deep and widespread appeal. In early years antislavery leaders avoided political involvement, turned to the evangelical church, and relied on moral support.

A major shift came with the annexation of Texas and President James K. Polk's Oregon boundary compromise, his veto of a River and Harbor Bill favorable to the West, "his Mexican War," and the lower tariff of 1846. Each of these seemed to favor the slaveholding South. The Wilmot Proviso of 1846 and the organization of the Free-Soil party in 1848 marked the beginning of open northern resistance to the "slave power," which would climax after the passage of the Kansas-Nebraska Bill in the birth of the Republican party.

The forces that had produced both the Kansas-Nebraska Bill and the sharp reaction against it centered largely in the Old Northwest. They came to focus ultimately in the state of Illinois, where Stephen A. Douglas, seeking re-election to the Senate, was forced not only to justify his bill but also to state his position on the whole slavery-expansion issue. In doing this, he spoke for himself as well as for the whole northern Democracy. That permitted his opponent Abraham Lincoln to emerge as a national spokesman for Republican principles and as a politician capable of holding his own in any campaign. It set the stage for 1860, when the Republicans nominated and elected a man with no administrative experience, a local politician who had served only one term in Congress, had failed miserably and returned home with his political career seemingly ended. Just now, however, all the party needed was a moderate spokesman who could, in good Old Testament language, reveal the moral weakness in Douglas' program regardless of its practical results—a man who could view northern economic demands as steps toward national greatness and the threat of slavery expansion as a barrier to America's obligation to all mankind, as a democratic experiment in government of the people, by the people, for the people. These were high ideals; but it should also be noted that no sooner had southerners left their seats in Congress than the Republicans passed a homestead bill, voted aid to transcontinental internal improvements, passed a higher tariff, and created a new National Banking System! Economic measures were also moral measures. Joshua Giddings had said as much and had acted on that assumption.[3] Morals and progress were one.

[3] See discussion in Avery Craven, *The Coming of the Civil War* (Chicago, 1957), pp. 178, 215.

V

For the student of Reconstruction, the significant fact is that the Republican party was born out of high moral indignation and bitter resentment against both the South and the Democratic party. It was strictly a northern party loosely constructed to oppose all that the South seemed to represent. It found no support for its economic demands or its moral values in the South, and its distrust and dislike of the South were deepened by four years of bloody war forced upon the North by southern refusal to accept Republican rule.

Furthermore, the Republican party, built on such foundations, lacked basic unity. It was composed of all kinds and shades of opinion. What unity it had consisted primarily of emotions, not basic agreements on all public issues. Its course both in war and Reconstruction would reveal a divided quality and often an aggressiveness born more of insecurity than purpose. Even after the war it was a party that was trying to find out just exactly what it stood for. It was, furthermore, a minority party and its first president-elect had been a minority president.

Much strife prevailed within the party all through the war, and Lincoln at times had been able to survive only through Democratic and army support. Yet with victory and peace, Republicans could forget the support given by loyal Democrats and claim full credit for saving the Union and freeing the slaves. The party could still boast of its moral superiority and lay the blame for all the nation's troubles on the Democratic party. The *Chicago Tribune* could editorialize: "The war of the Rebellion, on the surface a conflict between North and South, was in reality a conflict between the Republican and Democratic parties and principles."

In like manner, Senator Henry Wilson of Massachusetts could claim that there was more moral and intellectual worth in the Republican party than was ever embodied "in any political organization in any land." It had in fact been "created by no man or set of men, but brought into being by Almighty God himself and endowed by the Creator with all power and every office under Heaven."

The Democratic party, of course, would be the party of treason. As Governor Oliver P. Morton of Indiana commented, "In short, the Democratic Party may be described as a common sewer and loathsome receptacle. . . ."

Not only would the Republican party be the party that saved the Union and freed the slaves; it would be the party of progress in terms of the new age of industry and finance. It would have matchless advantage in being able to claim all that the war represented as it was related to the emerging age. Yet a temporary quality and a bit of exaggeration permeated much of this braggadocio.

Not all good and intelligent Americans accepted the Republican claims, nor had Thomas Jefferson ceased to walk American streets. What was equally important, the Republican party had absorbed the reforming zeal which the abolitionists had generated in opposing sin as it revealed itself in slavery—the greatest curse to both blacks and whites that ever existed on American soil. In Republican hands, however, that drive lost its religious flavor, and the race question, which now came to take the place of slavery, became primarily a political issue between Republicans and Democrats. Immediatism also lost its place in reform; not all northern Republicans were ready immediately to accept the Negro as an all-out equal and to grant him equal rights. Expediency as well as morals was involved.

THE WAR
AND RECONSTRUCTION

I

The Civil War was not a war between distinct peoples and nations. Both parties in that struggle were good Americans firmly convinced of the soundness of their cause and of the evil intentions of their opponents. They were not separated from each other by any physical barrier, difference in language or traditions. Differences had developed between them over economic policies and over the interpretation of the Constitution, but these differences represented largely selfish ends and rationalizations to support them. It is even somewhat difficult to explain why the existence of slave labor in the South, which some critics said was less exploitative than the "wage slavery" in northern factories, should have produced an "irrepressible conflict." Opposition to slavery was evidently at first more against the abstract idea than against exploitation of the Negro. For in the North, as well as in the South, he was viewed as an inferior creature who could not safely be granted equal rights. Perhaps, as had been said, "The wars that have not happened are the best to study."

Nor was states' rights a strictly southern doctrine; nor was support for the right of secession lacking in a portion of the northern press in 1860. Both Abraham Lincoln and Jefferson Davis, in their efforts to achieve the central efficiency necessary for the waging of war, met bitter opposition from local authorities. Lincoln was forced at times to suspend the right of habeas corpus and to repress a newspaper, while Davis faced governors who openly defied his orders and a Vice President who remained at home to criticize and obstruct.

The final acceptance of war as unavoidable came slowly, and the difficulties of choosing sides and getting into a fighting mood were forced upon unprepared thousands. That was particularly the case along the border, where reluctance ran as far south as North Carolina and Tennessee. Nor was it entirely lacking in other parts of both North and South. It is probably true that a small minority made the decisions by which war became inevitable but which a whole people had to accept as their cause. That is not to say that this was a needless war. Rather, that there is a difference between starting a war and a whole people getting into it—a wide difference between the causes of a war and the multiple reasons for which individuals and even sections fight and give their lives.

That is why, when the firing began at Fort Sumter, Americans of every shade of opinion, or none at all, suddenly responded in a burst of emotion, often more of indignation than hatred, but which passed for patriotism. As one moderate southerner wrote, "The voice of reason is stilled. Furious passion and thirst for blood consumes the air. . . . Nobody is allowed to retain and assert his reason. . . . The very women and children are for war." From Washington, Henry B. Stanton wrote that he could "hear Old John Brown knocking on the lid of his coffin and shouting 'Let me out, let me out!' The doom of slavery is at hand. It is to be wiped out in blood. Amen!"

Then men began to fear and hate. The *New York Times* told of the intense hatred and indignation that greeted Jefferson Davis's letters of marque and reprisal. "Our people," it commented, "begin to realize the real character of the foe. . . . They cannot even make war in the spirit of civilized nations."

When the fighting actually began, partisans were willing to believe almost anything said against the enemy. One *New York Herald* reporter told of southern atrocities at Bull Run, where "rebel fiends" thrust their bayonets and knives through the hearts of "our wounded and dying soldiers"; where "rebels" severed the heads of the Union dead and used them as footballs; and where from Yankee bones they carved bracelets for southern belles. He concluded his story by stating that such barbarities, "unworthy of the Christian era," were but samples of the boasted chivalry of those "worse than fiends," the national product of a slaveholding society.

Such extremes, of course, diminished as the soldier learned to respect the qualities of the men he faced in battle, but attitudes of civilians changed little.[1] They accepted without question reports of willful neglect and abuses in prison camps, the charge of disease germs scattered abroad in enemy territory, and the refusal to allow medical supplies to reach enemy hospitals. Thus, when the war ended with "victor and vanquished," the spirit of revenge stepped forward. The demand that all leaders of "the rebellion" be driven from the land or buried in it became general. The soldiers' attitude, however, delayed and softened the demand, and in the end Jefferson Davis became a kind of sacrificial offering for most of his section's sins. On May 23, 1865, the *New York Herald* reported:

---

[1] George M. Fredrickson, *The Inner Civil War* (New York, 1965), pp. 170–171.

At about three o'clock yesterday all that is mortal of Jeff'n Davis, late so-called President of the alleged Confederate States, was duly, but quietly and effectively, committed to that living tomb prepared within the impregnable walls of Fortress Monroe. The 22nd of May, 1865, may be said to be the day when all the earthly aspirations of Jeff'n Davis ceased. . . . No more will Jeff'n Davis be known among the masses of men . . . he is buried alive.

With a guard of seventy men, shut away in a deep inner cell with only one small window well above his reach, denied sleep by a lamp burning night and day at his head and by guards constantly walking back and forth a few feet away, with heavy iron weights for a time riveted to his legs, denied all communication with the outside world, Davis was indeed buried alive. Not until his health threatened death and European newspapers shamed the American people into action was his torture lessened.

All these things might gladly be forgotten if they did not constitute the atmosphere in which Reconstruction began. Neither North nor South could forgive and forget all the bitterness and all the distrust that had been generated between the sections for decades before it culminated in open war, or the blood and anguish that four years of fighting had entailed. They did not always hate, but they always distrusted. There would be no blood bath during Reconstruction, but much caution and a long-held belief in fundamental sectional differences.[2]

---

[2] It is true that only one "war criminal," Commandant Henry Wirtz of Andersonville prison, was hanged, and that only a few of the southern political leaders were imprisoned, but this does not mean that there was a kindly, understanding, forgiving spirit abroad in the North. Too much talk of forced exile and too many demands for blood enough to "satisfy poetic and national justice" existed to be ignored. A middle ground on the subject is nearer the truth than either extreme. See *The Independent*, May 18, 1865, before reaching a conclusion. ". . . We have learned to hate one another as no people have ever hated."—Thomas A. Hendricks of Indiana, *Congressional Globe*, 39th Cong., 1st sess., p. 876. See also *Congressional Globe*, 37th Cong., 2d sess., pp. 175–179, where Bull Run charges are repeated.

II

The Civil War was not an effort on the part of a handful of individuals to seize control of the government. It was the climax of an unsettled dispute over the character of the government itself and its use by one geographical portion to deny the other what it considered its constitutional rights. It was a war between two ideologies that could not coexist. Each side, being American, proved its case by appeal to logic and history and relied on the very same documents for support. The line between the two sections was never sharply drawn, nor was the character of the struggle defined, but for all practical purposes the war was waged between two American nations observing the rules of international war. In spite of some rather labored rationalizing to justify the term rebels, intelligent northerners soon saw the absurdity of dealing with individual southerners as traitors. Yet that necessity did not change their feelings toward men who would destroy the Union and deny the Negro his rights as a human being. They were bitter enemies. As victors at the end of the war, northerners went as far as legality, human decency, and the traditions of their culture permitted. Even Wendell Phillips exclaimed, "What, cover the continent with gibbets. We cannot sicken the nineteenth century with such a sight!"

In fact, there has remained ever since Reconstruction an air of guilt and half-apology on the part of many Americans for what *was done*. Along with it has lingered an undercurrent of sectional feeling that has, on occasion, quickly risen to the surface.[3]

After four years of bloody fighting both sides were desperately war weary, and until something might occur to reveal the fact that old differences were still there,

[3] Even as early as February 11, 1875, E. L. Godkin wrote in *The Nation*, "That the chapter which tells the story of reconstruction should have to follow the chapter which tells the story of the war and of emancipation, is something over which many a generation will blush."

North and South could relax. Yet the wounds which the past had left on their very souls had not healed. The North would soon discover that it was in no mood to yield the "security" which it had won in a costly all-out war, and the South, although accepting defeat, would feel that it was unnecessary to yield to a hated foe any more of its values than defeat made necessary. There was too much of what makes an American about each of them for things to be otherwise!

No parallel really prevailed (as some have suggested) between the forgiving and forgetting possible in the world-wide wars of the twentieth century and the emotions arising out of our Civil War. In the latter case, the opposing forces had long lived together as one people, faced each other day after day in Congress for long bitter years, and would now return to a forced coexistence in which one was in complete control. Everyday domestic interests, not distant foreign affairs, had to be considered. Suspicions and fears, not necessarily hatred, demanded caution and no relaxation. Old political parties were still in existence, and the victorious Republican party, never a real unity, could always be in danger of defeat. Southerners, and even a goodly number of men in the North, were still Democrats. The parties might still represent competing values worth fighting for. Only brutal absolutes, not sweet material compromises, would suffice after a civil war. The whole future course the nation was to take was the issue. It could still be phrased in terms of right versus wrong.[4]

III

One thing to be kept in mind was that the Civil War came just at the time when the North as a section was catching the full sweep of the industrial revolution. As J. F. C. Fuller, the English military authority, stated:

---

[4] "Let us hold on to the power we now have to do right, to protect the loyal, to rebuild the state, to re-establish society, to secure the liberty of the peoples and the safety of the Union. Let

The first of the unlimited industrialized wars was the Civil War in America. It was the first great conflict of the age of steam, and the aim of the Northern or Federal States, was unconditional surrender, that is, total victory. Its character was, therefore, that of a crusade, and because of this, as well as because it put to test the military developments of the Industrial Revolution, it opened a radically new chapter in the history of war.[5]

What is of equal importance, the Civil War marked the end of an old social and economic order and the beginning of a new one. As Allan Nevins [6] has said, "The war measurably transformed an inchoate nation, individualistic in temper and wedded to improvisation, into a shaped and disciplined nation. . . ." Under the demands of war, the North entered the modern world of planned production, organized social action, and concentration on efficiency. The industrial revolution fought on its side. "The resultant alteration in national character was one of the central results of the gigantic struggle." The South for its failure to keep step paid in defeat and in years of "backwardness." That meant that sectional differences, conflicting demands, and values that had led to the war were far greater at the end of it than they had been at the beginning. The sections were further apart in the ability to understand each other, to tolerate, to discuss rationally, and to compromise than they had been before. The democratic process would have little to do with Reconstruction.

The direct and immediate effect of the new technology on the fighting itself was to increase its destructiveness. Men could kill more efficiently than ever before in history. In spite of the well-known reluctance of the military mind to accept change, the old muzzle-loading, smoothbore

---

it be used with parental kindness and in the temper of conciliation. But hold on to the power and in the fear of God let it be used."—Governor John Andrew, in the *New York World*, June 23, 1865.

[5] J. F. C. Fuller, *The Generalship of Ulysses S. Grant* (Bloomington, Ind., 1958), pp. 1–12.

[6] Allan Nevins, *War for the Union* (New York, 1959–1960), vol. 1, pp. v–vi.

muskets were gradually replaced by rifles with greater range and accuracy. "Brown Bess" had been dangerous at only about one hundred yards, whereas the new Springfields and Endfields in the hands of a sharpshooter could kill at half a mile, and were effective as an infantry weapon at some 250 and 300 yards. That should have put an end to the old mass infantry charge with fixed bayonets, with artillery support that could be checked only by massed cavalry charges to saber the gunners. Yet old tactics, with sickening slaughter, persisted in the romantic charges at Gettysburg and Cold Harbor. Only gradually did the military leaders learn that artillery support and the cavalry charge had lost their effectiveness when sharpshooters could pick off the gunners more effectively at long distance. Then the cavalry was used more for scouting and screening, and the artillery became a more mobile and more deadly instrument. The spade became as important as the rifle, and the beginnings of trench warfare developed. Observation from the air came into use, and the ironclads and crude submarines were developed as products of the new machine age.[7]

What these technical changes meant, while the old fighting tactics lagged behind, is revealed in the frightening casualty figures. Out of a total male population of some 6,000,000, some 618,000 men gave their lives. In some battles each army lost a fourth of its complement. Some regiments in battles suffered 70 to 80 percent casualties. In all, the best estimates that historians have been able to make show that the Union deaths were over 360,000; Confederate deaths, uncertain, but something over 258,000—or a fourth of Confederacy men in arms.

Losses of the South were proportionately much heavier than those of the North, both in killed and wounded in battle. Had the North lost as many in proportion as the South, it would have suffered more than a million casualties instead of 360,000. The South paid a fearful price for

[7] Bruce Catton, *America Goes to War* (Middletown, Conn., 1958), pp. 14–27.

its experiment in rebellion. This was due in part to the fact that its armies had not profited to the same degree as those of the North from the technology of the industrial revolution, and in part to the character of its men.

The British historian J. F. C. Fuller wrote that "except for his lack of discipline, the Southern soldier was probably the finest individual fighter of his day." But, as General A. P. Hill pointed out:

> Self-reliant always, obedient when he chose to be, impatient of drill and discipline, he was unsurpassed as a scout or on the skirmish line. Of the shoulder-to-shoulder courage, bred to drill and discipline, he knew nothing and cared less. Hence, on the battle field he was more of a free-lance than a machine. Whoever saw a Confederate line advancing that was not as crooked as a cow's horn? Each ragged rebel yelling on his own hook and aligning on himself. . . . In battle he fought like a Berserker—out of battle he ceased to be a soldier—straggling was an inalienable right.

Fuller's conclusion is that the Union soldier was a semi-regular, the Confederate a semiguerrilla.[8]

Now if this were true in war—how could it have been different in Reconstruction? Could the South have achieved an orderly procedure of well-disciplined and cooperative action, or could the orderly, disciplined North have expected or understood anything else? All we know is that both proceeded in Reconstruction as they had in war, with about the same results.

Another thing about this modern war was that it was a war on a whole people by a whole people. Efforts were not confined to battlefields. Railroads were torn up and everything about them systematically destroyed; bridges wherever found were burned; foundries, regardless of product, were left in ruins; fields were devastated and the very earth scorched. Medical supplies were cut off from the wounded and from prisoners; destruction of homes and personal property was regarded as a war measure.

---

[8] J. F. C. Fuller, *Grant and Lee: A Study in Personality and Generalship* (London, 1933), pp. 52–53, and his *Decisive Battles of the U. S. A.* (New York, 1942), p. 181.

Authorities have hailed General William T. Sherman as the greatest of modern generals because he made a whole people suffer. As Sherman moved across Georgia, he declared, "If the people raise a howl against my barbarity and cruelty, I will answer that war is war, and not a popularity seeking. If they want peace, they and their relatives must stop the war." Prior to his famous march across the South Sherman commented:

> Until we can repopulate Georgia, it is useless to occupy it; but the utter destruction of its roads, houses and people will cripple their military resources—I can make the march and make Georgia howl . . . we are not fighting hostile armies, but a hostile people, and must make old and young, rich and poor, feel the hard hand of war. . . . The truth is, the whole army is burning with an insatiable desire to wreak vengeance upon South Carolina. I almost tremble for her fate!

Sherman later estimated that he did $100 million worth of damage, of which only $20 million inured to the North's advantage, the remainder being simple waste and destruction. This made him a modern-age general in a modern war. All this was involved in Reconstruction as a purpose to be fulfilled and as something to be remembered by those who endured.

IV

These were the more spectacular influences that the war imposed on Reconstruction. There were others, perhaps more significant, that the carrying forward of the war effort had set into motion. They were the factors that carried the war objective far beyond the simple purpose of saving the Union. They did not create a single economic pressure, but taken together they were all on the side of the modern business world.

Wars are expensive luxuries. In a nation like ours, primarily agricultural in the 1860s, personal incomes were low and savings had gone back heavily into land purchases. Taxes had been light, and the government had largely depended on customs and land sales for its revenue. Credit, banking, and borrowing were primitive enough to have scattered panics at regular intervals through the years to 1860. A quick expansion of revenue was impossible. Debts rose by leaps and bounds as expenditures mounted to unprecedented heights. The government was, therefore, forced to turn in any direction where help might be found. Its interests were soon linked to those few banks and bankers, particularly Jay Cooke & Company of Philadelphia, whose knowledge and resources not only enabled them to dictate present policies but gave them the power to shape the whole financial course of the nation in days ahead.

The first step of major concern was the decision that the war generation should not attempt to carry the load alone. Future generations should pay their share. That meant borrowing at high rates. It began in July 1861, when Secretary of the Treasury Salmon P. Chase was authorized to borrow up to $250 million at 6 and 7 percent through the house of Jay Cooke in Philadelphia and at other banks in New York City and Boston. Soon a 7.3 percent rate became the rule on bonds and treasury notes. By 1865 the total indebtedness was over $2,680,000; a powerful financial interest had been created, largely centering in the East and definitely conservative in attitudes.

Taxation naturally followed, but neither borrowing nor taxing solved the problem. The final step was forced loans from all the people in the form of "greenbacks"—promises to pay without security or interest. In all, some $430 million in greenbacks were issued and made legal tender save for duties on imports. They quickly drove metal out of circulation and depreciated at times to as low as thirty-nine cents on the dollar. Yet there were also times when they could be used to buy bonds, later to be redeemed at face value in gold.

By 1863 war expenses reached $2,500,000 a day, and the national debt had risen to over a billion dollars. Banks had suspended specie payments, and the government was some sixty million dollars in arrears on soldiers' pay. That gave Chase an opportunity to establish what he had long desired, a national banking system that would create a market for government bonds, give the nation a more stable currency, and link the small bankers out in the byways to the central government and its financial policies.

As a result, Lincoln could say in his message of December 6, 1864, that, in the preceding month, 584 national banks had been organized, many of which had been conversions from state banks. He then noted that "changes from State systems to the national system are rapidly taking place, and it is hoped that, very soon, there will be in the United States, no banks of issue not authorized by Congress, and no bank-note circulation not secured by the government." [9] At which Andrew Jackson must have turned over several times in his grave!

Both the greenbacks and the new banking system had been justified to the public largely as war necessities. Many had believed both to be unsound, at least the greenbacks if not the banking system itself. So when Lincoln, to Chase's surprise, accepted one of his hasty resignations, and when the end of the war seemed to be a possibility, pressure for the contraction of the greenbacks began to be felt. It reached the point of action when Hugh McCulloch, a conservative western banker, took over the Treasury Department. He had opposed the National Banking Act and believed that the greenbacks were unconstitutional. He thus began, early in July 1865, to contract the volume of greenbacks as a step against the growing inflation. He would set the course along conservative lines.

The reaction to this move was quick and positive. Any policy that touched the currency or the payment of the huge war debt involved the well-being of every American. The reaction, therefore, was one dictated primarily by self-interest. Men reacted as bankers, merchants, manufacturers, farmers, or citizens of the older East or the newer West. Yet reform was in the air; the drive for more

[9] Abraham Lincoln, *Collected Works* (New Brunswick, N.J., 1953–1955), vol. 8, p. 332.

justice and equality for the Negro when applied to finances made soft-money anticontractionists out of the
so-called Radical Republicans and hard-money advocates
out of conservative Republicans. The same impulse would
make some Radicals favor the high tariff and turn opponents into free traders. Meanwhile, western Democrats
would take sides with the Radical Republicans while
many of their fellows in the Northeast would be in opposition. Not until Reconstruction was well out of the way
would Republicans as a whole unite on gold and tariffs,
and Democrats find unity in opposition. That would come
only when Republican commitments to the Negro weakened and the commitments to northern and modern-world
business interests predominated. That shift in emphasis
would, in turn, have a part in the abandonment of Reconstruction.[10]

In this connection, southern finances also became important. The Confederacy had issued notes, laid a direct
war tax, and borrowed abroad. Interest rates ran to 8
percent, and a provision tax of 10 percent was ultimately
laid. Depreciation in the end sent flour to $1,000 a barrel,
coffee to $40 a pound, a dinner in a hotel to $100. The
South's final debt was about $2,350,000,000—all to be
repudiated, along with state debts of $67,000,000. So
here was a section whose total wealth in 1860 was only
$3,405,796,607 forced to accept repudiation of well over
$5,000,000,000. A whole section was thus rendered ab-
solutely bankrupt. That, too, has a place in Reconstruction.

V

Another side of war finance was the tariff. That had
been one of the most bitterly contested issues between
North and South. Seemingly everything that could be said

[10] Robert P. Sharkey, *Money, Class, and Party: An Economic
Study of Civil War and Reconstruction* (Baltimore, Md., 1959),
pp. 56–134, 276–311; Irwin Unger, *The Greenback Era: A Social
and Political History of American Finance,* 1865–1879 (Princeton, N.J., 1964), *passim.*

for or against protection had been said, and something of understanding had been reached by 1860: the Government would only use tariffs to raise such funds as it might wish, and rates were to be adjusted so as to aid young industry where such adjustment seemed to be in the national interest.

As a Republican in 1859, Lincoln said that while he believed in a moderate protective policy, he was of the opinion that just then the issue could not be raised. "We have been beaten on it," were his words. The tariff then stood at 19 percent.

In the wake of the panic of 1857 certain interests became active; and in 1860 the House passed what came to be called the Morrill Bill (though the Senate did not readily approve the measure). The Republicans in the 1860 convention did favor this bill but with no particular emphasis. That was the situation when the war called for revenue and especially for some way to compensate for higher domestic taxes. Rates were up to 37 percent in 1862 and to 47 percent in 1864.

The idea was that these duties were only temporary measures, war measures which war-Democrats had favored. They were passed hurriedly and without careful debate. No effort was made to give them a scientific character, and raises were unusually in lump terms. These tariffs did confer matchless favors on certain interests and often granted a monopoly market. Although never favored by all, they soon became a permanent part of Republican doctrine. That brought sharp protest from Democrats and those who were beginning to be called "Liberal Republicans." Many called it favoritism.

At any rate here again was an interest group granted extravagant favors. Already economists under the lead of David A. Wells had begun to question the high tariff's value in a democracy. The tariff had about it a modern age quality and was in time accepted as good Republican doctrine. Liberals who favored more justice for the Negro in turn favored protection of the American laborer from foreign competition.

The war thus left a nation that would never be the same again. The government itself had been altered, as both Lincoln and Davis, at times, turned dictator to secure efficiency. As W. A. Dunning has argued: "The general concurrence in avowed ignoring of the organic law emphasizes the completeness of the revolution which was in progress."

The balance of power had shifted radically, and the North and its Republican party would dictate the national course as the modern world would have it. A new industrial and financially minded American would henceforth dwarf the politician of old. There would be no more Websters, Calhouns, and Lincolns. A new age emerged through war; the tragedy lay in the fact that America entered it through war and reconstruction.

THE SOUTH
AFTER THE WAR

I

It must be understood that before the war there had been no one South; instead, there were many Souths. Geographically, the region was divided into several distinct units. Some faced the Atlantic, some the Gulf, some the Mississippi River system, and some were effectively isolated by swamps and mountains.

A series of great ridges and valleys stretching from Pennsylvania to Alabama divided the East into two parts, while the Mississippi River did the same to the South as a whole. Texas, Missouri, and Arkansas never quite knew whether they were southern or western, and parts of southern Indiana and Illinois do not know even today. From 10 to 15 degrees of latitude separated the South's northern and southern borders, and the rainfall varied from 70 inches on the Allegheny watershed to 2 inches in the far Southwest.

Within these larger divisions were sharp lines of cleavage. There were tidewater regions and peoples, and up-country regions and peoples. The only mountain folk in the United States were the southern highlanders, tucked away in the coves and ridges, differing even in speech from those of the lowlands. The bayou people of Louisiana were just as unique, with a tongue and name of their own, the Cajuns. Then, on poor lands and in isolated corners, were some southerners who even bore the word poor before the designation of their color or lack of it.

Some parts of the South were old, as old as any English settlements on the continent; some, in 1860, were the rawest of frontiers. Virginia with its tobacco and its English country ways differed sharply from South Carolina, which formed almost a city-state with its rice and its Charleston. Between them lay North Carolina, whose plain, self-supporting farmers formed what some spoke of as "the valley of humility between two mountains of conceit." Georgia still bore the stain of prisoner-debtor beginnings, which probably inspired it to become by 1850 the most progressive state in the South—progressive enough sometimes to be called the South's Yankee state. Louisiana, with its Creoles, its great sugar plantations, its Cajuns, and its New Orleans with the river trade, was just something else, as was Texas, recently arrived.

To add to the diversity and confusion, there were three Kentuckys, three Tennessees, two Alabamas (if not three), and as many Mississippis. Sectionalism had always been a part of the South, and its internal quarrels had forever threatened the division of state after state into two parts. The only example of such a step in our history came in Virginia with the outbreak of war.

The Civil War had not improved the situation. The border states delayed joining the Confederacy until Lincoln pushed them in with his call for troops, and even then some never joined. The Confederacy never acquired even the degree of unity arrived at in the North and none of the efficiency. As Frank Owsley once observed, "If a monument is ever erected as a symbolic gravestone over 'the lost cause,' it should have engraved upon it these words: 'Died of States' Rights.'"

Wartime governors made life miserable for Jefferson Davis, and even Vice-President Alexander H. Stephens sat on "the seat of the scornful" throughout the war. H. J. Eckenrode insists that the removal of the capital from Montgomery to Richmond sealed the fate of the Confederacy, although he admits that it had to be moved there to hold Virginia in the fold.

With so little to build on in the beginning and with so much turmoil throughout the war, it seems only a modest statement to assert that the Confederate States of America never developed anything that can be called a national spirit. It never found a spokesman who, like Lincoln or Churchill, could lift its cause to such sublime grandeur that a whole people would respond and be welded together in a great cause. It left no great presidential messages or great speeches from its battlefields. It never was given a great inspiring song, like the "Battle Hymn of the Republic." All it had was an old minstrel tune written by a Yankee and with only doggerel words. The Confederacy never found its soul. It produced great individual fighters who served their commanders, not their nation. It was for Lee and Jackson, not Jefferson Davis, that they fought. The "lost cause" was lost before it ever became a cause.

II

At the end of the war the Confederate States of America no longer existed. The southern states, in spite of differing theories, were for all practical purposes just eleven badly beaten and helpless units. Most of the war had been fought on their soil. Most of the material damage had been inflicted there. The northern armies had been thorough and often wanton in their destructiveness.

Across Georgia, Mississippi, South Carolina, and Virginia —the states most hurt—one writer told of "blackened chimneys" standing guard above charred rafters where once had stood a mansion, a substantial farm house, a trim town house. Much of Jackson, Charleston, Mobile, Richmond, and Savannah, and many smaller communities had been burned. Atlanta and Columbia lay in ashes. A correspondent of the *New York Herald* who was with Sherman in Atlanta wrote:

> On Sunday night a kind of long streak of light, like an aurora, marked the line of march and the burning stores, depots, and bridges, in the train of the army . . . everything in the way of destruction was now considered legalized . . . ruffians ran with brands, to fire churches, hotels, depots, and stores, pillaging as they went. "The streets" were soon in one fierce sheet of flame, houses were falling on all sides, and fiery flakes of cinders were whirled about. Men plunged into the houses, broke windows and doors with their muskets, dragging out armfuls of clothes, dressing themselves with some, and flinging the rest into the fire. Occasionally shells exploded, excited men rushed through the choking atmosphere to escape the ruin. At a distance the burning city seemed overshadowed by a cloud of black smoke. The sun looked like a blood-red ball of fire; and the air for miles around, felt oppressive and intolerable. The lyre of the South was laid in ashes, and the "Gate City" was a thing of the past.[1]

This correspondent reported that wherever the Union armies had passed, the homes of the well-to-do and the middle classes were left almost bare of silver, paintings, books, and even clothing—anything of value or any trifle that attracted the pillager's eye. Trees, fences, and shrubbery were felled or uprooted. Not enough ginhouses were left standing to accommodate even the small crop of 1865. Men in creaking wagons drove their gaunt mules for miles to find fords across bridgeless rivers.

Two years after his march, Sherman described conditions:

---

[1] David P. Conyngham, *Sherman's March Through the South* (New York, 1865), pp. 236–238, 243–269.

Look to the South, and you who went with me through that land can best say if they too have not been fearfully punished. Mourning in every household, desolation written in broad characters across the whole face of this country, cities in ashes and fields laid waste, their commerce gone, their system of labor annihilated and destroyed. Ruin, poverty and distress everywhere, and now pestilence adding the very cap-sheaf to their stack of miseries; her proud men begging for pardon and appealing for permission to raise food for their children; her five million of slaves free and their value lost to their former owners forever.[2]

Sherman knew whereof he spoke, for the New York newspaperman who was with him on his march to the sea told of the vandalism that had been openly encouraged and seldom punished. On one occasion the correspondent reported that he:

. . . came up to a retired plantation house, just set on fire. The soldiers were rushing off on every side with their pillage. An old lady and her two grandchildren were in the yard alarmed and helpless. The flames and smoke were shooting through the windows. The old lady rushed from one to another beseeching them at least to save her furniture. They only enjoyed the whole thing, including her distress. . . . The scenes I witnessed in Columbia—scenes that would have driven Alaric the Goth into frenzied ecstasies, had he witnessed them—made me ponder a little on the horrors of war.[3]

He might have said "civil war."

Nor were there funds with which to rebuild or restore the damage. One editor described the situation:

It is difficult, for those who are away to understand the utter pecuniary prostration in which the war has left this section of the country. It is as if at a single word and in a single moment the issues of every state and national bank and of the government should prove without value or effect, and the people instead of currency that they had as representative of toil and years of labor and hard-earned competency had only pieces of waste-paper.[4]

[2] Quoted in Hodding Carter, *The Angry Scar: The Story of Reconstruction, 1865–1890* (New York, 1959), p. 33.

[3] D. P. Conyngham, *op. cit.*, pp. 313, 335.

[4] Francis B. Simkins and Robert H. Woody, *South Carolina During Reconstruction* (Chapel Hill, N.C., 1932), p. 11.

Nearly every mode of investment shared the same fate. Confederate securities had absorbed the greater part of the gold, so now all that was left of wealth in the country was mere lands. Even these had suffered. In a region of heavy concentrated rainfall, erosion and harmful microorganisms had always been a problem. The end of war found galls and gullies on every side, and wide acres abandoned to sorrel and sedge. Fences were gone, farm buildings tumbling down, seed lacking, stock depleted. It is estimated that from a third to a fourth of all the horses, mules, and hogs had vanished. In places, if a plow was to be used, men and women would have to drag it through the fields. Farm machinery was worn out. Even shovels, spades, and hoes were lacking. Actual starvation threatened.

Human losses were far more serious. Manpower was heavily depleted. The population was now around five million, of whom one million had been in the armies. Many of these were crippled and maimed, more a burden than an asset. More than a quarter of a million had died in the war, so that from a fourth to a third of the able-bodied white men were gone. In South Carolina, of some 44,046 arms-bearing population, 44,000 had volunteered, and in all some 71,000 men had seen service. Of these, nearly 13,000 (23 percent) had been killed. Of Alabama's 126,587 white men between the ages of 15 and 20, over 122,000 had ultimately been in the army and over 35,000 were lost in the war.

The section had been bled white, and those lost were its best—young men who would leave no descendants. Never before or since in modern times has any people suffered such proportionately high casualties. To the South's 258,000 dead must be added at least 100,000 who were wounded, with an additional 60,000 taken prisoners. When an already bankrupt people were forced to spend as much as a fifth of their total revenue to buy artificial arms and legs for their veterans and even more for the support of their widows and orphans, one can begin to realize something of the human wreckage.

"It is, therefore," as Paul H. Buck writes, "a false impression to assume that the South of 1865 was much concerned with politics" or that it was interested in anything of reconstruction.

> The North itself was so preoccupied with the issue of deciding a Reconstruction policy that everything Southern was distorted. Purveyors of Southern news to the North were curious as to what the South thought, especially about the negro and the political situation. They pried into the minds that would never otherwise have expressed opinions, and opinions were relayed North to be printed in newspapers, reports, and books.[5]

The North was interested. The South was passive. It had had its fill of politics. The North could solve the problem of the nation's future but the South needed all its energy and thought to salvage out of the general ruin the bare necessities of life. Its social problems were equally great.

The plight of the Negro at war's end was even more tragic. He, too, was a war casualty with an uncertain future. He had escaped where possible or remained on the land as a slave in the first years of the war. Emancipation did not everywhere affect his everyday life or set him free. That would come for most only near the end of the fighting or when the Union Army would come their way. A few had gone to war with their masters, and some had been used to work on fortifications and other defenses. Both Davis and Lee were ready to put Negroes into the ranks of the Confederate army near the end, and thousands did join the Union army as opportunity opened, and proved their worth as soldiers. Many fell in, as refugees, as the Union army swept through the South, becoming a serious problem for its officers. The first Freedmen's Bureau was the product of this situation, as were the experiments with the independent Negro farm-

---

[5] Paul H. Buck, *The Road to Reunion* (Boston, 1937), pp. 36–37.

ers on the South Carolina Sea Islands and along the lower Mississippi River.[6]

With peace, freedom everywhere became a reality. Many, especially the old and infirm, remained where they were; others began to move toward the cities and the West. All had to learn to care for themselves, an experience which slavery had too often denied them. In Charleston, the mortality of Negro adults was soon twice that of white adults, and of Negro children, three times that of white children. The Negro had to shake off the habits of a slave system that had not always accepted his right to legal marriage, where stealing was no sin, and the truth was just what he was expected to say. He, too, was in for a social, intellectual revolution. He would become the race question of the days ahead.

Therefore, southern reconstruction was, from the purely material angle, not only the task of rebuilding a wrecked and ruined section, but of moving along the road toward modern urban industrialism and a more humane, democratic social order. To make even a start would require a social, intellectual revolution and the acceptance of capital-labor obligations that two hundred years of habit and thought had totally unprepared southerners, both black and white, to accept.

Most certainly this south was in no condition to produce a Washington, a Jefferson, a Madison, a John Marshall, or even another Jefferson Davis. It really did not need them. It required men who could set the plows to work, who could scrape enough money together to plant a field where food with perhaps a little surplus to sell could be raised. It needed hands—black hands as well as white—to get the basic, primitive processes going again. It could for a time dispense with statesmen.

[6] James M. McPherson, *The Negro's Civil War* (New York, 1965), pp. 143–148, 173–181, 183–192; Willie Lee Rose, *Rehearsal for Reconstruction: The Port Royal Experiment* (Indianapolis, 1964), pp. 203–216, 282–296; George R. Bentley, *A History of the Freedmen's Bureau* (Philadelphia, 1955), pp. 6–12, 21–29.

III

Such were the effects of the war on the physical South and its social structure. What the war had done to the southern "mind," however, is not so clear. Defeat can do strange things. The writings of northerners who went south, asking questions and talking to people, are well known. These travelers usually saw what they expected to find and intended to report. What the great body of the southern people thought and felt is still something of a mystery. Their reaction to Reconstruction measures still puzzles the historian.

The first thing to be noted is that defeat and surrender came as a sudden shock. In spite of overwhelming odds and a growing realization that these were increasing, southerners somehow kept their faith in the army and its leaders to perform miracles. They had done it so often that when disaster came few were prepared. A kind of numbness mixed with fear and hatred took over. Even soldiers in the ranks were stunned. After four years of fighting they thought of themselves more as part of an army than as citizens of the Confederacy. For that reason, they thought little of the political consequences of what had been transpiring. They had no thoughts of having been traitors. They simply accepted defeat. They had been beaten by superior numbers and equipment. They would go home and start over again. No wonder the northern visitors found the army men, high and low, to be "behaving splendidly—an honor to the American name."

As a young Virginia soldier told his mother:

> Citizens generally are taking the Amnesty oath—the most prominent setting the example. Though it is exceedingly repugnant both to my taste and feelings to assume any such obligation, as there is no longer any reason against it, I expect to succumb in a week or so and take the oath in good faith. It is impossible to do otherwise.

He advised one who was thinking of emigrating to Mexico to "stick by Old Virginia," and confessed that if he were migrating he would seek a home among the Yankees.[7]

Some who had not known the discipline of the army felt differently. In a family letter a young soldier reported that "Uncle Jim has suffered so terribly on account of the South that his hatred and abhorrence of Yankees amounts to a monomania. I can not in a letter convey to you the remotest idea of the fierce condition of his emotions." A northern-born Texan at the same time wrote of "the fairest portion of God's heritage turned into worse than a wilderness" by the brutal Yankee soldiers who were setting free "four million helpless, ignorant, lazy, thievish human beings to fight their way against a superior race." Once proud of being a Yankee, he now had nothing but "contempt and hatred for the place and its people." [8]

Meanwhile an exile in Amelia County, Virginia, ended his diary—and his life—with these words:

> I here declare my unmitigated hatred to Yankee rule—to all political, social and business connections with the Yankees and to the Yankee race. Would that I could impress these sentiments, in their full force, on every living Southerner and bequeath them to every one yet to be born! ... And now with what will be my latest writing and utterance, and with what will be near my lastest breath, I here repeat and would willingly proclaim my unmitigated hatred to Yankee rule ... and all connections with Yankees, and the perfidious, malignant and vile Yankee race.[9]

In sharp contrast, as if to reveal the southern mind to be as uniquely American in defeat as in victory, a good Virginia woman who had given her five sons to the Confederate army confided to her diary:

> A new era has dawned. ... Slavery has been abolished? Too suddenly for the real good of the Slaves, as they are not prepared to enjoy and appreciate the great boon of national

---

[7] L. Minor Blackford, *Mine Eyes Have Seen the Glory* (Cambridge, Mass., 1954), pp. 240–244.

[8] MS. in possession of the author.

[9] Avery O. Craven, *Edmund Ruffin, Southerner: A Study in Secession* (New York, 1932), p. 259.

freedom after being kept so many years in abject Slavery and in profound ignorance. . . .

She added, however:

> I have this morning witnessed a procession of nearly a thousand children belonging to colored schools. It was to me the most interesting public occasion I ever witnessed. For when I thought that this was the anniversary of the day when these little ones were no longer shut out of God's truth, that the fetters of ignorance were broken, and that they might not be forced from their parents and sold at auction to the highest bidder, my heart went up in adoring gratitude to the great God; not only on their account, but that we white people were no longer permitted to go on in such wickedness, heaping up more and more wrath of God upon our devoted heads.[10]

The simple truth seems to be that there was no uniform southern mind, nor one that remained constant. Reactions seem to vary from man to man, time to time, and place to place. Like that of the North, insofar as either ever reach an equilibrium, it would evolve with events.

IV

Yet whatever the "Souths" were in 1865 after four years of civil war and utter defeat, they constituted "a South" with a long and unique past. It had always been a land primarily rural and much of it was still frontier in character. Only one generation had occupied the vast Indian country that stretched from middle Georgia to the older Spanish-French region around and above New Orleans. Texas, beyond, was even more an American West and had come only recently out of revolution. Taken as a whole, southern society was much inclined to be highly personal and individualistic. That gave it a bent toward violence. What might elsewhere be left to the law, men took into their own hands. Those in the upper class fought duels or "horsewhipped" offenders. Lower-class whites fought each other with their fists or with dirks.

[10] L. Minor Blackford, *op. cit.*, pp. 249–250.

and accepted their white skins as conferring the privilege of dealing with the Negro as passion might dictate. Lynching might be expected where crimes were serious. Masters on plantations, meanwhile, were inclined to mete out physical punishment to their slaves as "necessary," in a system that was a tangle of labor, race, and everyday living together. Violence had even been a part of the struggle between the low-country and the up-country, and filibustering against weaker neighbors had enlisted wide support.

Violence, of course, was only one feature of a society that had great virtues as well. Many northerners apparently expected the South in defeat to assume the characteristics of a quiet New England village. That it did not do what it was expected to do is one of the tragedies of Reconstruction. The existence of violence suggested to outsiders only continued resistance to northern demands and threats to Negro security. This hid the reality of social chaos in which "men demoralized and faced with poverty, turned to stealing and plundering their neighbors"; where the courts had not met for two or three years and criminals, if arrested, found escape from dilapidated jails easy; and in which "a poverty-stricken and utterly subjected people [were] now only anxious for the restoration of authority of whatever description." [11]

[11] William C. Harris, *Presidential Reconstruction in Mississippi* (Baton Rouge, 1967), pp. 34–35.

CHAPTER

6

APPROACHING
RECONSTRUCTION

I

The Civil War came to a sudden end in the spring of
1865 with no negotiations of any kind and no treaty of
peace that might have given some hint of what might be
expected of victor and vanquished. Southern soldiers
simply quit and went home. The Confederate States of
America ceased to exist. Union generals set such terms of
surrender as soldiers who had learned to respect a worthy
foe might choose to make. They were, as a rule, more than
generous, but they had no legal or political base on which
to rest. Sherman's terms even had to be repudiated. A
permanent settlement with the southern people and the
southern states was another matter and would be in other
hands. The only thing generally agreed upon was that the
Union would be restored—by whom and how, no one

seemed to know. The Constitution said nothing about how to deal with such a situation.

The first and largest fact was that everyone, both North and South, was glad that the fighting and bloodshed were ended. Soldiers, as they expressed their feelings in song, were "tired of war" and "longed for home and friends so dear." But something other than just quitting and going home was required. The soldier was through. A problem new to Americans had somehow to be solved. A dissatisfied section that for four years had maintained a separate government of its own had to be molded back into a harmonious part of a common nation. It had been brought back by force, and no one seemed to know what demands the victor might make and the defeated willingly accept. As General George Meade wrote to his wife:

> We of the Army have done our work, the military power of the rebellion is shattered. It remains for statesmen, if we have any, to bring the people of the South back to their allegiance and into the Union. In the meantime I presume our armies will have to occupy the Southern States. I am myself for conciliation as the policy most likely to effect a speedy reunion. If we are going to punish treason, as perhaps strict justice would demand, we shall have to shed almost as much blood as has already been poured out in this terrible war. These are points however for others to adjust.

Rebuilding began in confusion. For four years a wide gap had existed between Lincoln's legal theory that secession was impossible and that the southern states had never been out of the Union, and the steps required to fight a war. Rebellion was indeed treason, but Lincoln had been forced to treat Lee's men as soldiers not traitors. He had by implication also been forced to accept the Confederacy as a political entity.

With peace and the Confederacy gone, southerners were now only a badly beaten and disorganized body of fellow Americans, and Lincoln was realist enough to know that they and their states could not immediately resume their place in the Union. He therefore bluntly said it was well to forget all theory. Thaddeus Stevens, on the other hand, viewed the South as conquered territory, and Charles Sumner insisted that the states had committed suicide. Each demanded both punishment and social reconstruction. Nevertheless, all of them knew that some day the Union must be restored, and the problem was one of finding a way, not too un-American, by which all groups could be satisfied. There must be an air of legality and constitutionality about what was done, but it must be accomplished in such a way as to allow Radical Republicans to have what they called security and satisfaction.

More important than the effect of theory on the future was what the war had done to Americans North and South by leaving one section victor, the other a totally beaten loser. Economic, social, political, and moral differences had led to the breakdown of the democratic process, and war had followed. Now that the war had ended, what about those interests and values? Was any room left for differences? Did northern victory mean that Republican interests and values were to become the national interests and values? Or did the Republicans have obligations to the nation as a whole—even to Democrats who opposed them? Would the Confederates have anything to say about how they and their states were to return to the Union? Had the democratic process returned with peace, or was force still to be applied? These all-important questions would sooner or later have to be faced. What could, and would, be done would depend largely on which theory of the condition of the southern states was accepted.

No procedural precedents existed. The immediate situation most certainly rested on force—force in Republican party hands. Yet this nation had a mission; it had obligations to Christianity, to democracy, and to the future. The war had been something of a crusade as well as an effort to beat down a dastardly foe. The Declaration of Independence which Abraham Lincoln loved to quote said that all men had certain inalienable rights, and southerners were men. So were the Negroes. Perhaps that made a difference. It certainly added confusion.

II

To begin with, the North had come out of the war with most of its economic demands more than realized—tariffs, homesteads, internal improvements, and finances beyond all expectations. The war had settled these matters and opened the way for whatever else might be asked. It had done even more to create the new America which the South had been holding back. The North had come out of the war vastly stronger along all lines than when it began. As Eric F. Goldman has observed:

> Except in the battered South everybody and everything seemed on the move. The drain of the Civil War was over, the backward looking planters were crushed. The Industrial Revolution, wheeled ahead decades by five years of war, was creating new careers by the thousands, turning thistle-patches into whistle-stops, towns into cities, and cities into metropolitan centers. In the East a rampant prosperity touched every venture with the "every-thing-is-possible." In the West, the tide of emigration swept out in proportions unequaled in man's restless history. West and East, virtually every index of activity—the number of steel ingots produced, the number of trees felled, the immigrants arriving for a farm, the gentlemen leaving for a spin around Europe, the churches built—almost any statistics showed a wild surge upward.[1]

The old America given to improvisation was no more.

It would thus seem that the Republican party, as victor, had achieved all the material things it had ever wanted or had gone to war to gain for the nation. Its social demands had been achieved by the freeing of the slaves, for that was all they had initially asked. There would, of course, never again be any question of slavery in the territories. Victory had been complete.

But war had added something of its own. The Republicans were victors, and victors, we are told by psychologists, have certain "spiritual requirements." A deeper satisfaction is demanded. As Senator Jacob Collamer of

---

[1] Eric F. Goldman, *Rendezvous with Destiny: A History of Modern American Reform* (New York, 1952), p. 3.

Vermont remarked, "It is not enough that they should stop their hostility and are repentant. They should present fruits meet for repentance." Eric L. McKitrick explains what this implied:

> The victor needs to be assured that his triumph has been invested with the fullest spiritual and ceremonial meaning. . . . He must know that his expenditures have gone for something, that the righteousness of his principles had been given its vindication. The assurance must be accorded him in terms that go well beyond the physical and objective; he must have ritual proofs. The conquered enemy must be prepared to give symbolic satisfaction as well as physical surrender . . . he must act out his defeat.[2]

According to this view, the victorious Republicans would not receive the assurance required for restoring southerners to national equality until they ceased to be southerners, admitted that all they believed and had fought for was wrong, that they repented in sackcloth and ashes for all their crimes, and were completely made over in mind and spirit to a prescribed pattern. Moreover, in complete sincerity, they must act out these changes by a complete repudiation not only of what had been southern mores and beliefs, but also of all that allegiance to the Confederacy had implied. Republican demands, of course, could not be stated in these blunt terms, perhaps not even considered in these terms (except by a few so-called Radicals), but they could be felt well down below the level of expression by the many. It would take some southern action, some expression of southern humility, some sign of a revolutionary change of heart, and a complete rejection of all old values as evidence of repentance.

At first war-weariness and the fact of peace kept what lay beneath the surface from rising to men's consciousness. Attitudes and demands would develop only when the real problem of adjustment was faced. Then, in the light of what the psychologist foretold, it might be of interest to note that in 1860 the South itself had made almost

---

[2] Eric L. McKitrick, *Andrew Johnson and Reconstruction* (Chicago, 1960), pp. 15–41.

these same demands for a revolutionary change of heart on the part of the North, and a guarantee of performance in regard to slavery. As a southern editor commented:

> Without a change of heart, radical and thorough, all guarantees which might be offered are not worth the paper on which they would be inscribed. As long as slavery is looked upon by the North with abhorrence; as long as the South is regarded as a mere slave-breeding, slave-driving community; as long as false and pernicious theories are cherished respecting the inherent equality and rights of every human being, there can be no satisfactory political union between the two sections.[3]

This was in fact asking northerners to cease being northern, to admit that they had ever been in the wrong and were now ready to repent. The northern answer had been a firm refusal. That was asking more than any northerner, perhaps any American, could grant. Now that the tables were turned would history repeat itself? Only two things might interfere: the temptations and opportunities now open to enjoy the fleshpots of the new industrial age might turn interests away from the South; and a strange American dislike for kicking those who are down might soften the blows—that is, after the victor had done a satisfactory amount of kicking. Both things would happen.

III

As for the South, all evidence seems to indicate that the same war-weariness, combined with a consciousness of total subjection, prevailed. The practiced eye and analytical mind of Whitelaw Reid saw clearly in the grievous hour of defeat the chastened southern spirit:

> The first feelings were those of baffled rage. Men who had fought four years for an idea smarted with actual anguish under the stroke which showed their utter failure. Then followed a sense of bewilderment and helplessness. . . . I speak

[3] Quoted in Avery Craven, *An Historian and the Civil War* (Chicago, 1964), p. 214.

advisedly, and after a careful review of our whole experience through the months of May and June, in all the leading centers of the Southern influence, when I say that the National Government could at the time have prescribed no condition for the return of the Rebel States which they would not have promptly accepted. They expected nothing; were prepared for the worst; would have been thankful for anything.[4]

Some southerners had already anticipated the tragic consequences of defeat. In his fast-day address to the Legislature of South Carolina in December 1863, the Rev. Benjamin M. Palmer told his listeners, "The contest in which we are embarked is a struggle for existence, in which defeat means simple destruction." The northern purpose all along, he said, had been to reduce the South to "a state of political vassalage" and with a "refinement of cruelty" and "with suicidal madness to overthrow her domestic economy.... To suppose the enmity of the North appeased just at the moment it is tasting the sweetness of revenge, is to give it credit for a generosity which would have forbidden it ever to arise.... Nothing is less desired by the dominant party of the North than the reconstruction of the old Union if the South shall ever lie at its feet as helpless prey, to be devoured at will."

Lincoln, too, had been thinking of what lay beyond the war. William B. Hesseltine, in *Lincoln's Plan of Reconstruction*, suggested that Lincoln foreshadowed his ideas when he secured satisfactory governors in Maryland, Kentucky, and Tennessee, and used military force to see that conditions remained satisfactory. As more and more areas fell under Union control, the President began to experiment with more elaborate procedures. In December 1863, he issued a proclamation offering pardon (with some exceptions) to any Confederate who would take an oath to support the Constitution of the United States. Moreover, when these loyal citizens in any state equaled one-tenth of the vote cast by the state in the 1860 presidential election,

---

[4] Whitelaw Reid, *After the War* (New York, 1866), pp. 206–207, 295–296.

they could establish a state government, abolish slavery, and then receive executive recognition. Yet Lincoln did not guarantee that Congress would recognize it.

Two nights before his assassination, Lincoln elaborated his ideas.

> We all agree that the seceded states, so called, are out of their proper practical relation with the Union, and that the sole object of the government, civil and military, in regard to those states, is to again get them into the proper practical relation. I believe that it is not only possible, but in fact easier, to do this without deciding or even considering whether these states have ever been out of the Union than with it. Finding themselves safely at home, it would be utterly immaterial whether they had even been abroad. Let us all join in doing the acts necessary to restoring the proper practical relations between these states and the Union, and each forever after innocently indulge his own opinion whether in doing the acts he brought the states from without into the Union, or only gave them proper assistance, they never having been out of it.[5]

Such a proposal for reconstruction was immediately rejected by other Republicans who, under the leadership of Henry Winter Davis, Benjamin F. Wade, Thaddeus Stevens, Charles Sumner, Zachariah Chandler, and George W. Julian, introduced their own plan. This, passed by Congress, left state reconstruction to a majority whose past conduct alone should be considered. Then, with the oath accepted, an appointed provisional governor could arrange a convention providing for a government in which no one who had held state or Confederate office under "rebel usurpation," or had borne arms against the United States, should vote or serve as a delegate. Slavery should be declared ended, and rebel debts repudiated; and

---

[5] Abraham Lincoln, *Collected Works* (New Brunswick, N.J., 1953–1955), vol. 8, pp. 403–405. It is interesting to note that Charles Sumner wrote on April 18, 1865, "It is probable that the policy towards leading rebels will be modified. President Lincoln was so essentially humane and gentle that he could not make up his mind to any severity, even to Jefferson Davis."—Edward L. Pierce (ed.), *Memoir and Letters of Charles Sumner* (Boston, 1877–1893), vol. 4, p. 239.

no persons who had held Confederate office should vote for or be a legislator or governor. Lincoln pocket-vetoed this so-called Wade-Davis Bill. With his appointment of military governors in different states, the reconstruction struggle began in earnest. The issue between "resumption" and "reconstruction" had been clearly revealed. Lincoln's death checked action temporarily, yet the Democratic *New York World* had written in September 1865 that "the real leaders" of the Republican party "see that unless the South can be trodden down and kept under foot for long years, or unless they can give the negroes the ballot, and control it in their hands, their present political supremacy is gone forever."

Charles Sumner completed the story in a letter to his colleague, Salmon P. Chase:

> On the main question [Lincoln] is reticent. But he saw with his own eyes at Richmond and Petersburg, that the only people who showed themselves were negroes. All others had fled or were retired in their houses. Never was I more convinced of the utter impossibility of any organization which is not founded on the votes of the negroes.

Thaddeus Stevens, who believed that "there can be no fanatics in the cause of genuine liberty," had already advocated the seizing of "every foot of land and every dollar of their property as our armies go along" and sending soldiers there "with arms in their hands to occupy the heritage of traitors." He now rejected Lincoln's program of reconstruction as absurd. The idea that the "rebel states," four years at war as a separate power and with no representation in Congress, were all the time still in the Union, did not make sense. It was "merely a pernicious abstraction." The South was conquered territory, and the Republican party could do with it whatever it saw fit.[6]

Some Republicans were evidently determined to have their "spiritual requirements," "the deeper satisfaction required," the necessary "vindication," and the "initial

[6] *Congressional Globe*, 37th Cong., 2d sess., p. 3127.

proof." The conquest of the southern spirit had begun. Southern people had not quite known before, nor did they now understand exactly what was required in conduct.

Republican "needs" certainly ran deeper than some immediate material gain. What the Republicans required as a party, and what they considered a national necessity, was both absolute security against reaction and clear evidence of a contrite spirit. The South restored and northern Democrats revived, with their old traditions and policies, would be a serious threat to party and nation. Fear, distrust, and uncertainty made a slow and careful procedure absolutely necessary. Yet a united effort in this direction would be difficult. Already members of Congress were being designated as "Radical Republicans" and "Conservative" Republicans." Furthermore, the new President, Andrew Johnson, was a southerner who had once been a Democrat. It would be well to watch him, even to distrust and to fear him. Nor was it clear as yet who was to shape the reconstruction program. Lincoln had taken the initiative, but opposition had already appeared. With the Executive, the South, the Democratic party, and even the Supreme Court able and willing to thwart any program vital to Republican control, the Radicals were in no mood to take chances.

Opposition to Lincoln's reconstruction efforts began at once. To grant self-rule to a southern state without requiring solid guaranty of equal Negro rights was to return to 1860. It was giving the states "the power to prevent every colored man from voting," said the *Boston Commonwealth*, "and in the present state of public opinion in all the slave States, *they will prevent it*. . . . Besides being a burlesque upon popular sovereignty, the thing is impossible." Wendell Phillips was more specific:

> Never will this nation be a unit until every class God has made, from the lakes to the Gulf, has its ballot to protect itself. . . . The negro has earned land, education, rights. Before we leave him, we ought to leave him on his own soil, in his own house, with the right to the ballot and the schoolhouse within reach. Unless we have done it, the North has let the cunning of politics filch the fruits of this war.

Thaddeus Stevens told the House that he was unable to comprehend "the idea that the loyal citizens, though few, are the State, and in the State municipalities may overrule and govern the disloyal millions. . . . When the doctrine that the *quality* and not the *number* of voters is to decide the right to govern, then we no longer have a republic, but the worst form of despotism." [7]

It is thus clear that no program for reconstructing the nation had been accepted as yet. It is equally clear that certain unanswered questions would have to be faced sooner or later: Had the southern states been out of the Union? If so, had they committed suicide by seceding? Were they now simply conquered territories? Regarding their status, who was to decide—the Executive? the Congress? the Court? What about the Negro, his rights and his place in the nation's future life? Should reconstruction aim only at restoring the Union, or should it include a social reordering that would bring our national professions and practices closer together?

In 1860 the democratic process had broken down, and civil war had come because men had been unable to solve the problem of peaceful coexistence. After four bloody years, could they expect to do any better?

[7] *Boston Commonwealth*, Jan. 1, 1864, May 6, 1865; *New York Tribune*, Dec. 25, 1863; *The Liberator*, Jan. 1, 1864; *New York Herald*, Dec. 13, 1865.

CHAPTER

7

PRESIDENTIAL RECONSTRUCTION BEGINS

I

As the war was coming to an end, Lincoln began experimenting with his plan for quick reconstruction. In southern states where federal troops had established a firm foothold, he appointed military governors who were to encourage and organize Union sentiment and bring loyal governments into being under his 10 percent proposal. In this way he soon had military governors at work in Tennessee, Arkansas, and Louisiana. He had no final, fixed program; he was just experimenting. He told his officials in Louisiana, which was to serve as a test case, to follow the forms of law as far as convenient, but at all events to get the expression of loyalty from the largest number of people possible. The situation was, he said, "so new and unprecedented . . . that no exclusive and inflexible plan can be prescribed as to details and collaterals."

So uncertain was Lincoln of the final course to be followed that he frankly said that if any loyal southern state wished to follow the Wade-Davis procedure (which he had pocket-vetoed), he would be "fully satisfied." He evidently would have one plan for one state, a different plan for another state, as practical circumstances dictated.

Any attempt to echo what was in Lincoln's mind is, of course, only conjecture. As an astute politician, he may have realized that his party had been, and probably still would be, a minority party when the nation resumed a normal course. By a quick and generous restoration of the southern states, he may have been aiming at the building of a southern Republican wing on old Whig foundations. He may have been only expressing the deep human qualities which were part of a man to whom war had brought much of sorrow but little of hatred.

At any rate, under his 10 percent plan reconstruction in Louisiana proceeded rapidly. The test oath was administered, a convention was called, a constitution was formed prohibiting slavery, and a governor and United States senators were chosen. Internal affairs were left largely to the people, yet Lincoln suggested to Governor Michael Hahn that the vote be given to qualified Negroes. He noted that only the United States Senate had the right to decide on the admission of the Louisiana senators. This matter was, therefore, referred to the Senate Judiciary Committee. On February 17, its chairman, Lyman Trumbull, reported a joint resolution: "That the United States do hereby recognize the government of the State of Louisiana as a legitimate government of the said state and entitled to the guarantees and all other rights of a State Government under the Constitution of the United States."

Charles Sumner, who had been demanding the vote for all Negroes, bitterly opposed this resolution and started a filibuster to prevent its adoption. Caught with the necessity of passing an army and navy bill, the Senate yielded and the resolution was set aside. Louisiana would have to wait.

After much confusion and uncertainty, both Tennessee and Arkansas also held conventions and framed constitutions abolishing slavery and repudiating secession. The government of Virginia under Francis Harrison Pierpont was recognized as the legitimate government of that state. With Lincoln's death and with growing resistance in Congress, none of these three states was admitted. Further steps toward reconstruction thus fell to President Andrew Johnson, who came from a state not yet a member of the Union. It should be noted that many who had opposed Lincoln's southern experiments welcomed Johnson's accession to the Presidency. They agreed with Indiana Senator George W. Julian that Lincoln's removal "would prove a godsend to the country." They had already met to urge a new cabinet and "a line of policy less conciliatory" than that of Mr. Lincoln, "whose tenderness to the Rebels" and views on reconstruction were as "distasteful as possible."

Historians have generally been reluctant to evaluate Lincoln's reconstruction efforts. They were never brought to a final test, nor did they represent his final thinking on the whole subject. Yet even if we view Lincoln's efforts at reconstruction simply as experiments and not as parts of a well thought-out plan, one simple fact remains: although Lincoln had an efficient army to carry out his program, he failed completely.

Not a single state was brought back into the Union and the bitterness and confusion—both North and South—was increased. Granting Lincoln all the qualities of diplomacy, adroitness, and ability to get along with others, which supposedly would have prevented all that subsequently happened, he still failed to accomplish anything and, at the same time, created enemies in his own party who rejoiced at his death far more than did intelligent southerners.

Why did Lincoln fail so completely and why this angry

opposition? The answer seems to lie in the fact that he was too conservative to satisfy the deep but as yet unexpressed demands of his party for "security" and "repentance." [1] In his first message to Congress in December 1861, he had talked of compensation for states that freed their slaves. In his message of December 1, 1862, he had proposed an elaborate plan for ending the war by "delivering" interest-bearing government bonds to any state that would free its slaves, immediately or gradually, up to the first day of January 1900. In each case Lincoln favored colonizing the freed Negroes "at some place, or places, in a climate congenial to them." In his muchquoted letter of August 1864 to Charles D. Robinson (written but not sent), Lincoln reaffirmed his willingness to save the Union "without freeing any slave" if necessary. He then went on to assert that his statement that "reunion and abandonment of slavery would be considered, if offered" was not "saying that nothing *else* or *less* would be considered." He closed the letter by commenting that "if Jefferson Davis wishes, for himself, or for the benefit of his friends at the North, to know what I would do if he were to offer peace and re-union, saying nothing about slavery, let him try me." [2]

All this was consistent with Lincoln's declaration that the war was being waged solely for the purpose of saving the Union. He held firmly to the constitutional theory that secession was impossible and that no southern state had ever been out of the Union. It had only been out of its "proper practical relation" to it. He had once said that he "thought the act of secession" was "legally nothing and needs no repealing." He had even been a bit lax about the loyalty oaths, advising one official to have the loyal as well as the disloyal take them because it "did not hurt them" and would swell the aggregate number required for this

---

[1] James D. B. DeBow had observed, "I may *think* treason any day of the year, but without an *overt act*, there can be no traitor."

[2] Abraham Lincoln, *Collected Works* (New Brunswick, N.J., 1953–1955), vol. 7, pp. 499–501.

purpose. So when a reasonable number of the citizens of a state had taken the oath, incorporated into its constitution the fallacy of secession, accepted the abolition of slavery, perhaps given deserving Negroes the franchise and every chance for an education, renounced Confederate debts, and ratified the Thirteenth Amendment, it should resume its full rights as a state in the Union.

Two things in such a program were lacking. It did not provide adequate punishment for "unrepentant rebels," and it did not offer sufficient guaranty of justice and equality for the Negro. Lincoln had not learned to hate. He most certainly lagged far behind the "radical" element of his party in racial attitudes. He had seemingly accepted conditionally the existing system when he said that if the new state governments "recognized and declared [the freedmen's] permanent freedom, [and] provided for their education," the Executive would not object, "as a temporary arrangement," to "their present condition as a laboring, landless, and homeless class." Furthermore, he had earlier remarked that he did not favor "bringing about in any way the social and political equality of the white and black races . . . qualifying them to hold office, nor to intermarry with the white people. . . ." He had said repeatedly that he believed there were physical differences which would "forever forbid the two races living together on terms of social and political equality." [3]

Lincoln had never in his own state attempted to remove the bar against Negroes voting, holding office, or attending the public schools. He had checked the army officers who had attempted to free the slaves in conquered areas, and, at all times, he had advocated the removal of the Negro, when freed, from the United States. He had never gone further than to say that slavery was morally wrong and that the Negro had a right to eat the bread his labor created. Lincoln would free him from slavery and grant

---

[3] In debate with Stephen A. Douglas. See Paul M. Angle (ed.), *Created Equal: The Complete Lincoln and Douglas Debates of 1858* (Chicago, 1958), pp. 39–42.

him all the rights of a human being; but beyond that he conceded no plans for a social revolution. He had not even carried out the seizure of Confederate lands that the confiscation acts of 1861–1862 had authorized. Nor had Lincoln required the southern people either to humiliate themselves or to undergo a complete social and intellectual revolution. He had ignored Congress, and, as the nation's executive, he had attempted to secure a quick return to normalcy in any state where conditions permitted. Lincoln's purpose was to put an end to bloodshed and to resume a national life. In other words, Lincoln had acted like a practical, pragmatic American politician taking what could intelligently be got. On the grounds that it was essential to maintain state identity in reconstruction, he even rejected Stanton's proposal to combine Virginia and North Carolina into a single military district. As one critic wrote: "If there was a grievous fault in Mr. Lincoln's administration it was in the fostering of enemies, and the discarding of friends . . . in fattening rebels and starving those who had elevated him to power." This he thought had been carried to the point where rebellion had been made respectable. Lincoln had attempted the impossible. He had tried to run "the Train of Freedom with slavery conductors . . . giving them plenty of money if they would not smash the cars." The only true policy of government, he insisted, was "to the victors belong the control," and no man should be employed unless known "as the enemy of the rebellion." Only then would the nation be entirely safe.

II

How each and all of these things contributed to Lincoln's failure would become clear only when Andrew Johnson, as President, took over the job with the approval of those who opposed Lincoln. These two men had much in common yet differed radically in personality. Lincoln had learned to work with others; Johnson had learned only to oppose. Yet now all responsibility for a permanent reconstruction fell to Johnson. Lincoln had been experimenting before the war ended. Johnson would be required to offer a definite plan, to live under Lincoln's shadow and to suffer from comparisons at every step with a Lincoln becoming more mythical with each day of martyrdom. Johnson would be forced to adopt as his own what he believed was Lincoln's program. He would even have to work with what had been Lincoln's cabinet. He could not escape.

As a person Johnson was rough, rugged, honest, blunt, and as stubborn as the East Tennessee that had shaped him. He was strictly a self-made man, proud of his accomplishments, and intensely dedicated to the democratic institutions that had enabled him to rise from lowly beginning to marked success. Charles Dickens thought that his face indicated "courage, watchfulness, certainly strength of purpose." In manners, he had acquired a degree of polish and was always neat in person and dress, as might become a tailor by trade. But it was a polish and a poise acquired, and won through conscious effort. Under pressure, he could quickly revert to the crude and violent in both speech and action. Johnson was never quite sure of himself, always more sensitive than necessary, always in danger of losing his acquired surface qualities. He was completely lacking in a sense of humor. He was always in dead earnest. Moreover, Johnson was ever conscious of his humble origins and always talking about them.

Johnson was southern-born in common man's North Carolina. His parents were poor but respectable and well liked. His father had lost his life from exposure in rescuing two men from drowning, and his mother had found it difficult to support her little family. At fourteen Andrew was apprenticed to a local tailor, to whom his older brother William had earlier been apprenticed. In the next two years, he apparently acquired some skill as a tailor, but after getting into difficulty with some neighbors, he and his brother ran away. Mr. Selby, the tailor, inserted an advertisement in the Raleigh newspaper offering a $10 reward for capture of the fleshy, freckled-faced, light-haired, fair-complexioned Andrew. He was evidently glad to be rid of William, whom he described as dark in most ways, including habits. Selby certainly did not know his apprentices well, for his descriptions of their physical appearances were reversed.

The boys were not captured, but Andrew later, and of his own free will, returned to Raleigh, only to find both Selby and his shop gone. He then set out for Tennessee as thousands were doing, and at the age of eighteen entered the little town of Greeneville. There he set up his tailor shop, married the girl who improved his ability at writing, and began broadening his understanding by having the newspapers read to him as he sat cross-legged plying his needle. He even pushed himself into the debating societies of two little colleges nearby.

Gradually Johnson's shop became the center of gatherings to discuss and argue the issues of the day. As alderman in Greeneville, he began a political career that had run to the state legislature, the U.S. House of Representatives, the governorship of Tennessee, the U.S. Senate, and the Vice-Presidency of the United States. It was a course in which every step was a bitter fight. There were three Tennessees, with East Tennessee the least prosperous, the most lacking in culture, and the most democratic. It always had to fight bitterly for everything it wanted and for every value it held. The aristocratic planters on the limestone soils about Nashville in the center, and the new cotton and tobacco men to the west, where Memphis looked down the Mississippi, viewed the lesser men of East Tennessee with condescension and contempt. It took courage for a poor man from East Tennessee to make headway against entrenched interests and superior advantages. Hard blows had to be taken and returned. A sharp tongue capable of rough words was required, and sometimes resort to physical force. It was an uncompromising battle all the way. One never yielded an inch. It was always a personal matter: a personal triumph or a personal defeat.

For this reason, Johnson was incapable of cooperation.

His experience had always been one of combating opposition. He took his stand and expected to be attacked or at least opposed. To defend a position and to combat opponents was all he knew, all he expected. A capacity for consulting, adjusting, yielding, or compromising was almost lacking. He could only defend a position taken and doggedly maintain that it was sound and right. To stand alone was a virtue.

The same conditions that fixed Johnson's personality also fixed his political principles. His fight (and it was always a fight) was with, and for, common men against what he called "the stuck-up aristocrats" who were running the country. He would be the successor to Andrew Jackson. He would secure economy in government, build public schools, and distribute the public lands as homes for common men. Isham Harris, one of his opponents, once commented that if Johnson had been a snake, he would lie in the grass to bite the heels of rich men's children.

Johnson was a Democrat, especially after 1840, but he was too independent, too much Andrew Johnson, to wear party harness well. His respect for the Constitution as he interpreted it was proverbial, and this determined, to a degree, his attitude toward the Negro and slavery. He accepted slavery's rights where the institution legally existed, disliked slaveholders thoroughly, viewed the Negro as an inferior, and had no use whatsoever for abolitionists. To him, John Brown was simply a murderer.

Few knew Johnson intimately. They saw him primarily as a sincere, hard-working man, careful of details but too narrow to be a statesman, much less a pragmatic politician.

He was without question an ardent Union man, as were most of those who lived in that halfway house between East and West. He viewed the United States as the place where common men might be free and have the chance that he himself had had. He had stood by the Union in 1860 and talked of the "hell-born" and "hell-bound" secessionists. They must not be allowed to destroy the people's government. As he declared, he would "defend and maintain the supremacy of the Constitution . . . preserve the Union with all the dignity, equality, and rights of the States unimpaired. . . ."

So in 1860 Johnson returned to East Tennessee to fight for the Union, then back to the Senate "bereft of a state," for Tennessee had seceded. As parts of Tennessee were cleared, Lincoln appointed him war governor of Tennessee on the firing line where danger was real, where stubborn courage was demanded. When Lincoln invited Johnson to be his running mate in 1864 on the Union ticket, Johnson could say—on somewhat dubious grounds —that Tennessee was now reclaimed and ready to resume its place in the Union.

III

Such was the man whom the Union ticket had made Vice-President and whom an assassin now made President of the United States. He was, as his career to date indicated, no simple personality. There were many contradictions here—conflicting elements, much strength, much weakness, and now, much uncertainty. He was finding his way and looking for advice. He was willing to listen, and in the present conflict of opinion on reconstruction men with every shade of opinion found some excuse for talking with him. Each, it seems, came away quite certain that the President agreed with him. This was probably because most of his visitors came with such fixed ideas of what should be done that they could not conceive of rejection. It was Gideon Welles, Secretary of the Navy, who said that unless Johnson emphatically disagreed with some opinion, he was inclined to listen and say nothing. "They make statements themselves which he does not deny and dispute, and he is consequently represented as entertaining the views of his auditor or adviser." This was especially true of Charles Sumner.[4]

[4] Writing to F. W. Bird, April 25, 1865, Sumner reported that he "had seen a good deal" of Johnson and found his manner "ex-

At any rate, some were convinced that Johnson intended to carry out Lincoln's "program," that he considered himself the trustee of Lincoln's policies. Others were emphatically saying that he would have none of it, and would go the whole way, hang Davis and Lee, expatriate some, disfranchise the rest and teach them that "treason is a crime." Sumner, Wade, Stevens, and Chase were therefore certain the Negro would be given the vote and the South properly punished.

At first it seemed that the "radicals" were right. Johnson's remarks to Governor Oliver P. Morton of Indiana were widely circulated as proof:

> The time has arrived when the American people should understand what crime is, and that it should be punished, and its penalties enforced and inflicted. . . . If you take the life of one individual for the murder of another, and believe that his property should be confiscated, what should be done with one who is trying to assassinate the nation? Treason must be made odious . . . traitors must be punished and impoverished . . . their social power must be destroyed. I say, as to the leaders, punishment. I say leniency, conciliation and amnesty to the thousands whom they have misled and deceived.

On another occasion Johnson said:

> I shall go to my grave with the firm belief that Davis, Cobb, Toombs, and a few others of the arch-conspirators and traitors should have been tried, convicted, and hanged for treason. . . . If it was the last act of my life I'd hang Jeff Davis as an example. I'd show coming generations that, while rebellion was too popular a revolt to punish many who participated in it, treason should be made odious and arch-traitors should be punished.

---

cellent" and even "sympathetic." He was "well disposed" regarding negro suffrage." On May 1, Sumner reported "a long conversation" with Johnson on "the theme" of "justice to the colored race, stating that the President "accepted this idea completely" and said "that there is no difference between us."—Edward L. Pierce (ed.), *Memoir and Letters of Charles Sumner* (Boston, 1877–1893), vol. 4, pp. 241–242.

As he then continued, it seemed almost like another man talking:

> ... if rebellion had ... set aside the machinery of the state for a time, there stands a great law to remove the paralysis and neutralize it, and put it on its feet again. ... Life breath has been only suspended, and it is a high constitutional obligation with them to secure each of those States in the possession of enjoyment of a republican form of government. ... I care not how small the number of Union men, if enough to man the ship of state, I hold it, I say, a high duty to protect and secure to them a republican form of government.

Here was the old Tennessee Johnson in a fighting mood against vile enemies. Here was the Johnson who believed that Abraham Lincoln "was the greatest American that has ever lived." He had already begun to find out what it meant to be the President of the United States and not just Andrew Johnson of East Tennessee. He was also beginning to learn that the possession of power carries with it responsibility. He was, in one way, a man without a party. He had been a Democrat all his life but now he owed his position to a hybrid political organization that functioned through Republican party machinery. It was a period, moreover, when both the Democrats and the Republicans were beginning to assert themselves again as parties—a time when their basic political aims and philosophies would give conflicting approaches to the reconstruction of the South, as they had to the war.

IV

The temptation to compare Andrew Johnson with Abraham Lincoln is almost irresistible and seldom resisted. Yet the dice are so heavily loaded in Lincoln's favor that simple justice is seldom done. The two were so much alike in origin, ambition, devotion to principles and common men that the striking difference in their personalities tends to dwarf the one and magnify the other. One lived to fail; the other died to achieve unblemished success. One worked in an atmosphere of hatred, fear, and distrust in which meanness and distortion were as common as virtue and truth, and where the end was failure. The other played his troubled part where patriotism, noble ideals, and sacrifice brought a great victory. The one came to office through the regular democratic political process; the other inherited his office through pure chance. Comparisons, in this case, are at best odious. Nor is there profit in speculating on what Lincoln might have done had he lived. Reconstruction could not be delayed, and Andrew Johnson, whatever his qualifications, had to assume the responsibility.

CHAPTER

8

JOHNSON "RESUMES"

I

In his first days as President, Andrew Johnson only talked and listened. His visitors seem to have been largely, but not entirely, those who were opposed to Lincoln's reconstruction program—men such as Charles Sumner and Salmon P. Chase who were particularly interested in securing the vote for the Negro. Each visitor had the impression that Johnson was in agreement with his views. Secretary of the Navy Welles noted that Johnson listened more than he talked and that his silence was often interpreted as approval, when it was not so necessarily.

At any rate, when Johnson began to act, it soon became apparent that he was in the main following—or trying to follow—Lincoln rather than those who had opposed him. Johnson no longer insisted that "traitors should take a back seat in the work of restoration." He seemed to have forgotten that he had once emphatically stated that the traitor had ceased to be a citizen and had forfeited his right to vote when he sought to destroy our government, "and [that] it was his [Johnson's] judgment that such a man should be subjected to a severe ordeal before he is restored to citizenship." He had even said that "their great plantations might be seized and divided into small farms, and be sold to honest, industrious men."

Neither the "severe ordeal" before the granting of citizenship nor the confiscation of property had been a part of Lincoln's efforts as applied to Louisiana, Tennessee, and Arkansas. So if Johnson were to proceed from the point where Lincoln left off, charges of betrayal would be added to the already angry opposition that Lincoln himself had faced. The disagreement forecast in the Wade-Davis Bill would fall upon Johnson with added force.

Here the question as to whether Lincoln really had a program becomes important. He had most certainly adopted a few general principles that looked forward to the rapid return of the southern states to their normal place in the Union. However, his methods had varied according to each situation, and he was constantly suggesting new approaches. Nothing was fixed or frozen. Johnson would therefore be forced to create a program out of considerable confusion. He began, on May 29, 1865, by issuing a Proclamation of Amnesty. In it he accepted Lincoln's purpose "to induce all persons to return to their loyalty and to restore the authority of the United States" so that peace, order, and freedom might be established.

For these purposes he granted to "all persons who have directly participated in the existing rebellion . . . amnesty and pardon, with restoration of all rights of property, except as to slaves" or "where legal proceeding . . . providing for confiscation of persons engaged in rebellion" had already been instituted.

This pardon and restoration was granted on condition that each person take an oath to "henceforth faithfully support, protect and defend the Constitution of the United States and the Union of the states thereunder, and abide by and faithfully support all laws and proclamations which have been made during the existing rebellion with reference to the emancipation of slaves."

From the benefits of this document Johnson exempted all those, civil and military, who had served the Confederacy as officers or who had left the service of the United States to aid the rebellion. To these were added a long list of others who might have rendered significant service to the Confederacy or done damage to the Union. The proclamation ended by excluding any person who had in 1860 owned property with a taxable value of over $20,000 and who had voluntarily participated in the rebellion. This was a blow at the hated planter aristocracy. With this addition, a majority of persons who had been of any public or private importance in the antebellum South were excluded or forced to seek a special pardon from the President himself.

Johnson's emphasis on oaths and pardons grew out of his firm constitutional theory that, as he stated, "there is no such thing as reconstruction. These states have not gone out of the Union." The citizens alone were the guilty ones. Their oaths and his pardon constituted the basic steps to what he now called "restoration." Some believe that it was here that Johnson's failure began—that the oath and the pardon, as the only required evidence of repentance, were his undoing.

II

Having taken care of questions of individual loyalty, Johnson turned to the institutional side of restoration. Since those who would be punished were eliminated and the remainder had taken an oath of loyalty and been pardoned, it was only necessary for the resumption of statehood that a provisional governor be appointed, a constitutional convention called to correct past errors and to accept the new requirements, a legislature elected, and state officials chosen. Then reconstruction would be completed and the Union resumed.

To have done otherwise would have required a different legal position regarding secession and civil war. Johnson would have been forced to say that the states had committed suicide or that they had been what southerners claimed, a separate nation, which now, in defeat, was conquered territory. Under either of these approaches the South could be dealt with as severely and as arbitrarily as the victorious North chose. A social and economic revolution could be demanded that would eliminate all restraints which accompanied the idea that the southern states were still states simply out of their "proper practical relation to Union," as Lincoln had said.

The long recess of Congress, which did not end until December 1865, permitted Johnson to go ahead on Lincoln's assumption that it was the President's business, as chief executive and commander of the army and navy, to frame and carry out the work of organizing and restoring the southern states and the Union. He began with North Carolina, his native state.

On May 29, 1865, he issued a proclamation stating that the Constitution guaranteed to every state in the Union a republican form of government. Since the rebellion, waged "in the most violent and revolting form," had now been almost entirely overcome and had left the people of North Carolina without any civil government, he as President was "bound by solemn oath to take care that the law be faithfully executed and the people of North Carolina secure the enjoyment of a republican form of government."

Therefore, "in obedience to the high and solemn duties imposed on him by the Constitution," Johnson appointed William W. Holden provisional governor of North Carolina. "At the earliest practicable period," Holden was to prescribe such rules and regulation as were necessary and proper for convening a convention of delegates to be chosen by the loyal people for the purpose of altering or amending their existing constitution. These delegates would have "authority to exercise within the state all powers necessary and proper to enable such loyal people to restore their state to its Constitutional relations to the Federal Government." They would recommend a republican form of government and thus ensure its people against invasion, insurrection, and domestic violence.

Then followed the provision that all persons chosen to the convention must have taken the May 29, 1865, oath of amnesty, and have been qualified voters by the federal and state laws in force before May 20, 1861 (the date of North Carolina's secession). The state legislature should then assume its usual functions.

The military commander of the department and other federal officials were directed to assist in establishing the normal federal postal, judiciary, taxation, and all other governmental machinery in the state. Johnson also insisted that the "resuming" state repeal secession, repudiate Confederate debts, and ratify the Thirteenth Amendment. He brought pressure for each of these where necessary.

It should be noted that with all his supposed constitutional scruples Johnson did not leave the "sovereign state" officials to go their own way. He required them to meet certain conditions and he imposed his own authority when they did not comply. He was not accepting his own theory of their status.[1]

What is even more significant about Johnson's program for reconstructing the South is that it aimed only at political restoration. The southern people themselves were permitted to carry out the program.

In the next few months the same process was extended to Mississippi, Georgia, Texas, Alabama, South Carolina, and Florida. Johnson did suggest to Governor William L. Sharkey of Mississippi that certain Negroes be given the vote, but Sharkey alone was left to decide.

---

[1] J. G. de Roulhac Hamilton, *Reconstruction in North Carolina* (New York, 1914), pp. 106–147.

If you could extend the elective franchise to all persons of color who can read the Constitution of the United States in English and write their names, and to all persons of color who own real-estate valued at not less than $250 and pay taxes thereon, you would completely disarm the adversary and set an example the other states will follow. This you can do with perfect safety, and you would thus place Southern States in reference to free persons of color upon the same basis with the free states. . . . And as a consequence the radicals . . . will be completely foiled.

It was a suggestion, not a command.

III

When Congress met in December, 1865, Johnson could announce:

I have . . . gradually and quietly and by almost imperceptible steps, sought to restore the rightful energy of the General Government and of the States. To that end, provisional governors have been appointed for the states, conventions called, governors elected, legislatures assembled, and senators and representatives chosen to the Congress of the United States.

He advised the southern senators and representatives not to apply until after Congress had organized. He then added that courts of the United States had been reopened so that the laws of the United States could be enforced through their agency. Blockages had been removed, custom houses re-established, postal service restored, and the Thirteenth Amendment abolishing slavery ratified by "each one of these states." All had gone better than could possibly have been expected.

Had reconstruction been only a problem of restoring the Union and bringing peace to a war-weary people, Andrew Johnson's report would have indicated real progress. Under existing conditions it served only to show that the war had become the carrier of a social, political, and moral revolution and had left its early impulses far behind. The great masses may have gladly seen the army disbanded and looked forward to a quick return to normal living, but there were persons in Congress and out who would not believe the war had come to an end until those who had caused it were adequately punished, the Negro set on the road to first-class citizenship, and the Republican party assured of perpetual dominance. This group regarded Johnson's report as merely a statement of an unsuccessful experiment. As early as May 5, 1865, *The Independent*, which spoke for what came to be called the Radical Republicans in Congress, was asserting:

> There is one, and only one, sure and safe policy for the immediate future, namely: *the North must remain the absolute Dictator of the Republic until the spirit of the North shall become the spirit of the whole country.* . . . The South is still unpurged of her treason. Prostrate in the dust she is no less a traitor at this hour than when her head was erect. . . . They cannot be trusted with authority over their former slaves: they cannot be trusted with authority over the re-cemented Republic. . . . The only hope for the South is to give the ballot to the Negro and in denying it to the rebels.

In like spirit George W. Julian of Indiana would "indict, convict and hang Jefferson Davis in the name of God; as for Robert E. Lee, unmolested in Virginia, hang him too. And stop there? Not at all. I would hang liberally while I had my hand in." Senator Benjamin F. Wade of Ohio suggested that "if the negroes by insurrection could contrive to slay one-half of the Southern whites, the remaining half would then hold them in respect and treat them with justice." Thaddeus Stevens would wipe out southern state lines and reduce the section to a territory where rebels would learn to practice justice to all men. Charles Sumner would seize all rebel property and distribute it to the Negroes, give them the vote, and let them rule the section.

On the other hand, such moderates as James R. Doolittle of Wisconsin, James Dixon of Connecticut, and Edgar Cowan of Pennsylvania backed Johnson's program even in the face of party pressure. William P. Fessenden of Maine, John Sherman of Ohio, James W. Grimes of Iowa, and others asked only for cooperation and enough balance to keep their party in control and the nation on the right course.

Republican attitudes acceptable to a working majority would thus emerge gradually—vague and uncertain at first, but becoming increasingly harsh under Andrew Johnson's refusal to cooperate or to yield, and under a growing inclination of southerners to look after their own interests. Only when it became politically necessary did the Republicans close ranks and vote as Republicans because they were Republicans. Differences among members that might have led to compromise were then forgotten and the more "radical," or "realistic," element permitted to have its way.

The course that the Republican party traveled from cooperation to an open break with President Johnson is not clear. Most Republicans had realized from the first that nothing would ever be the same again. They had assumed a heavy moral responsibility, but they did not know until faced with reality what they meant by "security," "southern humility," "a change of heart," and "southern repentence." These were very uncertain terms. The South in turn never knew exactly what was being demanded. It acted accordingly. It was not until President Johnson had taken the initiative, and the South had responded, that the Republicans as a party gradually realized what they had, perhaps from the beginning, required of the South and what they in the end would take. That turned the quarrel into one between the Republican Congress and the President. It made the South and the President one—perhaps even the President and the Democratic party one.

IV

Meanwhile much had been going on behind the scenes to complicate matters. William H. Seward, with his mind on the political future, had in 1864 and 1865 organized a powerful lobby to forward adoption of the Thirteenth Amendment and the elimination of slavery. He had converted a number of conservative Democrats to the cause and had taken steps to cement and perpetuate the alliance of conservatives from both parties, especially in New York. This faction had served Lincoln well in the election of 1864, and it now gave support to Johnson's reconstruction efforts. The idea of a new conservative party in which Seward would play a dominant role was clearly evident. Johnson, of course, would be its figurehead.[2]

The Francis Preston Blair family, meanwhile, was back in the Democratic fold and had developed similar ideas for a new party. It, too, courted Johnson and became an open rival of the Seward-Weed group for his support. Together they represented a political effort to build a new conservative party in which Republicans and Democrats would fuse for the purpose of pushing the Radical Republicans aside. Three things stood in their way: Johnson did not respond openly; he would not remove such critics as Secretary of War Edwin M. Stanton or limit his appointments to conservatives. Either Johnson was too lacking in decisiveness or too clever a politician to make the break. Both reasons have been offered for his failure to act and for the ambiguity in what he said. Was he, too, in his own way, playing a clever game to create and lead a new party in the next election? Or was he just a weak and vacillating person possessed only of stubbornness and a liking for flattery? Both explanations have been given. Did it not, however, all add up to a revival of Democratic influence and a quick return of a nonrepentant south unless Republicans bestirred themselves? Were not the great moral obligations involved being ignored?

V

Republicans now began to see that the old political conflict with the Democrats still existed. They saw again the South which they feared and distrusted being restored to national life with its attitudes toward the Negro still those born of slavery. They realized that economic interests

[2] LaWanda and John H. Cox, *Politics, Principle, and Prejudice, 1865–1866* (New York, 1963), pp. 1–30.

which measured the difference between progress and backwardness were also at stake. The Declaration of Independence, which they had brought back into American life, was again being pushed aside. They therefore began to understand what they wanted reconstruction to do. It must include a social revolution that would give the Negro security in southern life and gain his support for the Republican party. Johnson and the Democrats were clearing the air. It was not just the Negro, as some say; it was the whole modern world that must be made secure. The Negro was only one item in it, but just now the important one. Under such conditions, Republicans would find themselves more united than even they suspected.

VI

In 1865 the southerner represented the only white American who had ever known total defeat, absolute poverty, and subjection to an armed enemy. This was a new and unprecedented American experience. The southerner, both as an individual and as a member of a "conquered nation," had to learn what was expected of him. He, too, had a very vague notion of the meaning of the words being used by the Republicans. He did not interpret them as requiring a social and economic revolution. He did accept the fact that he had been conquered by superior numbers and resources, but he was certain that he had fought well for a cause which he had thought worthy. He would accept it as a lost cause and meet the demands of the victor, though he was not inclined to grovel in the dust. He was not acting in a spirit of defiance; like any American, he felt awkward at playing humble and repentant. He was not sure he was either.

Furthermore, his people were more sharply divided in attitude than were the Republicans. They were badly divided before, during, and now after the war. There was in reality no South, nor was there one attitude. Much debate would ensue among southerners as to what defeat entailed, how to deal with the Negro, what to do about

Confederate debts, and how to proceed with economic recovery. Conservative and radical opinions were expressed, as might be expected in any assembly of Americans anywhere, at any time. But in this case, as a people recently in rebellion and now totally defeated, did they have the right to opinions that ran counter to those of the North? Such opinions, even if held only by a few, sounded like defiance, insolence, and anything but "repentance." As Judge J. W. C. Watson told the Mississippi convention delegates, they were conquered people and had no right to dictate terms. "Gentlemen talk as if we had a choice," said another Mississippian, "but we have no choice. . . . The only course we can pursue is that dictated to us by the powers at Washington. . . ." A compatriot added, "As men of sense let us endeavor to remedy what we can alter, and gather together whatever may tend to palliate our misfortunes." They had no right to quibble over things. Yet that was what some were doing while a suspicious North listened. They did not come clean on the repudiation of Confederate debts, the repeal of secession, the abolition of slavery, or the ratification of the Thirteenth Amendment. Johnson had to bring pressure to end their debates.

The economic situation, however, was something else. In some places people were starving. Delay was impossible; some economic stability was absolutely and immediately necessary. A crop had to be raised and sold before any recovery was possible. Yet this involved the most important and the most emotion-charged issue in all reconstruction—the southern belief in Negro inferiority and the need for rigid control for efficiency. Most Republicans united in opposition to this attitude.

For solution of this problem, either the North or the South would have to undergo a psychological revolution! A social, economic, and intellectual revolution was also involved, yet few had been thinking in terms of revolution. Perhaps security required it. Perhaps repentance did also.

9

THE SOUTHERN STATES RESUME

I

Under Johnson's "provisional governors" the southern states began the task of carrying out the President's plan for "restoration" amid difficult circumstances. In the states three different authorities were now exercising a degree of control. Besides the newly appointed provisional governors, there was the army, with its own acting governors who had already taken a hand in running civil affairs, and the Freedmen's Bureau, established March 3, 1864, to feed and care for the refugees who had drifted along with the army, and to take charge of lands abandoned by the owners as they served the Confederacy or had fled before the approaching invaders. By its right to seize property under the Confiscation Acts, and to settle refugees thereon, the Bureau had an unusual influence with the Negroes.

Under such a distribution of powers, conflict of authority was inevitable. The situation was made even more difficult because at no time did there exist a clear understanding of just what the Republicans of the North demanded of the South. The people knew in a general way what Johnson had requested, and he had encouraged them to think that he spoke with authority for the nation. It was soon clear, however, that he spoke only for himself and that he did not have the undivided support of Congress. Moreover, it was increasingly apparent that the Republicans did not agree among themselves. It took considerable time and a lot of pounding from Thaddeus Stevens and Charles Sumner to pull them away from Johnson. As long as things remained fluid and what Johnson was doing could be considered an experiment, the more conservative members would avoid a dangerous split in the party. Until the Republicans reached some agreement on basic demands, or until developments in the South under Johnson's plan ran counter to their deeper feelings, there was no reason to see Johnson and the South on one side, and the Republican party in Congress on the other.[1]

The difficulty of "restoration" increased at this time also because of the quality of the individuals involved. The work of reconstruction was now strictly in Andrew Johnson's hands. As President, he had taken charge, and his personality became an important factor. Few have ever questioned Johnson's honesty or his courage, but even these qualities in a proud, stubborn, sensitive man did not always serve a situation where tact, firmness, and common sense were essential. Moreover, opposition and unfair criticism brought his crudeness and prejudices to

[1] It is the historian's task to weigh the evidence and explain how and why the situation now assumed such a pattern. In the answering of this question, as we shall see, the historians of the so-called Dunning School and the revisionists of our day part company. Here the historian again proves that each generation must write its own history; that facts do not change, but that the emphasis does.

the surface. In handling what was perhaps from the beginning an impossible situation, Johnson chose to work alone. He became the victim of his own constitutional theory, and so lost control over the southern states. As soon as they were newly reorganized, he left them in the main free to act as sovereign states and to ignore even his own preorganization demands. He could then only beg them for compliance.[2]

It should also be remembered that some Republicans had bluntly opposed Lincoln and that Congress had been openly resentful of the way he had taken charge and relegated Congress to a secondary role. It now seemed that Johnson was doing the same in reconstruction. As a result, an inflexible executive now faced a Congress gradually coming increasingly under the influence of more radical leaders, many of whom matched or surpassed the President himself in bizarre qualities. It is almost unbelievable, except for the abnormal condition following a civil war, that such a group as Charles Sumner, George W. Julian, Benjamin F. Wade, Thaddeus Stevens, and Salmon P. Chase could have obtained great influence. Each presents a personal tangle that no biographer has yet completely solved. Their dedication to abstract justice was unquestionably intense and sincere, and it seems equally certain that they were engaged in no sinister conspiracy to forward some hidden ends. They were just abstractionists oblivious of practical politics and certain that ends justified means where a cause was just. We need such men in a democracy, but they contribute nothing to its stability.

Chaos in the South added to the difficulties. Most of the old and experienced leaders had been refused amnesty and forced to apply personally for pardon if they wished to play any part in public affairs. That meant a flood of

[2] See an excellent discussion in Eric L. McKitrick, *Andrew Johnson and Reconstruction* (Chicago, 1960), pp. 186–212. Here Johnson not only allowed Governor William L. Sharkey of Mississippi to override his own wishes, but to defy a Union general and mislead the southern states as to the power they possessed.

requests, made for all kinds of reasons, which could not be carefully scrutinized and judged. Some men, it was charged, applied only in order to be elected to the conventions or legislatures; some applied only after they had been elected. It left many, perhaps the best men, outside. In the confusion many ex-Confederates (pardoned or not) were elected by the people. This alarmed the North. It looked like defiance. Yet as Governor John A. Andrew of Massachusetts—one of the South's bitterest enemies— observed, "Unless we give those who are by intelligence and character, the natural leaders of the people, and who surely will lead them by and by, an opportunity to lead them now, we cannot reorganize political society with any proper security."

To weaken even more the quality of those expected to put Johnson's plan into effect, many capable southerners had left the broken South and moved to Mexico and to Central and South America, particularly to Brazil. There they acquired land, established colonies, and resumed cultivating cotton. The South needed just such men, and it could most certainly have made use of such leaders as Judah P. Benjamin, who now gave his great talents to England.

Thus with many superior men barred from office or in exile, the South was in for trouble. It had never developed a large, politically active or socially minded middle class. Only a comparatively few small farmers or tradesmen had entered politics or shared in the shaping of public policy until quite recently. Although three-fourths of the southerners held few or no slaves, the nonslaveholder, even more than the planter, viewed the Negro as an inferior and a potential rival. This group was usually race conscious, and often given to violence. From the planters, the lawyers, the editors, and the men of wealth had come those who had ruled the old South and who when once in office had remained there as by right. With this element now partly gone, Johnson was supposed to depend to a large degree on a rather limited group of middle-class, racially conscious men who had opposed the war and who could easily qualify for pardon. Unless they asked for pardon, he could not turn to the more experienced men who realistically accepted defeat and northern demands, and only wanted to get on with a new start. It was good theory to reward the Union men of the South, but in practice this could not replace the old leadership.

Another factor that clouded the atmosphere in which presidential reconstruction took place was the presence, throughout the South, of agents of the U.S. Treasury Department who were seeking and seizing Confederate property under the Confiscation Acts. Cotton, of course, was the great object. The Confederacy had built its diplomacy and hopes for European recognition on cotton, and it had accumulated stores of this scarce and valuable article throughout the war. Much still remained unsold. However, no way existed of always distinguishing government cotton from that which was privately owned. Agents working on a 25 percent commission were inclined to see all cotton as Confederate cotton. Wholesale robbery resulted, and southerners with nothing of value to sell except cotton were the bitter victims. Agents made fortunes, and fake agents, in the uncertain confusion, joined in the plunder. Agent jobs were bought and sold at high prices—even an assistantship bringing as high as $25,000. One agent in Demopolis, Alabama, later boasted that he had made $80,000 in one month.

So wild did the game become that planters were forced to pay from $5 to $10 a bale on their own cotton against threats of seizure. In all, according to government records, something like $500 million worth of cotton was seized, but the government itself received only $34 million; or, of over 3,000,000 bales seized, the government got only 114,000 bales. Even Secretary of the Treasury Hugh McCulloch later denounced the whole business, and some 40,000 persons were reimbursed. Yet the immediate effect was to produce contempt for all government officials and a reckless determination on the part of southerners to look out for themselves and their interests.

II

Under such conditions Johnson's plan of reconstruction began its trial, first in North Carolina, then in the other states. As North Carolina's provisional governor, he had chosen William W. Holden, a man who had been something of an erratic editor before the war, a master of sarcasm, a Democrat who was extreme in his denunciation of what he called the "Black Republicans." [3] However, Holden had shifted his position on the eve of secession to one of violent opposition. Throughout the war he had been a harsh critic of President Jefferson Davis and had spread defeatism widely in the last years. With peace he had quickly seen the advantage in cooperating with the victors. He immediately took the oath and gave loud support to Johnson's plan.

Although hardly popular, Holden was able to organize a convention which declared and ordained that "slavery and involuntary servitude . . . shall be and is hereby forever prohibited within the state"; that the Constitution of the United States and all its amendments had at all times since its adoption back in 1789 been in force and effect, regardless of secession; that all debts created to aid the rebellion were repudiated finally and forever. The Convention then declared that all laws in force before secession were now again "in full force," as were all judicial proceedings and all contracts. Furthermore, no person who had been in the civil or military service of the state or of the Confederate states should be held for any act performed in the discharge of duties required by these bodies. Reluctantly and only under Johnson's pressure did the convention repudiate the Confederate debt.

[3] Walter L. Fleming (ed.), *Documentary History of Reconstruction* . . . , *1865 to the Present Time* (Cleveland, 1906–1907), vol. 1, pp. 25–33; J. G. de Rouhlac Hamilton, *Reconstruction in North Carolina* (New York, 1914), pp. 3, 106–145; William C. Harris, *Presidential Reconstruction in Mississippi* (Baton Rouge, 1967), pp. 36–140.

This done, the convention provided for the election of a governor and a legislature by the qualified voters. However, social and economic matters were passed on to the new governor and his legislature. It had not been difficult to reorder a state where middle-class men predominated, where Union sentiment had always been strong, and where secession had been delayed until Lincoln asked for troops to help fight their neighbors. But even in North Carolina there had been quibbling and too many questions asked. Holden himself had written Johnson, "I regret to say that there is much of a rebellious spirit still in this state." [4]

III

Meanwhile, other provisional governors had been busy. A brief glance at two will reveal the important fact that reconstruction was a unique matter for each state. As provisional governor of South Carolina, Johnson named Benjamin F. Perry, who had refused to follow the state's delegation out of the 1860 Democratic convention at Charleston, had opposed secession to the very end, but had gone with his state and served it in various capacities during the war. Unfortunately, Perry had made a speech in his up-country town just before the arrival of his appointment as provisional governor reached him. In the speech he had told his people that the sorrow and devastation all around them was the bitter fruit of secession, and he denounced the secessionists for their madness and folly. He insisted that the Confederacy was defeated because the heart of the southern people was never in this revolution. But now that the war was over it was their duty to accept the President's proclamation and return

---

[4] "We . . . grieve to say that the President's North Carolina measure cannot receive the approval of abolitionists, nor does it deserve the acquiescence of the practical statesman." It denied the ballot "to men who have battled *for* the Union, and granted it to men who have battled *against* it."—*The Independent*, June 8, 1865.

their allegiance to the United States. In closing he confessed that no man in the southern states "feels more bitterly the humiliation and degradation of going back into the Union than I do." [5]

This may have been Perry's way of telling his neighbors, who knew that he had always been a Union man, that he was also a South Carolinian who understood their feelings. Yet to the northern Republicans, who distrusted "all rebels," it proved what they wanted proved—no southerner was really "repentant."

For Johnson's program, it was a bad start. Matters grew worse when the elected convention contained twelve men who had sat in the seceding convention of 1860, twenty-five or thirty, including four generals and six colonels, who had been officers in the Confederate Army, and one man who had sat in the Confederate Congress. Nor were things improved when a few immediately urged clemency for Jefferson Davis, when the Ordinance of Secession was not "nullified" but "repealed," and when the convention announced that since their slaves were already emancipated by the action of the United States authorities, neither slavery nor involuntary servitude "would ever be reinstated" in South Carolina. It said nothing about repudiating Confederate debts, as Johnson had advised, and it left all economic and social matters for the legislature, soon to be elected.[6] One Northern newspaper man wrote, "They are all Rebels here—all Rebels."

That part of the northern press which was hostile to Johnson's plan made the most of South Carolina's actions. It paid scant attention to the sane and sober men who had opposed most of what had been done or to the fact that what had been done represented a compromise. The fact that there was quibbling and debate was, to the northern press, evidence of continued disloyalty and the absense of repentance. As a result Republicans in increasing num-

---

[5] Lillian A. Kibler, *Benjamin F. Perry, South Carolina Unionist* (Durham, N.C., 1946), pp. 379–380.

[6] Francis B. Simkins and Robert H. Woody, *South Carolina During Reconstruction* (Chapel Hill, N.C., 1932), pp. 29–63.

bers questioned the South's willingness to grant either "security" or "repentance." Yet the Republicans were being forced to understand what they really had in mind when they used those terms.

IV

Mississippi, too, got the Johnson plan under way. The state was fortunate in its provisional governor, one of the best men appointed to office in the South. Judge William L. Sharkey had served for more than twenty years in the courts of the state, had been a Whig in politics, and had remained a strong Union man. In 1860, he had told the people they were engaged in rebellion, not peaceful secession. As soon as appointed, he reinstated all local officers who had been in service and directed sheriffs to hold elections for members of the new convention. He even organized a state militia to keep order. In asking all to take the required oath, he remarked:

> The people of the South were in rebellion; the President has the right to prescribe terms of amnesty. . . . It is the part of wisdom and of honor to submit without a murmur. The negroes are free—free by the fortunes of war, free by the proclamation, free by common consent, free practically as well as theoretically, and it is too late to raise the technical question as to the means by which they became so.

Sharkey went so far as to say that southern success in the late war would have been the greatest calamity that could have befallen the country, "the greatest to the cause of civil liberty throughout the world." That was a good beginning, and as the most important newspaper in the state observed: "We think a decided majority of the convention (now assembling) will ignore quibbling and meet the issue of the hour like men of sense and candor." [7]

As elected, the convention contained a majority of old-line Whigs, most of whom had opposed secession. Sharkey

[7] James W. Garner, *Reconstruction in Mississippi* (New York, 1901), pp. 75–81, 82–96; William C. Harris, *op. cit.*, pp. 36–140.

advised them to adopt the constitutional amendment abolishing slavery and extend the franchise to all persons of color who could read the Constitution in English, write their names, or owned real estate valued at not less than $250.

The convention declared the institution of slavery to be at a permanent end in the state. Secession was declared null and void, and an amendment to the Constitution of the state was adopted "making it the duty of the legislature at its next session to provide by law for the protection and securing of person and property of the freedmen, and to guard them and the state against any evils that should arise from their sudden emancipation." The vote was granted only to whites, however, and the matter of the Confederate debt not decided. All else was left to the incoming legislature.

The work of the convention had not been done without debate and difference of opinion on all issues. Yet men who recognized that they were "now vanquished and helpless" had their way, and were disposed to return to their allegiance, and to make out of the disasters that have befallen them the best that they could. They were embarrassed when the people in the election that followed chose as governor a man who had not even applied for pardon or taken the oath! They would also discover that in taking things into their own hands so completely they had offended officials of both the Army and the Freedmen's Bureau.

In the meantime, provisional governors in the other southern states had called conventions, which in turn had taken action that in a general way fell in between that of South Carolina and of Mississippi. Nowhere did the Negro receive the vote, while the Confederate debt, and even the proper wording regarding secession, aroused debate. There was also in some corners talk of this being a white man's country! [8]

[8] "The Alabama State Convention has adjourned. Better for President Johnson's plans had it never met. . . . The South is out-

In Washington, President Johnson was having his troubles. The flood of amnesty petitions continued and since he had taken the position that "resumption" was the Executive's job, southerners had assumed that what he said and did constituted the national program. He had held to the constitutional doctrine that "a State cannot go out of the Union," and he had accepted advice on local conditions from southern delegations composed of men from old aristocratic ranks. The result was near home rule for the southern states and a free interpretation of the conditions he had imposed. Where Johnson brought pressure, it was often taken simply as advice. Soon southern Unionists complained of being pushed aside.

At first, approval of Johnson's course was quite general among both conservative Republicans and Democrats. His statement that Congress had complete control over the admission or rejection of its membership seemed to imply, at least, the acceptance of some joint cooperation between Executive and Congress. Critics noticed, however, a kind of vague and ambiguous quality that was gradually creeping into Johnson's actions and words. Meanwhile, northern men such as Sumner, Chase, Stevens, and perhaps Stanton were gaining wider Republican support for what W. E. B. Du Bois viewed as the greatest social revolution ever possible—"that of giving the negro the franchise and uniting the workers as such, against the capitalists." Johnson replied that if he forced the southern states to do that, he would be forced to make Pennsylvania, Connecticut, and other northern states do the same. So reconstruction awaited the southern legislatures. The Negro and his future had become the important issue.

In this connection, it is difficult to ascertain Johnson's personal attitude toward the Negro and his future place

---

generaling the Administration. . . . The President's policy gave the South an opportunity to demand too much. But the South abuses the too liberal privilege, and demands much more than too much. . . . The South is yet to learn . . . that she is to win no victories over the Union, either through war or through peace."
—*The Independent*, Oct. 5, 1865.

in American life. Johnson came from a border state where slavery existed, and he himself had once held a few slaves as domestic servants. He had waged a continuous battle against the slaveholding planter element and had aggressively opposed secession and the slavery values behind it. Now, as President, he faced the race issue in concrete form as the southern states set up their governments and a "radical" element in the North and in Congress demanded the franchise for the Negro. Johnson had suggested to the provisional governor of Mississippi that he could "with perfect safety" extend the franchise to the literate and property-holding freedmen and thereby "set an example the other States will follow." This suggestion had not been accepted, and the whole matter of disfranchising Confederates and enfranchising Negroes became tangled with the growing dispute between Johnson and the Republicans.

In the light of what happened later in the Reconstruction story, some modern historians see in Johnson's veto messages, which were to follow, and in a few chance remarks someone claims to have heard him make, that he was hostile to the Negro.[9] Others have stated that Johnson always ranged himself on the side of the racists and, in effect, demanded that the South remain a "white man's country." Support for this is found largely in Johnson's third annual message in which he opposed granting the Negro the vote on grounds that "no independent government of any form has ever been successful in [his] hands." Yet Johnson's point was that Negroes just out of slavery knew so little of public affairs that their voting would consist of nothing more "than carrying a ballot to the place where they were directed to deposit it."

If we had found it necessary, he argued, to require the intelligent foreigner who makes our land his choice for a home to establish residence of five years, gain a knowledge of our institutions, and prove his good moral char-

[9] LaWanda and John H. Cox, *Politics, Principle, and Prejudice, 1865–1866* (New York, 1963), pp. 151–171.

acter before he be admitted to citizenship, why should not some such period of "probation preparation" also be required for the Negro? He affirmed:

> I repeat, the expression of my willingness to join in any plan within the scope of our constitutional authority which promises to better the condition of the Negroes in the South, by encouraging them in industry, enlightening their minds, improving their morals, and giving protection to all their rights as freemen. But the transfer of our political heritage to them would, in my opinion, be an abandonment of a duty we owe alike to the memory of our fathers and the rights of our children.

Johson was frank to admit that he opposed any effort to give the Negro the vote and at the same time to disenfranchise such a number of white citizens that the former would be given a clear majority in all elections in the southern states. He was opposed, he said, "to Africanizing the South." [10]

Johnson was most certainly not an advanced advocate of racial equality, nor did he vary greatly in his attitude toward the Negro from the average American. But unfortunately he was President of the United States, a land in which the Declaration of Independence, with its assertions of equality and unalienable rights, has a way of becoming more important than the legalities of the Constitution; a land in which Evangelical Christianity and democracy at times become hopelessly tangled together; and where even politicians are willing to go to war for the preservation of human rights.

[10] James D. Richardson (ed.), *A Compilation of the Messages and Papers of the Presidents* (Washington, 1909), vol. 6, pp. 558–567.

CHAPTER

10

THE BLACK CODES

I

By the time the southern legislatures began convening, it was quite clear that something was wrong. Southerners, as they were supposed to do, were taking the oath and asking for pardon by the hundreds. Robert E. Lee had done so and had urged all southerners to do the same as a national obligation. If the oath was what was required to get back their citizenship and their property, they were willing to comply. Lincoln had said that it was necessary, and had said absolutely nothing about its being only a war measure: "We all agree that the seceded states, so called, are out of their proper, practical relation with the Union, and that the sole object of the government, civil and military, in regard to those states, is to again get them into that 'proper practical relation.' "

He made no mention of a social revolution. Johnson, in turn, had talked about "treason being odious" and about making southerners realize "the enormity of their crime." Yet, like Lincoln, he apparently believed that taking the oath and begging for pardon met the requirements. With that, the states could organize and enter the Union. Certainly Johnson thought that such pardon should be personally scrutinized and enough delay imposed to cause worry and thought. At first, this was possible; but events crowded, and Johnson could not do the job alone. Help was never adequate, and in the end even the provisional governors were at times allowed to grant the pardons. To the critical observer, "treason" was not being made exactly odious, nor was the "enormity of the crime" of rebellion being properly impressed. On the other hand, Lincoln's "sole object," that of getting the states back into their "proper practical relation to the Union," was making marvelous headway. What was wrong? Who was to blame? Johnson? His constitutional theory? The southern people? The provisional governors? The "radical" element in the Republican party? No one seemed quite sure.

To throw some light on the southern peoples and the part they might be playing in producing the growing uncertainty and unrest, a number of observers went South to inspect and report on conditions. Historians as a rule are very skeptical of travelers, who, they know, take prejudices with them on their journeys and find largely what they went to find. The difficulty, of course, was that in this South anything and everything could be found. It might be fact, yet not tell the entire story.

Such was the case in this instance. Observations were limited and reports varied greatly. Their chief importance is that they strengthened the opinions and prejudices already existing in the North and revealed the general confusion and contradictions to be found in the South. What is probably of equal importance is that they have provided later historians with quotations to buttress whatever point of view they have already accepted.

Two or three samples will suffice. General Ulysses S. Grant went South at President Johnson's request. He talked largely to persons in official positions, then reported: "I am satisfied that the mass of the thinking men of the South accept the present situation of affairs in good faith. . . . I was pleased to learn from the leading men whom I met, that they not only accepted the decision arrived at as final . . . but as a fortunate one for the whole country." Grant found the citizens "anxious to return to self government within the Union." [1]

Benjamin Truman, a New Englander and probably the most competent investigator of the lot, found the soldiers of the rebel army even more wearied, disgusted with war, and desirous of peace than were the northern soldiers.[2] He saw the Negro as better off under the planter class, and the wild reports of disorders in the South as badly "over done," Truman concluded that the southern states were fully ready to resume their places in the Union. The substantial element of the South was more loyal now than before the war. Harvey Watterson,[3] also sent by Johnson, reached practically the same conclusions. His report, like that of Truman, was small in size and completely devoid of sensational material. Both had a strong, forward, businesslike quality, and justified President Johnson's procedure, as did reports of many military officers.

In sharp contrast to these, both in character and size, was Carl Schurz's report. Schurz was anything but a modest man and anything but a man without a mission. He had once told Abraham Lincoln how to win the Civil War, and he now told Johnson what was needed for reconstruc-

[1] *Senate Executive Document*, 39th Cong., 1st sess., no. 2, pp. 106–108.

[2] *Senate Executive Document*, 39th Cong., 1st sess., no. 43, p. 6. John T. Throwbridge (in *The Desolate South, 1865–1866*, New York, 1956) and Whitelaw Reid (in *After the War*, New York, 1866) both comment on the willingness of Confederate soldiers to accept defeat and give loyal support to the Union.

[3] Library of Congress, Johnson MSS, Watterson to Johnson, July 8 and Oct. 3, 1865, vol. 1, p. 266.

tion. Johnson may have sent him South as much to get rid of him as to get information, for he paid no further attention to him. Perhaps the fact that Schurz had written letters for a Boston newspaper while on an official trip and had also tried to meddle in a quarrel between a governor and a general had had its effect.[4]

At any rate, when on his return Schurz attempted to talk with the President, he received a cold reception after a long wait, and was not asked for his report or for any details of his trip. Schurz, however, was not to be denied. He had undertaken the trip with the advice and financial assistance of Sumner, Stanton, and the other Republican leaders. He had accomplished a mission. He had seen what he and his friends wanted seen, and he would be heard. As he wrote his wife, "I found all of my preconceived opinions verified most fully—no more than that," and it was his intention now "to open the eyes of the people of the North."

It took Schurz a month to write his long report, and he did not deliver it to the President until after Congress had assembled. His request that it be published at once was refused, but it appeared later with an introduction noting that Johnson had neither read nor endorsed the document. The main thesis was that southerners had yielded only because they were obliged to do so, or in order to obtain control of their own affairs. Many still swaggered about, persecuting Negroes and Union men, while the rest were too ignorant to do anything but follow. Southerners refused to fraternize with northern soldiers and viewed outsiders as intruders or Yankees. Treason, Schurz felt, had not been made odious in the South, and any expression of "hearty attachment to the great republic" was pure insincerity. Southerners were still rebels at heart. In many places where the army was not in control Ne-

---

[4] Schurz had appeared in Mississippi at the time when Governor William L. Sharkey was having trouble with General Henry W. Slocum over the militia, and Shurz had evidently favored Slocum.

groes were being reduced virtually to slavery. Hence, there was much racial conflict, with most of the blame on the whites.

Schurz summed up by observing that "a good many planters are at present more nervously jealous of their authority than before, while the freedmen are not always inclined to forget that they are free men." He was certain the Negro should have the ballot. This should be a condition to "readmission."

Schurz had seen, and now said, the things the Radical Republicans wanted seen and said. Sumner had the report printed and distributed by the thousands at public expense.[5]

Thus both President Johnson and Senator Sumner and his friends were given the picture of the South which justified the attitudes and the course each was taking. Neither saw any reason for a change because of the information received. The difficulty was that a total picture of southern conditions and what course of action should be adopted had not been given. The road ahead was not clear.

As the southern people began to elect their governors, legislatures, congressmen, and senators, they quickly altered the entire picture. In this connection it must be remembered that in 1862 an act had been passed requiring from any elected or appointed federal official, an "iron-clad oath" that he had never directly or indirectly had any part in armed hostility to the United States government. That law was still on the books.

Yet when the new southern bodies began choosing the men to represent them in Congress they completely ignored both the law and President Johnson's warning. Georgia elected as senators Alexander H. Stephens, late Vice-President of the Confederacy, just paroled from prison, and Herschel V. Johnson, who had rendered the

[5] Carl Schurz, *The Reminiscences of Carl Schurz* (New York, 1907–1908), vol. 3, pp. 157, 159. His prejudices even before he reached the South are evident in this work, vol. 1, p. 268. See letters in the *Boston Advertiser*, July 17, 21, 25, 31, and August 8, 1865.

Confederacy invaluable service. Other states did just as badly. Mississippi's James L. Alcorn had been a Confederate brigadier-general; South Carolina's John L. Manning, a member of General Pierre Beauregard's staff; North Carolina's William A. Graham, a member of the Confederate Congress. Only one senator chosen could sign the oath. Those elected to the House included four Confederate generals and twice as many colonels, to say nothing of lesser officers.

What did this actually mean? The answer, of course, depends on the peculiar interests and prejudices of the observer. To the Republicans, already alarmed at the increase of southern political strength through the ending of the three-fifths rule and indignant at the quibbling over what they considered reasonable demands made on southern conventions, it meant defiance. It proved that "the Confederacy, though beaten, refused to die." It even seemed to some that southerners had come to think that they were now free to do whatever they pleased. Johnson had spoiled them. He had demanded too little and had not always enforced that little.[6]

On the other hand, it could be said that southerners, in their haste to return to a normal condition and surrounded by economic and social chaos, had no time or inclination to plot defiance. Without the slightest reference to the Confederacy or any effort to keep it alive, they chose as their representatives men with political experience and those who, by merit proved in war, deserved their confidence.

Regardless of motives, in this situation where economic, social, moral, and political interests were at stake, where there was question as to who was to reconstruct, where the defeated South had no choices but those permitted by the victors, any move that could be interpreted

[6] "The humiliating tone . . . with which they recognized a few months ago their state as conquered, and their fate as victims, is fast passing away. The Government has thrown open the gates of political power to unrepentant rebels."—*The Independent,* Aug. 10, 1865.

as defiance or as an effort to return to ways that had been struck down in battle was a serious mistake. The southern states had blundered at a critical time, and Johnson, with his questionable constitutional theory and his cure-all oaths, had permitted them to do things that both he and they seemingly should have known the North would never accept. Yet did they know it? Could one group of Americans, battered and beaten, struggling to get enough to eat and literally beginning all over again—a scattered, divergent, rural people—possibly have understood other Americans living in peaceful villages and on prosperous farms and now rushing madly into the most extravagant economic era in all our national life?

The next step would prove an even greater blunder. The newly elected southern legislatures, wrongly assuming that reconstruction had been completed when constitutions had been altered, oaths of loyalty taken, and state and local machinery again established, now tackled the serious problem of restoring their chaotic social and economic order. This primarily involved land, capital, and labor. The result was what came to be called the Black Codes.[7]

Approached from any angle, the hope for permanent recovery and the resumption of normal life within the national pattern depended on the rebuilding of southern agriculture and a satisfactory rural way of life. Habit and opportunity both pointed in that direction. In fact, the sale of cotton accumulated in the towns during the war had saved the day as far as it had been saved.

To restore this rural agricultural order required, first of all, control and possession of the land. Planters often found their lands confiscated or seized while they were away. These could be recovered only after seeking and securing pardon. Even then there were difficulties. To whom should they apply for recovery? Would compensa-

[7] For a good summary, see Edward McPherson (ed.), *The Political History of the United States During the Period of Reconstruction* (Washington, 1875), pp. 29–44.

tion be given for damage done where the northern army had been responsible? Was it necessary to retain and care for the old or infirm Negroes who were still on the land? Where was the money to be found with which to buy seed, replace tools, and pay wages now required? Most important, what about labor? Any large-scale effort to produce a surplus for market required an organized and supervised force. Would the Negro, now a free man, accept such a system, with so much about it to remind him of slavery? As one man wrote, "They seem to have lost all attachment to, and confidence in their former masters. They will take the advice of the meanest Yankee or citizen in preference to their master. . . . They have in the main left the plantations and flocked to the cities and towns . . . and those not in the towns . . . are roving the country." The transition to a new order would be hard on both whites and Negroes. Both had much to learn.

Until now aiding the freedman had been the responsibility of the Freedmen's Bureau, created by act of Congress in March 1865 to care for the refugees who had flocked to the army and to supervise the use of what was called "abandoned lands." The Bureau assumed the task of furnishing supplies and medical service, set up schools, and soon was acting as a kind of labor bureau to arrange and supervise contracts between freedmen and employers. Following the end of hostilities, it spread as a kind of network across the whole South, with General O. O. Howard at its head and local agents in far-flung districts. It cared for the destitute and hungry, whites as well as Negroes, but its task became more and more that of protecting and guiding the Negro. Often it was closely linked with the army; many of its agents were army men.

In spite of the valuable work the Bureau did, southerners more and more viewed it as an outside factor operating as a force in race and labor relations beyond their control. Thus, when the southern legislatures began attempting to adjust race and labor relations to their own needs and prejudices, they found themselves facing this outside Bureau representing all that the Civil War had done and all that the victorious Republican party wanted in social terms. As one authority wrote, they "despised it more for what it stood for than for what it had done." [8]

Convinced that the Freedmen's Bureau, like the army, should now withdraw (reconstruction being ended and home rule instituted), the southern legislatures set to work to do the labor-race job as they thought it should be done. They started with two inherited preconceptions: that the Negro was an inferior individual and that he could be efficient only under white supervision. So universal were these conceptions among southerners and so much alike were their common social and economic problems that the codes now independently enacted were surprisingly uniform. Yet, did a defeated south have a right to such preconceptions when the victors were equally united in believing that the Negro under the Declaration of Independence was an equal and enough of a man to direct himself? He had proved this on the Sea Islands of South Carolina and on the lands assigned to him on the lower Mississippi.

Nevertheless, in good American fashion these new "legally" constructed legislatures set to work, as legislatures should, to solve their local problems. The laws they enacted unquestionably had as their purpose restoration of the absolutely necessary agricultural order and a more orderly social situation. In practice, however, they meant primarily the regulation and control of the Negro as a necessary labor force. They gave the planter most of the benefits of slavery without the responsibilities involved in slavery, and reduced the Negro to a servitude that largely lacked the benefits of the "peculiar institution."

The Mississippi code may be taken as an example. It began with an apprentice law which required that all

---

[8] George R. Bentley, *A History of the Freedmen's Bureau* (Philadelphia, 1955), p. 104. "To most of them it was virtually a foreign government forced upon them and supported by an army of occupation. They resented its very existence, regardless of what it might do, for it had power over them and it was beyond their control. It was the enemies' agent."—p. 105.

Negroes or mulattoes under eighteen years of age who were orphans or whose parents could not support them be bound out to some white person—preferably their former masters. The white man was to provide them with sufficient food, clothing, and medical care, and teach them to read and write. He could administer corporal punishment and could hold males until they were twenty-one, females eighteen. This took care of the young Negroes.

In addition, a vagrancy law was passed that applied not only to beggars and wandering minstrels but to all Negroes not in regular employment—to all who did not have a lawful home or employment, with written evidence of same by January 2, 1866. It could apply also to persons guilty of irregular conduct such as adultery, drunkenness, or petty thievery. Vagrants were to be fined and on failure to pay were to be hired out, preferably to former masters. It thus was clear to any Negro, desirable or undesirable, that he could be arrested as a vagrant and be bound out.[9]

Negroes were forbidden to lease land outside of an incorporated town, and anyone practicing a mechanical trade had to serve an apprenticeship and obtain a license. Similarly, a license was required for job work. Thus, the Negro was largely confined to agriculture.

All labor contracts had to be in writing and carefully explained before witnesses. If a contract was broken by a Negro, he forfeited his wages and could be hunted down and fined. As further protection for the employer, heavy penalties were laid against any efforts by others to lure his workers away.

Negroes not in military service were forbidden to keep

---

[9] In this connection it is interesting to note that in places where the United States army had been in control, officers charged with establishing order had instituted regulations for the control of freedmen strikingly like the Black Codes. As James E. Sefton writes, "There is a remarkable similarity in the measures of the Army, the bureau, and the states, which highlights the magnitude of the problem and makes the passage of the Black Codes more understandable."—*The United States Army and Reconstruction, 1865–1877* (Baton Rouge, 1967), pp. 42–50.

or carry firearms, or to possess ammunition, dirks, or bowie knives. For disturbing the peace, preaching without a license, or selling intoxicating liquor, heavy fines were provided, and hiring out was the penalty for nonpayment.

Furthermore, on the social side, the Negro was given the right to sue and be sued, to acquire and dispose of property, and to marry under the same laws as whites. All men and women living together were to be considered legally married. Interracial marriages were prohibited. Negroes could testify in courts where they were a party to the case, and all Negroes of age were taxed to provide a pauper fund for their own.

To the North these laws, of course, appeared as an effort to return to slavery, not just to establish social and economic stability. As the *Chicago Tribune* commented, "We tell the white men of Mississippi that men of the North will convert the State of Mississippi into a frog pond before they will allow such laws to disgrace one foot of soil in which the bones of our soldiers sleep and over which the flag of freedom waves." A Phi Beta Kappa speaker asked, "Shall the horrors of Salisbury and Andersonville prison, the murder of innocent persons be forgotten and forgiven to unrelenting, life-serving, lying rebels, whose oath is as naught under compulsion?" Charles Sumner shouted, "Strike at the Black Codes as you have already struck at the Slave Codes. There is nothing to choose between them. Strike at once; strike hard. You have already proclaimed Emancipation; proclaim Enforcement also." [10]

It is perfectly clear that the passage of such codes as that in Mississippi was an unpardonable mistake. This was no time for southerners to reveal their racial preju-

[10] *Chicago Tribune*, Dec. 1, 1865; *New York Times*, Dec. 1 and 7, 1865. Speaking of the South Carolina code, *The Independent*, Nov. 23, 1865, wrote, "This code, from beginning to end, is inequity framed into law—an outrage upon Liberty—a revival of 'chivalry'—a piece of malice aforethought against the negro—a scroll of injustice which we hold up to the contempt of mankind."

dices and their ideas regarding Negro inferiority. Too much was at stake. It may have been an effort on the part of desperate people to do something about the chaotic social and economic condition in which they found themselves, but it looked too much like an effort to deny the Negro the civil rights Republicans, whether radical or moderate, were determined he should have.

This being the case, why did the southern states make such a fatal blunder? Why did they so tragically fail to anticipate the northern reaction? The simple answer is that neither northerners nor southerners understood the thinking of the other. One group faced a society in economic and social chaos; the other, a society madly reveling in prosperity and progress. One viewed the freedman as a Negro who in the past had required, for efficiency, both control and supervision; the other saw him as a man immediately capable of working and voting as a citizen, if given an equal chance. Both were partly in error, but neither had yet learned that fact. Neither had as yet reached a clear understanding of its own thinking, let alone that of the other. Each was capable only of frustrating the other.

II

Such a situation in itself was bad enough. It became worse as stories of racial violence poured in from the South. The mail of every northerner of public importance who might be expected to sympathize was filled with reports of Negro whippings and murders as everyday occurrences. Much was fact; some was not. The effects, however, were the same. Abnormal conditions and attitudes were assumed to be normal and permanent. Northerners took it for granted that the southern people as a whole approved. The absence of government, the social and economic chaos, the uniquely personal character of southern society, and the widely varied rural and near-frontier character of much of the South were not considered. The reports indicated only "a South that was beaten but not yet conquered."

In this connection the report of "Union Officer" John De Forest, serving in the Freedmen's Bureau, is of interest. He noted that southerners differed completely from one another in attitudes and ways. He spoke of "the low-down people," of the "Semi-Chivalrous Southrons," "Chivalrous Southrons," and "More Chivalrous Southrons." He referred to the first group as "that wretched caste" and described their drunkenness, idleness, and improvidence, yet he found them possessed of a strange self-pride. He ascribed most "of the murders of the Negroes in the South" to these poor-whites. He found the upper groups, while somewhat "noddled by the results of the war," to have shown a "surprisingly general satisfaction over the accomplished fact of abolition. . . . 'I am glad the thing is done away with' was a frequent remark; 'it was more plague than pleasure, more loss than profit.' "

As to the Negroes, he found that "they wasted much of their time in amusement. What with trapping rabbits by day and treeing 'possims' by night and prayer-meetings which were little better than frolics, they contrive to be happier than they had 'any call to be,' considering their chances of starving to death." In the matter of honesty, he found that the freedmen were doing as well as could be expected. Stealing was still more common among them than among even "the low-down whites." He noted that "planters still complain that their hogs and hens disappear." This was not surprising since in slave days it was considered "no harm 'to put Massa's chicken into Massa's nigger.' " De Forest closed with the hope that the time would soon come when all our citizens would feel that they were Americans, and nothing but Americans.[11]

There were evidently still many widely differing Souths.

[11] John William De Forest, *A Union Officer in the Reconstruction*, edited and with notes by James H. Croushore and David Morris Potter (New Haven, Conn., 1948), pp. 99–106.

They neither acted, nor thought alike. None of them could be judged by the standards of a quiet undisturbed New England village.

CHAPTER

11

REPUBLICANS REACT

I

With passage of the Black Codes and the meeting of the 39th Congress in December 1865, the first phase of Reconstruction came to an end. One element in the Republican party had already been at work preparing for the second. From the beginning, an element in the Republican party had been interested more in social change than in political action. It had kept the Declaration of Independence in politics, objected to Lincoln's war aims because they did not include the abolition of slavery, and even attributed Union defeats to the fact that the generals were not abolitionists. This element had not been satisfied with the Emancipation Proclamation; it had openly opposed Lincoln's election in 1864 and had quickly launched a campaign against his reconstruction policy. Lincoln had rejected demands for calling Congress into extra session, and the day before his assassination had remarked to Secretary of the Navy Gideon Welles that it would be wise to have southern governments in successful operation and the Union re-established before Congress met.

The opposition, confident at first, had soon discovered that President Johnson would follow Lincoln, not his critics.[1] Then they began to worry and to plan. Charles Sumner and Thaddeus Stevens exchanged frantic letters. Stevens wrote:

> I see the president is precipitating things. I fear before Congress meets he will have so be-deviled matters as to render them incurable. I almost despair of resisting Executive influence. . . . Is it possible to devise any plan to arrest the government in its ruinous course? When will you be in Washington? Could we collect bold men enough to lay the foundations of a party to take the helm of government, and keep it off the rocks?

In another letter he asked:

> Is there no way to arrest the insane course of the president? Can you get up a movement in Massachusetts? I thought of trying it at our convention. . . . If something is not done the president will be crowned King before Congress meets.

For them, the Civil War was not over. Reconstruction had not begun.[2]

[1] Senator James W. Grimes of Iowa asked his colleague William P. Fessenden, "What do you think of Andy's reconstruction schemes? It strikes me that matters are getting complicated, and that the rebels are having it all their own way."—Bowden College, Fessenden MS, July 14, 1865. Charles Sumner added, "I insist that the rebel states shall not come back except on the footing of the Declaration of Independence, with all persons equal before the law . . . there shall be no discrimination on account of color."—Edward L. Pierce (ed.), *Memoir and Letters of Charles Sumner* (Boston, 1877–1893), vol. 2, p. 229.

[2] Stevens said in a speech at Lancaster on September 7, 1865, "It is intended to revolutionize their principles and feelings . . . [and] to work a radical reorganization in Southern institutions, habits, and manners."—Library of Congress, Stevens MS. "It appears," wrote *The Independent,* on December 2, 1865, "that this

Then began an intensive campaign for creating alarm and opposition. It began with a call for delay in southern reconstruction, moved on to open criticism of Johnson's policy, and ended with bitter attacks on the President himself. Johnson was not a legal President; he was ignorant and stubborn; he was, worst of all, a Democrat. The purpose was to gain control of Congress, give it a hand in reconstruction, and thus inaugurate a new program that would insure control of the South and justice for the Negro. As Stevens wrote Sumner, "Get the rebel states into a territorial condition, and [Negro suffrage] can be easily dealt with. That I think should be our great aim." Stevens even wrote pointedly to Johnson, "I have not found a single person who approves of your policy. Wait for Congress." [3]

Sumner was equally critical of Johnson and his program:

> It is difficult to measure the mischief which has already ensued from the "experiment" which has been made. . . . Looking at the distress which it has caused among loyal people by the revival of the rebel spirit, it is heart-rending. Looking at it anyway, it is a terrible failure. It will be for Congress to apply the remedy . . . nor do I doubt its duty to see that every pretended government organized by recent rebels is treated as a present nullity." [4]

That these men were ready for action as soon as Congress met was quite apparent when Speaker of the House

---

Congress has been in session during the whole of its vacation— that is, its members have been quietly busy all summer drafting laws, motions, resolutions, bills, and amendments—many of which are in unpacked trunks; but the present prospect is that they will be showered in double handfuls upon Congress day by day during the early days of the session."

[3] Library of Congress, Johnson MSS, Stevens to Johnson, July 6, 1865. A Faneuil Hall meeting in Boston resolved: "The true doctrine of reconstruction is that defeated rebels have no civil or political rights, which loyal men are bound to respect, and that all loyal men without regard to race or color, are entitled to equal rights as citizens."—*Chicago Tribune*, June 1, 1865.

[4] A letter published in *The Independent*, Nov. 2, 1865.

Schuyler Colfax arrived in Washington and addressed a clearly prearranged crowd in front of his lodging. In what was an apparent effort to smooth the path, and perhaps, to disarm the President, Colfax went out of his way to praise Johnson and express good will. He then made it perfectly clear that he was assuming Congress would not take hasty action in admitting the newly elected southern members. The Constitution, of course, gave each house the exclusive right to judge the qualifications of its members, and all knew that there had been certain things in the behavior of the southern states under Johnson's program that would cause Congress to move slowly. Colfax expressed the belief (how sincerely only he could know) that the executive and legislative bodies would cooperate in reconstructing the Union "wisely and patriotically" and that the South would accept the situation.[5]

Was this an announcement of what had already been planned, or was it just an offhand speech? Historians differ in their answers. At any rate, a caucus of arriving members had already agreed on a plan for setting up a joint congressional committee on reconstruction. That would be the first order of business.

When Congress assembled, the clerk, Edward McPherson, in calling the roll, accepted the fact that the House itself had not acted. He rightly omitted the names of the newly elected representatives of the southern states, passing over even those from the state of Tennessee. At which minority leader James Brooks asked, "If Tennessee is not in the Union . . . by what right does the president of the United States usurp a place in the White House?" It was indeed a pointed question.

Then even before the President's message was read, radical members moved to create a Joint Committee of Congress on Reconstruction. It was a way of serving notice that Congress was to have its say on what had been done and what would be done in the future.

The resolution to create a joint committee had been

---

[5] *New York World*, Nov. 20, 1865.

planned well in advance, drawn up in a preliminary caucus, and presented to the House by Thaddeus Stevens almost before it had come to order. The committee was to be composed of nine representatives and six senators and was to "enquire into the condition of the States which formed the so-called Confederate States of America, and report whether they or any of them, are entitled to be represented in either House of Congress." The resolution then declared that no senator or representative should be admitted into either branch of Congress from any of the eleven states that had been declared in insurrection, "until Congress shall have declared such State entitled to such representation."

When these resolutions reached the Senate, a majority of the Republicans favored their adoption, but Senator James R. Doolittle of Wisconsin objected. The resolutions, he observed, "read word for word like those which had been drawn up and published as the proceedings of a caucus of gentlemen in the city of Washington" on the preceding Saturday night. Then "within three minutes, by the clock, after the hour when [the House] met, Mr. Stevens had moved his committee on resolutions, and was withdrawing with his committee from that body to make his report." Then within ten minutes, "without any discussion, without any consideration whatever," it was by that "cool tact and talent" of Mr. Stevens "pressed through that body and declared to be unanimously adopted. . . ."

Why such haste?

Who does not know [said Doolittle] that the leader of that assemblage did not desire to wait, nor did he dare to wait until the President had spoken to the country in his annual message. Progress was being made in the South, and while there was much to give pain, no one last spring could have dreamed that such progress could have been made. Cooperation was what was needed and not the things Stevens represented. If this resolution as it stands, should be adopted and receive the signature of the President, you, have accomplished what the rebellion could not accomplish, what the sacrifice of half a million men could not accomplish in warring against the government—you have dissolved the Union by act of Congress.[6]

But the majority had its way. The Joint Committee, which opponents asserted could not have been formed at any other time than this, was set on its course. Senator William P. Fessenden,[7] chairman of the committee, described it as containing "a large majority of thorough men who were resolved that ample security should attend any restoration of the insurgent states, *come what will*, while they desire *if possible*, to avoid a division between Congress and the Executive, which can only result in unmixed evil." The doubt implied forecast trouble, as did the determination to achieve "ample security come what will."

While President Johnson considered reconstruction complete except for the admission of southern representatives to Congress, Fessenden spoke as though it had not begun. Thaddeus Stevens was saying that it was "the first duty of Congress to pass a law declaring the condition of these outside or defunct States and providing proper civil governments for them." He added, "It matters little . . . whether you call them States out of the Union or now conquered territories . . . they are . . . only dead carcasses lying within the Union. In either case it is very plain that it requires the action of Congress to enable them to form a State government and send representatives to Congress." [8]

The move to create the Joint Committee was not made without conservative protest. Democrats as well as more moderate Republicans restated the Lincoln-Johnson constitutional theory and their impression that the war was over and that it had been fought for the purpose of restoring the Union. Thomas A. Hendricks of Indiana asked:

[6] *Congressional Globe*, 39th Cong., 1st sess., pp. 24–26.
[7] *Ibid.*, pp. 26–27.
[8] *Ibid.*, pp. 72–75; Benjamin B. Kendrick (ed.), *The Journal of the Joint Committee of Fifteen on Reconstruction* (New York, 1914), pp. 138–140.

Why at the close of the war, Congressmen should adopt language which had not been used during the war in order to give a character to the rebellion which it had not had before? If they had fought to deny the right of secession, and insisted that it was only the people who were at fault, why now this talk of state suicide or conquered territory?

The answer, of course, was that there had been four years of fighting, of hating, of irremovable distrust and fear. The war would not be over until the southern people were "repentant" to the point of accepting intellectual, social, and economic changes, perhaps even a political rearrangement.

The symbol of these changes was to be the Negro. Just as slavery had in 1860 been the symbol of all that divided North and South, so now all differences had to do with the Negro.[9] The trouble with symbols is that they vastly oversimplify situations and tend unconsciously to stir emotions and to reduce material interest to the pattern of right versus wrong.

II

Important as was justice for the Negro and repentance for the South, these were but surface expressions. Back of them lay the larger fact that the Republican party was, and had been from the beginning, the carrier both of a moral, democratic mission and of all the vast changes and interests of an emerging modern world. The two had gone together, but in war days and in the struggle with Johnson, economic interests had received less public discussion. Now they had come together again in the reconstruction of the South. Equality for the Negro involved both the Declaration of Independence and the needs of the modern business world.

Put in the form of a single question, it might be asked:

[9] "The outside world has learned to comprehend far better than it did that this Rebellion means slavery—Nothing but Slavery. The conspirator against the Republic is SLAVERY. The hideous, ghastly Rebellion is SLAVERY."—*The Independent*, April 27, 1865.

Why did Congress now insist on taking a hand in control? The object, of course, was to give the legislature under Republican dominance the power to do with the South what the victor in the war thought should be done, and to secure for the Negro full justice. A powerful reform element in the party was not satisfied with what had been done so far. But there was more to it than this.

In the first place, Congress, as has been said, had long felt more or less slighted in the running of national affairs. The President had kept control throughout the war, and Congress had been asked only to provide the means. Wars make dictators. War might justify this, but peace called for a return to balance, or even to legislative dominance.[10]

Secondly, the Lincoln-Johnson program, now nearly complete, seemed not only to threaten Republican control but to ignore the social changes required. The Negro was now a five-fifths man, and his vote, if granted or refused, was a party matter. In either case it might determine party control. It could not be forgotten that Wade Hampton's brother had told Whitelaw Reid that if the Negro were given the ballot, "the old owners would cast the vote of their people almost as absolutely and securely as they cast their own. If Northern men expected in this way to build up a Northern party in the South they were gravely mistaken." Yet if it worked the other way, the future of Republican rule was assured.

As matters now stood, the Republicans could muster 141 votes in the House and 39 in the Senate. The old Democratic opposition controlled only 43 votes in the House and 11 in the Senate. But if from a restored South there were added 58 more votes in the House and 22 in the Senate, and to this a conservative Republican vote on some issues, then control could easily pass to the Democrats. As Benjamin F. Wade wrote in June 1865, "To

[10] Senator Fessenden admitted that "Congress in war accepted much," but he insisted that "these precedents do not now hold in peace."—*Congressional Globe*, 39th Cong., 1st sess., p. 279.

admit the [Southern] States on Mr. Johnson's plan, is voluntarily . . . to surrender our political rights into the hands and keeping of those traitors we have just conquered. . . . It is nothing less than political suicide."

What could Democratic dominance portend? Clearly, it could mean abuse of the Negro, the end of Republican dominance in officeholding, and the end of tariffs now yielding such matchless returns to the new age. The war debt, in which so many had a stake, might not be paid in gold; lavish gifts to railroads now bridging the continent could be checked and corporations in general restricted. The South might even ask its share in all this lavish "banquet." These things were not certain, but they were possible.

Thaddeus Stevens, always a bit more blunt and realistic than others, frankly admitted the purpose. He insisted that the southern states could not be restored until the Constitution had been so amended "as to secure perpetual ascendancy to the party of the Union." If this were not done, the South and the Democrats "will at the very first election take possession of the White House and of the Halls of Congress. . . . The Republican Party, and it alone can save the Union." "Do you aver the party purpose," he was asked, and he answered, "I do."

Republicans were without question interested in greater justice for the Negro, but that the Negro also had political value was not being overlooked. E. L. Godkin was afraid that the southern states, if readmitted, would oppose taxation for payment of the federal war debt. They would be "determined repudiationists" and impair the nation's credit.[11] One of Sumner's correspondents was certain that southerners would vote with the Democrats to reduce greatly the tariff to free-trade levels, and then demand repudiation. Sumner himself saw the ballot in

[11] Howard K. Beale, "The Tariff and Reconstruction," *American Historical Review*, XXXV (January, 1930), 276–294; *New York Tribune*, Feb. 26, 1879; Howard K. Beale, *The Critical Year: A Study of Andrew Johnson and Reconstruction* (New York, 1930), pp. 276–294.

the Negro's hand as the North's best guarantee against repudiation. "Only through him," observed Sumner, "can you save the national debt from the inevitable repudiation which awaits it when recent rebels in conjunction with Northern allies once more bear sway."

The *New York Tribune* went the whole way. "The cotton-planters," Horace Greeley editorialized, "were educated by Calhoun to the policy of keeping the Yankees from manufacturing, and confining them to raising cheap food for their slaves. . . . The failure of their Rebellion has not softened the temper of this education. The reconstructed South would vote solid to destroy the wealth-providing industry of the Loyal states." Their unprincipled slaves "in the 'copper mines' would lick their shoes while they voted for them." [12]

In other words, the power struggle was still being waged. The admission of the Southern states must not only satisfy the Republicans' emotional needs as victors in a bitter civil war, but it must be done in such a way as to guarantee both the economic and moral fibers that had been woven into the Republican pattern as a sectional expression from its very beginning. This is not to question, in any way, the deep sincerity and purpose of men who now believed that reconstruction was meaningless unless "security and repentance" involved a social, and intellectual change as well. It is only to suggest that the "steam engine" was, after all, the greatest fact of the day.

III

Johnson's message, which Congress soon received, made it clear that the President had been attempting to follow the Constitution as he understood it. Under it, he proclaimed the states were perpetual and as such had not through rebellion become conquered territory. Their vi-

[12] *The New York Semi-Weekly Tribune*, April 3, 1866, quoted in Howard K. Beale, *The Critical Year: A Study of Andrew Johnson and Reconstruction*, p. 275.

tality had been impaired but not extinguished; their functions suspended but not destroyed. His policy had aimed at the restoration, gradually and quietly, of normal state functions. He then explained the steps taken, the risks run, and the success achieved. He had granted pardons but had made sure that they were accompanied by unqualified acknowledgment of the changes wrought by the emancipation of the slaves. To have established military governments would have engendered hate, not affection. His policy had "made us once more a United people."

Each house of Congress could judge for itself the election returns and the qualifications of its members—a hint that it was now their duty to complete that unity. Johnson then explained that he could not have given the Southern Negro the vote without giving it to colored men everywhere. By patience and manly virtue, he thought, the Negroes would gradually win it for themselves. He closed by asking, "Who will not join me in prayer that the Invisible Hand which has led us through the clouds that gloomed around our path will guide us onward to a perfect restoration of fraternal affection that we of this day may be able to transmit our great inheritance of state governments in all their rights, of the general government in its whole constitutional vigor, to our posterity, and they to theirs through countless generations?"

The message was a moderate, well-written appeal for acceptance of what Johnson considered the completion of a most difficult task. It seemed to imply, however, that with the adoption of the Thirteenth Amendment and his own work of restoration, the major tasks of reconstruction had been completed. Whether Johnson was leaving room for Congress to do more than admit Southern representatives to Congress was not clear. The message could be interpreted one way as well as the other.

On the whole it was well received throughout the nation. Moderate Republicans and most Democrats accepted it as a statesmanlike appeal for national unity and a fair statement of the steps already taken. Yet Sumner and

Stevens saw it as a challenge. With their congressional committee they would check the growth of executive power as it had grown up during the war, and substitute what W. E. B. Du Bois called a modified English parliamentary form of government.[13] As Du Bois wrote, "It was the business of the Committee of Fifteen to see how the government of the United States was to be changed after the war, from its form before the war"—changed in the basis of popular representation, in the clarification of the status of the Negro, and in a modification of the relation of the national government to state government. "It was," Du Bois added, "a plan to set up, temporarily at least, a cabinet form of responsible government in the United States."

Whether Stevens clearly saw or planned this makes no difference. It was what was to happen as both the executive, by impeachment, and the Supreme Court, by partial avoidance of involvement, left Congress and the nation more or less in the hands of the Joint Committee. Presidential reconstruction at least was at an end.

To understand the next phase of Reconstruction, it is necessary to try to understand the men who took Johnson's place in shaping reconstruction. Regardless of whether Thaddeus Stevens was the all-powerful dictator he was once considered to have been, or just the symbol of the new era, we need to know a few basic things about him. At this time he was an elderly bachelor whose past had only hardened what seems to have been original qualities. Stevens was a realist with a queer strain of idealism which was as hard and unbending as was his rather cynical view of the world. Vermont-born, he had known poverty and strife; and after a rather unpleasant fling at Dartmouth College, he had moved to Pennsylvania to practice law and engage in politics. In that bundle of

[13] William Edward Burghardt Du Bois, author of *Black Reconstruction* (New York, 1935), was the first "revisionist." In spite of a rather extreme quality and a Marxian approach, his volume deserves a careful reading for an occasional penetrating grasp of basic problems.

sections known as Pennsylvania, he learned all about the political game of give and take, about political bosses, and the necessity of principles yielding to expediency. He had once exclaimed to a fellow partisan, "Conscience indeed! Throw conscience to the devil and stand by your party."

With no faith in his fellows, blunt in his honesty even where he had been dishonest, and ruthless and without scruples when the end justified, Stevens was brutally intolerant and unforgiving with those who opposed him. As to the South, he hated aristocrats and traitors even as much as did Johnson. He never saw but one side of the issue. "Do not, I pray you, admit those who have slaughtered half a million of my countrymen, until their clothes are dried, and until they are reclad. I do not wish to sit side by side with men whose garments smell of the blood of my kindred."

As to Johnson, Stevens said:

> I cannot begin to attempt to unfold the policy of that man, in whom the people confided as a true patriot, and whom we have now found to be worse than the man who is incarcerated in Fortress Monroe.
>
> You remember that in Egypt the Lord sent frogs, locusts, murrain, and lice, and finally demanded the blood of the first born of all the oppressors; almost all of these have been sent upon us. We have been oppressed with taxes, and debts, and he has sent us more than lice, and has afflicted us with Andrew Johnson.

Yet underneath was a sincere devotion to democracy—something to be practiced as well as preached. Stevens had early made his way into local and national politics from that German-pietist, Scotch-Irish Presbyterian region around Gettysburg and Lancaster on such issues as Antimasonry, Prohibition, Know-Nothingism, and antislavery. He was never a complete success either in business or politics, and his personal life always skirted the edges between philanthropy and scandal. He was a bundle of contradictions which he himself may have taken an impish delight in creating. But whatever he was or was not, he fitted so well into this era of uncertainty, where a sharp, positive tongue and clever tricks counted, that he either reflected or led the revolt of Congress against the Johnson program.[14]

Of only one thing about Stevens are we certain: his intense purpose to see that the Negro secured justice and security through the right to vote and to possess both land and education. Stevens did more than abuse Johnson. He saw the social problem behind it all. "We had turned, or were about to turn loose four million slaves without a hut to shelter them or a cent in their pockets. The infernal laws of slavery had prevented them from acquiring an education, understanding the commonest law of contract, or of managing the ordinary business of life. The Congress was bound to provide for them until they could take care of themselves. If we did not furnish them with homesteads, and hedge them around with protective laws; if we left them to the legislation of their late masters, we had better have left them in bondage."

Stevens charged that:

> Demagogues of all parties, even some high in authority, gravely shout, "this is the white man's government." What is implied by this? That one race of men are to have the exclusive rights forever to rule this nation, and to exercise all acts of sovereignty, while all other races and nations and colors are to be their subjects, and have no voice in making the laws and choosing the rulers by whom they are to be governed....
>
> Our fathers repudiated the whole doctrine of the legal superiority of families or races, and proclaimed the equality of men before the law. Upon that they created a revolution and built the Republic. . . . It is our duty to complete their work. . . . If we have not yet been sufficiently scourged for our national sin to teach us to do justice to all God's creatures, without distinction of race or color, we must expect the still more heavy vengeance of an offended Father. . . .[15]

[14] See Fawn M. Brodie, *Thaddeus Stevens: Scourge of the South* (New York, 1959) and Richard N. Current, *Old Thad Stevens: A Story of Ambition* (Madison, Wis., 1942). The first is more friendly, the second more critical, but both are scholarly and well written.

[15] *Congressional Globe*, 39th Cong., 1st sess., pp. 74–75.

So Stevens proposed confiscation of the planters' lands, forty acres for each freedman, and continued support for the Negro until he could support himself.

To say that Thaddeus Stevens was sincere is not to say that he was wise. To say that his aim was greater justice for the Negro is not to say that his methods were sound or that what he accomplished was, in the end, all of value. He was at least usually ahead of the times.

In sharp contrast to Thaddeus Stevens as a factor in the Republican revolt against Johnson's program was Charles Sumner, senior senator from Massachusetts. While Stevens was a realist, Sumner was a man who dealt primarily in abstractions. He seldom saw things as they were, but only as he thought they ought to be. The practical results of what he advocated never bothered him. He showed no regard for the consequences of what he said, and he was always saying something. Reared in Boston and educated at Harvard, Sumner had studied law and attempted practice. His interests, however, were too abstract for success, and he soon abandoned the effort. He then began dabbling in reforms of various types. With the Whig split on slavery, he was drawn into politics, a field for which his close friends thought he had "not a single quality."

Sumner's forte was public speaking. Here he was always the actor, playing a part, delivering an oration, losing himself in the role he was taking. He therefore never felt responsible for what the character he was impersonating said or did, and he was surprised that others thought he should be. When his friend Robert C. Winthrop voted supplies for the army in Mexico, Sumner denounced him bitterly and in flowery language talked of all the waters of the oceans never being able to wash away his guilt. Yet he was astonished when Winthrop resented the attack. After Sumner had delivered his famous speech on Kansas and insulted every man he passed on the way, he never understood why anyone should have resented his words. When he adopted a cause, it became "right," and all who differed were blind and evil.

His closest friend, Henry Hilliard, said that he did not have an honest mind; and Henry Adams declared that his mind "had reached the calm of water which receives and reflects images without absorbing them; it contained nothing but itself." John Hay, listening to his attack on Johnson, could only see "the blindness of an honest, earnest man, who is so intent on what he thinks right and necessary that he closes his eyes to the fatal consequences of such a course in different circumstances and different times."

Sumner had now adopted the theory that the southern states had committed suicide. Nothing could change his mind. He added to it the absolute necessity of the vote in Negro hands, and pushed it to the point where even Fessenden wrote, "If I could cut the throats of about half a dozen Republican Senators . . . Sumner would be the first victim, as he is by far the biggest fool of the lot." Sumner was always in morals; he was always right; he was always "in order," when he chose to speak.

But Sumner, like Stevens, in the troubled waters, could supply the most essential elements: emotion and high-sounding morality. To him, the Negro must have the equal rights with all men to participate in the government, which he was taxed to support. "This," he asserted, "is the great guarantee without which all other guarantees will fail. This is the sole solution of our present troubles and anxieties. . . . A failure to perform these promises is moral and political bankruptcy." Then he added a more profound truth: "The ballot is a school master. Reading and writing are of inestimable value, but the ballot teaches what these cannot teach. It teaches manhood. Especially is it important to a race whose manhood had been denied. The work of redemption cannot be completed if the ballot is left in doubt." [16]

[16] *Congressional Globe*, 39th Cong., 1st sess., pp. 674–687; Edward L. Pierce (ed.), *Memoir and Letters of Charles Sumner* (Boston, 1877–1893), vol. 4, pp. 76, 181–183, 275. For some of Sumner's later ideas of integrated schools for the South and free

So with Stevens insisting that "the whole fabric of Southern society must be changed" and that "it never can be done if this opportunity is lost," and with Sumner demanding the franchise for the Negro as an obligation to democracy and the Declaration of Independence, the stage was set for a re-evaluation of the whole situation. The lines were being drawn. Sides would have to be taken and acceptance of change of some kind would be inevitable.

Stevens and Sumner represented the rather small extreme element in the Republican party. They never dominated the party but by their intense zeal kept the moral, social side always before their more conservative fellows. They were thus always in a position to plead the Negro's cause and to raise the cry when his interests seemed to be in danger. They spread distrust of the South and kept alive the notion that only through the presence of the army was the Negro safe. They dealt in suspicion and hatred, two essentials for drastic reconstruction steps; and somehow, in spite of rebuffs, they saw much of their program enacted.

Stevens and Sumner, of course, did not work alone. They could always count on assistance from Jacob M. Howard, William Kelly, George S. Boutwell, Zachariah Chandler, Benjamin F. Butler, and others of like mind. Yet their ultimate success in securing votes remains something of a mystery. Perhaps they gained by always asking for more than they expected to receive, and by seeming to compromise, they won over men of more conservative temper—men such as John A. Bingham, Lyman Trumbull, William P. Fessenden, James W. Grimes, and others, who were as much in favor of justice and security as they themselves. There was always a common base on which Republicans as Republicans could agree. The terms Radical and Conservative somehow tell too much and too little.

---

homesteads for all freedmen, see *Congressional Globe,* 40th Cong., 1st sess., p. 49.

12

JOHNSON
VERSUS CONGRESS

I

President Johnson's course in the period preceding the
meeting of Congress is something of a puzzle. He was
conscious of the Radical Republican hostility to his southern program and even of the critical, if not disloyal,
conduct of Secretary of War Edwin M. Stanton. He was
also aware of growing approval on the part of Democrats.
The friendly attitude of James Gordon Bennett of the
New York Herald seems to have been especially welcome.
Yet Johnson did not remove Stanton from the cabinet,
and he did not openly court the Democrats. His public
statements continued to be vague in character, while his
dealings with southern leaders still indicated a liberal
course. Many have attributed his conduct to indecisive-

ness.[1] Some have thought he was playing a clever political game while waiting for events to prove him the leader of a new conservative party alone capable of giving the nation peace and justice.[2] Others have seen him as a confused man who honestly thought he had completed reconstruction. At any rate, as Congress assembled it was clear that Johnson would be forced to show his hand. Even though many thought cooperation between Johnson and Congress possible, Republicans as a whole were not to remain passive much longer.[3] Some, like Senator Benjamin F. Wade, were already fearful that "that golden opportunity for humiliating and destroying the influence of the Southern aristocracy" had gone forever.

Action began on January 5, 1866, when Lyman Trumbull introduced two bills in the Senate, the first soon to be known as the Freedmen's Bureau Bill and the second as the Civil Rights Bill. Both measures represented the determination of Congress to take a hand in southern affairs where the southern legislatures, under Johnson's

[1] Secretary of the Navy Gideon Welles commented, "But it had been the misfortune, the weakness, the great error for the President to delay—hesitate before acting. It has weakened him in public estimation, and given the impression that he is not strong in his own opinions. Yet I know of no man who is more firm, when he has once taken a stand. But promptness as well as firmness is necessary to inspire public confidence."—Howard K. Beale (ed.), *The Diary of Gideon Welles* (New York, 1960), vol. 3, p. 61.

[2] David Donald, *The Politics of Reconstruction, 1863–1867* (Baton Rouge, 1965), pp. 22–24; LaWanda and John H. Cox, *Politics, Principle, and Prejudice, 1865–1866* (New York, 1963), pp. 134–140.

[3] "The loyal men of the nation . . . regard his actions and his speeches with almost sickening anxiety . . . and many of them are apt to fear that the immense pressure brought to bear upon him, acting on habits of thought and prejudices almost unavoidable under the circumstances of his Southern birth and breeding, may work mischiefs which even the power of Congress may find hard to mend. And it cannot be denied that some of Mr. Johnson's words and actions have given not unreasonable occasion to disloyal hopes and loyal fears."—*The Independent*, Sept. 21, 1865.

program, were seemingly acting as though there had been no civil war and no "lost cause."

The Freedmen's Bureau Bill would extend indefinitely the temporary Freedmen's Bill, correct its faults, extend its functions, and increase its efficiency. The Bureau was to remain under control of a commissioner with aid from both military and civilian officials, as found necessary. It would continue to find "abandoned" land for the freedmen,[4] build asylums and schools for their use, and give military protection for civil rights. What was new was the extension of military jurisdiction over all cases where any civil rights and immunities belonging to white persons (including the rights to make and enforce contracts, to give evidence, buy, sell, and hold property), were refused or denied by local law, prejudice on account of race, color, or previous condition of servitude; or where different punishments or penalties are inflicted upon Negroes from those prescribed for white persons committing like offenses.

Then, to put teeth into the bill, it was made a misdemeanor—punishable by a fine of $1000 or imprisonment for a year or both—for anyone to deprive another of these rights on account of race, color, or previous condition of servitude. The act applied only to the states where war had interfered with the ordinary judicial proceedings. Northern discrimination of the same kind was not to be affected.

Thaddeus Stevens immediately attempted to enlarge the scope of the bill so as to confiscate some 3,000,000 acres

---

[4] The matter of "abandoned lands," lands bid on at tax sales, etc., is too complicated to be discussed here. For the problem on the Sea Islands of South Carolina, see the excellent study: Willie Lee Rose, *Rehearsal for Reconstruction: The Port Royal Experiment* (Indianapolis, 1964). In opposing the Bureau, Senator Garrett Davis called it "the largest and most expensive eleemosynary institution that ever existed, and adopts all the Negro population . . . as its wards." It was, he charged, designed as "political machinery."—*Congressional Globe*, 39th Cong., 1st sess., pp. 933–936.

of land to be sold to refugee families. He would have the government seize the entire property of 70,000 southern planters to create farms for Negro families. The 70,000 displaced, he hoped, would become exiles. The exchange of industrious Negro farmers for worthless southern aristocrats would be a good bargain.

Stevens' suggestion was too extreme for wide acceptance, but the Freedmen's Bureau Bill did express the deep distrust most Republicans entertained regarding the safety of Negro rights under southern control. It also expressed the determination that justice be done. Johnson's new governments, it must be remembered, had only grudgingly granted the minimum required. As the *Jackson News* (Miss.) had warned, "Negroes as a class must be excluded from the witness stand. If the privilege is ever granted it will . . . at last end in the admission of the negro to the jury box and ballot box.

Republicans as a whole, therefore, saw nothing extreme about the Freedmen's Bureau Bill. They were only being cautious. In this spirit it was passed by the House after sharp debate on February 6, and by the Senate three days later. It then went to President Johnson for his signature.

With the Freedmen's Bureau Bill in the President's hands, certain things need to be noted. Since there was already a Freedmen's Bureau in operation in the South and its tenure had not expired, this new move on the part of Congress indicated dissatisfaction with existing conditions. It was a move not only to assert Congress' rights in the matter, but specifically a blow at the so-called Black Codes. What is of equal importance, the bill put an end to Johnson's ambiguity on issues and any plans for a new party to ensure his re-election. He now had to come out into the open.

Furthermore, the Bureau had already proved to be the most objectionable feature of military occupation to southerners. Its interference with what they thought were absolutely necessary steps to economic recovery and its efforts to impose a degree of racial equality had more than offset the aid it had given in food and other supplies to their own people.

Perhaps more significantly the bill indicated that Congress had begun to demand a hand in reconstruction. Some were beginning to say that the President had acted only under his rights as commander in chief of the army and navy. What he had done was merely to establish a temporary military order, which must be quickly replaced by one created by the Congress acting for "the United States" as the only body under our Constitution responsible for guaranteeing to each state a democratic form of government. Johnson's duty had been done. Future steps belonged in the main to Congress—in reality to the Joint Committee of Congress on Reconstruction.

Accompanying the Freedmen's Bill had come a request from the Joint Committee that further presidential steps on reconstruction end until the committee was ready to act. Many historians have viewed this as a friendly move toward cooperation. It in fact amounted to an order for Johnson to step aside. Senator William P. Fessenden, who with two companions carried the message to Johnson, in spite of a well-deserved reputation for being personally a conservative, had worked steadily with Stanton, Wade, Stevens and even Sumner, whose self-righteousness Fessenden despised. It was Fessenden who appointed an all-Radical committee which checked the move to admit Tennessee and thereby destroyed any hope, if it ever existed, that Johnson would sign the Freedmen's Bill. Under his direction the Committee of Fifteen was never interested in cooperation but was primarily a creation to check Johnson and to produce "a more just reconstruction." [5] To speak of Radical Republicans and Conservative

[5] Fessenden held that a victor in war can do anything it chooses with the vanquished and that this applied to the Civil War. Southern States had forfeited their status and "may be utterly extinguished and swept out of existence by civil war." He had, moreover, demanded immediate action on the Stevens resolution to create the Joint Committee and had insisted on the right of Congress to shape reconstruction. *Congressional Globe*, 39th Cong., 1st sess., pp. 954–955, 987–990.

Republicans is to overlook the basic fact that on the question of reaping the benefits of the war in terms of justice to the Negro, Republicans were just Republicans. They voted almost as a body on all the important reconstruction measures.

II

Johnson, meanwhile, had seen enough of the Joint Committee to know that it was asking him to step aside, to admit that he had failed—that all he had accomplished was in vain. He had only his firm, even if mistaken, belief that he had done what Lincoln would have done and what the Constitution and the best interests of the nation demanded. Regardless of the cost, he could not, and would not, sign the Freedmen's Bill. He would not even accept William H. Seward's wiser veto wording. His reasons and objections were frankly and fully stated in the veto message he sent to Congress. He could not see any reason for a new measure since the old Bureau was still in force. Besides, the heavy increase of military strength and granting the Bureau such wide control over judicial and civil affairs were both unwarranted and unconstitutional. The original Bureau was adequate for its intended purposes; the heavy expense for what amounted to a new bureau was not justified. It would only harm the Negro by exciting false hopes of constant government favors and delay his own efforts at self-sufficiency. The Negro could best realize his hopes under civil authorities, not under military control.

Johnson further questioned the soundness of legislation affecting people who were not represented in the government. The southern states had no part in making law or in explaining their needs and points of view. In a time of peace this could not be justified. The Constitution did not support such action.

Johnson also insisted that the Executive, more than Congress, spoke for the whole nation and that the southern states had been duly reconstructed and were entitled to their rights in the Union. His argument carried enough weight to prevent the overriding of his veto. The vote was 18 to 30.

The President's veto message, which showed no inclination to compromise or even to cooperate, cleared the air. It revealed the situation as a conflict of two distinct attitudes toward the southern states and, consequently, two differing purposes and procedures in reconstruction. Johnson had been forced to speak out.

Now the Radicals, too, were being forced to reveal purposes which until now had not been clear.[6] The day after the veto was received, the Joint Committee unanimously passed Stevens' resolution to the effect that both houses of Congress, "in order to close agitation upon a question which seems likely to disturb the action of the government, as well as to uncertainty which is agitating the minds of the people of the eleven states which have been declared to be in insurrection, no Senator or representative shall be admitted into either branch of Congress from any of said states until Congress shall have declared such state entitled to such representation."

There it was, and there could be no mistaking the situation. The states were still "declared to be in insurrection"; they had not as yet been reconstructed. That would be accomplished only when Congress admitted their representatives. What Johnson had done did not count.

Then Senator Trumbull, who had introduced the Freedmen's Bill, made it doubly clear that the Republicans did not trust the southern people to deal fairly with the Negro. He introduced his Civil Rights Bill, thought necessary because the Negro would "be tyrannized over, abused, and virtually re-enslaved without some legislation by the nation for his protection." This was only saying that the

[6] Welles had said, "On Reconstruction, as it is called, there are differences and doubts and darkness. None of the Radicals have any clear conception or perception of what they want [except power and place]. No well defined policy has been indicated by any of them."—Howard K. Beale (ed.), *op. cit.*, vol. 3, p. 29.

army alone could secure what the Republicans thought would give "security," and force the "repentance," necessary for the national welfare. As a moderate Republican, Trumbull was saying that a second reconstruction, involving an intellectual and social revolution, was necessary. He thought Johnson had been wrong about what was constitutional, what was truly economical, and what gave "security."

These blunt attacks and the rejection of all Johnson's efforts and political plans now added to the bitter, unfair whispering campaign which the radicals organized against him and which tore away his acquired poise and dignity. It reconverted Johnson into the Tennessee politician fighting "unprincipled enemies." Stimulated by a crowd of sympathizers who gathered one evening before the White House and called for a speech, Johnson suddenly forgot he was President of the United States. He used the occasion to strike at his enemies and to justify himself as the successor of those great Americans who in the past had stood by principle. He allied himself with Washington and Jackson and boasted of the part he had played in the rebellion and the sacrifices he had made for the preservation of the Union. With peace and repentance, he added, his policy had been one of forgiveness and restoration.

A new rebellion had begun, Johnson warned. A little group in Congress, "an irresponsible central directory," had assumed the right to deny seats in Congress to duly elected members. What it had done was just as treasonable as what "the Davises and Toombes, the Slidells and others" had done in the past. When asked for names, he responded, "I say Thaddeus Stevens, of Pennsylvania, I say Charles Sumner; I say Wendell Phillips and others of the same stripe." [7]

[7] Historians who hold that Johnson's vague and ambiguous statements of the past months were intentional and for the purpose of winning support for his re-election, see his sudden explosion as due to anger when forced to show his hand. LaWanda and John H. Cox, *op. cit.*, pp. 88–102, 129–145.

With that, the lid was off. Taking his cue from the remark of Stevens that King Charles of England had lost his head for less than Johnson had done, the President asked what usurpation he had been guilty of—and answered in terms of duty always done, as a tailor, as a legislator, and as President of the United States. Yet what was his reward? An effort on the part of that "irresponsible directory" to be rid of him. In fact, he shouted, their "intention was to incite assassination: to remove this obstacle to their seizure of place and power." Had not "the murder of Lincoln" appeased the vengeance and wrath of the opponents of this government? "Do they want more blood? If my blood is to be shed because I vindicate the Union and the preservation of this government in its original purity and character, let it be shed." He would "stand by the Constitution of our fathers though the heavens themselves may fall." He would never desert the people.

This was the silly speech of an excited and wounded man. It served no purpose but to announce a complete break in the Administration, an open war on the Joint Committee of Congress. Johnson's conduct was in bad taste, and his critics made the most of it in the press. Even papers friendly to Johnson were critical. Under normal conditions Johnson's outburst would not have attracted national attention. At a critical time, it offered the Radicals an excuse to do what they evidently already intended to do—take over the leadership of government. Senator John Sherman, however, saw deeper:

> I ask you, Senators, whether the President of the United States, regarding him as he is: a man who never turned his back upon a foe, personal or political: a man whose great virtue has been his combative propensity: as a man who repelled insults here on the very spot where I now stand, when they came from traitors arming themselves for the fight: can you ask him, because he is President, to submit to insult? Every sentiment of manhood, every dictate of our nature, would induce a man, when he heard these words [the enumerated insults of Stevens, Sumner, and Phillips] uttered, in the heat of passion, to thrust them back. When a

man becomes President he had none the less the feelings of manhood.[8]

One man, at least, saw the tragedy then evolving.

III

The significance of what had happened ran far deeper than personalities. The stage was set for one of the most important periods in American life. The physical struggle between the sections was ended; the struggle between values was not. The built-in conflicts and national commitments to mankind were still there, and again the legalistic threatened to overshadow the moral and the human.

The so-called Radical Republicans insisted that they were not threatening a new political and social revolution—that revolution had already occurred. They were only asking the nation to be true to itself and to accept what had been won in the recent physical conflict. The war had of course settled the matter of nationalism, but something had gone wrong. In the reconstruction program now in effect, the southern states were being treated as normal states and were being returned, without repentance, to near self-rule. This threatened American commitments to Christian and democratic values, now faced concretely in our obligations to the Negro. Lands that had once been the property of aristocratic slaveowners but had come into northern hands through confiscation or tax sales were now being returned to their pardoned original owners, and Negro occupants were being thrust aside. Even the courts were in some cases questioning the new powers discovered in the Constitution. Was it not time to call a halt? Was not American respect for traditional political forms and for property rights robbing the North of its victory? Was not Andrew Johnson speaking for the past? Did not the Republican party stand for a new age—economic, social, political,

---

[8] *Congressional Globe,* 39th Cong., Appendix, pp. 124–133.

and moral? This was certainly not a simple matter having to do with "resumption" following a civil war.

Issues involving the future political and social character of the nation had developed. A power struggle between the executive and the legislative departments had reached the breaking point. "Johnson had encouraged the Southern people to think of him as their protector against the Black Republicans of the North." He had given the impression that reconstruction was in *his* hands at the very moment when Congress was about to take command. The issue, as Senator Fessenden observed, was whether Congress was a mere tool for looking over credentials presented by southern men to see whether they were in proper order, or whether its members had a right "to bring their deliberate judgements on great questions before the American people." If Congress had no such powers, it was time both to drop the pretense and for its members to become mere nobodies.[9] The political issue was clearly stated—in terms beyond compromise.

The social issue was also assuming rigid form. As *The Independent* saw things, "The only issue between Democrats and Republicans was to be not an old issue but a new —not Slavery, but Suffrage. . . . The Springfield *Republican* and the *Evening Post* . . . unite in saying that the Republican party cannot afford to load its back with the burden of Equal Suffrage." Senator J. R. Doolittle of Wisconsin and Governor Oliver P. Morton of Indiana were saying the same thing. But *The Independent* would stand by equal rights "while we live," and sound Republicans knew it was better to lose the government than to lose principles.[10]

Conflict was inherent in such a situation. It was not a simple case of Johnson declaring war on Congress, or of Congress declaring war on President Johnson. It was considerably more the struggle of a confused nation trying to find its way out of one age and into another. That

---

[9] *Congressional Globe*, 39th Cong., 1st sess., pp. 954–955.
[10] *The Independent*, Oct. 12, 1865.

was why Republicans did not agree on details and methods but did largely agree on "modern" democratic, humanitarian values.

Behind this, however, was the Civil War and what it had done to a whole people. The United States that came out of the war was not the one that entered it. This was just as true for the South as for the North. But the past was still there. Southerners, no more than northerners, could believe that their sons had died for nothing, or for something not worth dying for. These may not have been things of which the modern world approved, but they were the things for which men had fought and suffered. The ideals had not perished with the soldiers.

All this simply meant that the war of ideas still had to be won; that a social revolution would probably evolve slowly; and that agreement on what was good, what was progressive, and what was American for all Americans would take time, patience, and good sense, more so because some Americans were victors, some vanquished.

IV

Perhaps from the beginning the situation was an impossible one. Given unyielding President Johnson and the idealistic Republican Congress as they were; given the widely differing theories as to the status of the southern states and the conflicting policies they permitted; given the vague and elastic terms "security," "repentance," and "equality" to be used for expressing the demands made and the yielding required; given the misunderstanding that had led to war and was now magnified by four years of bloody fighting; given the emerging modern world that had largely ignored the now broken and beaten South; and given the political party situation with all its distrust and the power control it represented—perhaps "failure and abandonment" were inevitable. If so, assigning blame and seeking villains is unnecessary.

THE JOINT COMMITTEE
ON RECONSTRUCTION

I

The Civil Rights Bill, companion to the Freedmen's
Bill, passed the Senate on February 2 and the House on
March 13. It conferred citizenship on all persons born in
the United States and confirmed them in the right to make
and enforce contracts, to appear in court and to inherit,
purchase, and sell property. Negroes were to have the full
and equal benefits of all laws for the security of person
and property. It was a reasonable bill where so many distrusted the southern willingness to deal justly with the
Negro.

Many thought that Johnson, having made his point in
the first veto, would sign the Civil Rights Bill. Perhaps
Thaddeus Stevens' move to have the clerk read into the
House record a statement from a New York paper that

Johnson was "an insolent, clownish drunkard in comparison to whom Caligula's horse was more respectable" may have had some influence. At any rate, on March 17 Congress received Johnson's veto message, in which there was no recognition of need for additional legislation in behalf of the Negro. His rights were already secure under state and federal laws. This bill only placed under federal courts cases that belonged to local courts. By such action, Johnson pointed out, a state's jurisdiction over its own cases was being usurped. In all our history, he continued, in all our experience as a people living under federal and state law, no such system as that contemplated by the details of this bill had ever before been proposed or adopted. It established for the security of the colored race safeguards that went infinitely beyond any federal government had ever provided for the white race. In fact, the distinction of race and color in the bill operated in favor of the colored race. The bill interfered with the municipal legislation of the states, and with the relations existing exclusively between a state and its citizens, or between inhabitants of the same state. It proposed an absorption and assumption of power by the federal government which, if accepted, must sap and destroy the federative system of limited powers and break down the barriers that preserve the rights of the states. Most of all, Johnson objected to the creation of an indiscriminate national citizenship given by law.[1]

Johnson had made an able legal case, and one that the Supreme Court would later uphold. He had not, however, faced or removed the fears that had prompted the Civil Rights Bill. As conservative John Sherman said, "To have refused the negroes the simplest rights granted to every other inhabitant, native or foreign, would be outrageous."

Ends, it is said, justify means, and safeguarding the rights of the Negro justified the highly questionable move

---

[1] James D. Richardson (ed.), *A Compilation of the Messages and Papers of the Presidents*, (Washington, 1909), vol. 6, pp. 504–513. For Trumbull's defense of the bill, see *Congressional Globe*, 39th Cong., 1st sess., pp. 1755–1761.

in Congress to unseat Senator-elect John Stockton and the even more questionable steps taken by Senator L. M. Morrill to secure the votes necessary to override Johnson's veto. Stockton, once legally seated, was now unseated; Morrill, paired with a sick senator, on short notice absolved the pair, and the vote was taken before the ailing senator could come. Johnson and Congress parted ways, with compromise no longer possible.

This was the setting in which the Joint Committee of Congress on Reconstruction suddenly pushed its hearings toward a report on April 30, 1866.[2] Since its appointment in December, it had held hearings aimed, it sometimes seemed, at carrying out the radical purpose of killing time until the nation was ready to accept a congressional plan of reconstruction. Its members up to this time had shown little interest in learning the truth about the South. They assumed they already knew it. All they asked of witnesses, who were evidently chosen for the purpose, was a statement justifying the new program of reconstruction already more or less agreed upon. They heard much of southern disloyalty, of the mistreatment of Negroes, and of the necessity of retaining troops in the South. They heard these things because the questions asked were largely on these subjects. Only now and then were other matters introduced.

[2] The Senate members of the Joint Committee were: William P. Fessenden, James W. Grimes, Ira Harris, Jacob M. Howard, G. N. Williams, and R. Johnson. House members were: Thaddeus Stevens, E. B. Washburne, J. G. Morrill, H. Greder, John A. Bingham, Roscoe Conkling, George S. Boutwell, Henry T. Blow, and A. J. Rogers. Charles Sumner, who greatly wished to be chosen, was ignored. Fessenden wrote of the committee, "We are embarrassed by men of extreme opinions who think all ways but their own are necessarily bad ways, and by others who cannot wait until the proper time, through fear lest their own names may not be sufficiently known in connection with the work to be done."—F. P. Fessenden, *Life and Public Services of William Pitt Fessenden* (Boston, 1907), vol. 1, pp. 13, 20. For discussion of Sumner and the committee, see vol. 1, p. 20.

Howard K. Beale computed that of 144 witnesses called, 114 were men whose private interests and prejudices strongly biased them against southerners, while only 30 had an interest in restoration. Seventy-seven were northerners living in the South; 67 were southerners, many with personal grievances. The 114 who favored continued military rule included: 10 northern travelers in the South, 10 northern officeholders in the South, 38 northern army officers, 15 northern Freedmen's Bureau officers, 3 northerners then living in the South, 21 southern white loyalists, and 8 Negro loyalists. The rest were ex-Confederates; these were not given the usual questions, and were heard primarily so that they might be trapped into making damaging statements.[3]

The procedure used with most witnesses was to ask specific questions categorically phrased so as to draw out the answers desired. Opinions, not facts, were sought, so that the matter of truth or falsehood would not be involved. Often questions were worded so as to suggest the answers expected, beginning, for example, "Is it not true. . . ." As a rule, questions dealt only with such matters as could be used to discredit the South under Johnson's plan. The South, as such, was never heard. It had already been convicted.

It is interesting to note, too, that Jacob M. Howard and George S. Boutwell, the two most radical members of the committee, were allowed to ask most of the questions. Only on the rarest occasion did any others take part. In this connection, the biographical section of the history of the Joint Committee, described Howard as "a worthy protégé of his colleague Zachary Chandler, . . . one of the most vulgar and reckless of radicals [who] served consistently in the vanguard of extreme Negrophiles." Bout-

[3] Howard K. Beale, *The Critical Year: A Study of Andrew Johnson and Reconstruction* (New York, 1930), pp. 94–96. All quotes and other material used in dealing with the report are taken from *Report of the Joint Committee on Reconstruction, at the First Session, Thirty-ninth Congress* (Washington, 1866).

well is characterized as "perhaps the coldest, most calcu-
lating, and yet unreasoning fanatic on the Committee—
always urging colleagues to more radical action." [4]

The inquiry developed a set of stock questions. They
varied according to the group to which the witness belonged, and were shaped to build up a single impression.
Soldiers stationed in the South were questioned in such a
way as to show that the army was not welcome and that
its personnel was generally ignored. They were given the
opportunity to express the opinion that neither the Union
element nor the Negro would be safe without its presence;
that if a president such as James Buchanan should again
come to office, Southerners would again attempt secession;
and that if the United States should go to war with England or France, southerners would join the enemy. Such
questions appear repeatedly, with uniform answers given.
Specific evidence was not sought, only general impres-
sions.

From the particular witnesses summoned and the questions asked, it is perfectly apparent that the object of
the hearings was to inspire fear and distrust of the South,
to discredit Johnson's program, and to create an excuse
for continued military control and more severe action by
Congress.

For a southerner of some importance, the questions
followed a rather common pattern. He was asked regarding the present feelings of the people about the war,
toward the United States government, and toward the
army stationed among them. Then followed the rebuttal
questions: "Is there or not a bitter feeling between those
who supported the rebellion and those who supported the
general government during the war?" "Are these Union
men safe without army protection, or do they enjoy social
intercourse and business relations with former rebels?"

Southerners were also asked about their loyalty in case

----

[4] Benjamin B. Kendrick (ed.), *The Journal of the Joint Committee of Fifteen on Reconstruction* (New York, 1914), pp. 192–
193, 187–190.

of a foreign war, whether they expected pay for the slaves lost, and their preference for seeing in public office rebels or Union men. Especially were they questioned on their attitude toward the Freedmen's Bureau and their willingness, without force, to do justice to the Negro and to respect his right to vote and to education.

If the witness were a person who had ranked high in the Confederacy—for example, Robert E. Lee—he was questioned concerning his loyalty, his acceptance of defeat, his willingness to pay taxes, his attitude toward the Negro, and his conduct in case of a foreign war. He was given a whole series of loaded questions, prefaced, so as to raise doubts, by a statement that he might refuse to answer if he chose. Especially marked was the way questions were continually reshaped so as to produce contradictions and doubts as to the witness's complete repentance and sincerity.[5]

II

With supposedly sufficient evidence to justify rejection of all that Johnson had done and to establish the need for a second reconstruction, the committee compiled a final report of some 800 pages and distributed 100,000 copies at government expense. It was offered as an authentic picture of conditions and attitudes in the South, from which the nation could judge as to the fitness of the southern states for representation in either house of Congress.

By way of introduction, the report opened with a statement that the Confederate States, "reduced to obedience

[5] *Report of the Joint Committee of Fifteen on Reconstruction.* For questioning of Lee, see Part II, pp. 129–136; a good example of questioning is in Section II, pp. 141–144. The committee wanted damaging evidence and they found much. Conditions in the South were bad and there was disloyalty and brutality. Much that was reported was truth, but it was not the whole truth. The fault in the report was a lack of the balance necessary to give a sound picture on which intelligent action could be based.

by force of arms," were in an abnormal condition, without civil government, without commercial connections, without national or international relations, and subject only to martial law. By withdrawing their representatives from Congress "they had renounced the privilege of representation," and by waging war they had "destroyed their State constitutions in respect to the vital principle which connected them with the Union." So there was "nothing of those constitutions which the United States was bound to take notice." Therefore, at the end of the war they were without any civil government.

To remedy this condition, the President had relied only on his powers as commander in chief of the army. The men he had put in office had only military authority and no right to organize civil governments. That right belonged only to Congress, in whom was lodged, by the Constitution, the authority "to fix the political relations of the States to the Union. . . ."

What Johnson had done had been merely a temporary emergency move. He had not had the proper information to do anything else. Furthermore, there was no evidence of the loyalty of those who had participated in southern conventions; Union men had been defeated in elections, and men who could not honestly take an oath of loyalty had been elected.

These were the reasons for the formation of the Joint Committee, which had now acquired the sound and necessary information for action by the proper constitutional authority, Congress. The report eliminated Johnson and all his works.

Then followed a recital of what the southern states had done—insurrection, open rebellion, and war against the government. To quote:

> They continued this war for four years with the most determined and malignant spirit, killing in battle . . . destroying the property of loyal citizens at sea and on land, and entailing on the government an enormous debt. . . . And they only yielded when, after a long, bloody and wasting war, they were compelled by utter exhaustion to lay down their arms;

. . . not willingly, but declaring that they yielded because they could no longer resist, affording no evidence whatever of repentance for their crime, and expressing no regret, except that they had no longer the power to continue the desperate struggle.

The conclusion drawn from this was that "a government thus outraged had a perfect right to exact indemnity for the injuries done, and security against the recurrence of such outrages in the future. . . ." This, the report stated, was impossible under Johnson's constitutional theory. "Treason defeated in the field, has only to take possession of Congress and the Cabinet." It was absurd to think that the southern states had the entire right to resume at their own will and pleasure all their privileges within the Union, "to participate in its government, and to control the conduct of its affairs." That section of the report thus took care of the part which the late Confederate States should play in Reconstruction.

III

There remained for the committee only the task of showing what its recent investigation had revealed: that what southerners had so far done was insincerely and reluctantly performed, and proved that "justice and security" were still in danger.

First, there was the Negro, once a chattel, now a free man and a citizen. He had been loyal in the war, and he must not be abandoned. Yet his freedom could increase the representation of the South in Congress. The only way to prevent it from enlarging the power and influence of the old dominating southern class was to give the Negro access to the ballot box and to decrease the representation of any state that denied him the right. This would require a constitutional amendment, and the committee had one to propose.[6] Until justice for all was written into the law

[6] The fact that a constitutional amendment was already in the making, and its terms already decided, was apparent when southerners were asked whether they would accept Negro suf-

of the land, the Republican party had not met its obligations.

Then followed a detailed statement of the proof which, the report said, the committee hearings had afforded that the southern people were not sincere in their repentance and would repudiate everything as soon as possible unless further restrained. The committee therefore asked for further proof that southerners were prepared and disposed

> in good faith to accept the results of the war, abandon their hostility to the government, and to live in peace and amity with the people of the loyal States, extending to all classes of citizens equal rights and privileges, and conforming to the republican idea of liberty and equality. They should exhibit in their acts something more than an unwilling submission to an unavoidable necessity—a feeling, if not cheerful, certainly not offensive and defiant. . . . They should evince an entire repudiation of all hostility to the general government, by an acceptance of such just and reasonable conditions as the government should think the public safety demands.

Here, at last, was clearly stated the demand on southerners for a change of heart, a humble spirit of repentance, an admission of error, and a willingness to "act out" their defeat in such terms as the victor spiritually required.

The final part of the report is a detailed statement of what the many witnesses had said about the South's failure to evidence any of the attitudes and actions required for a return to the Union. Hardly had the war ended, the report stated, before the people in the insurrectionary states were haughtily claiming the right of participating at once in the government which the southern people had been fighting to overthrow. Encouraged by an executive who had no right to act, southerners had placed in power leading rebels, unrepentant and unpardoned, and excluded with contempt those who had been attached to the

---

frage if refusal resulted in the reduction of their state's representation in Congress.

Union. Professing no repentance, glorying apparently in their crime, they had refused to submit to any conditions whatever as preliminary to a resumption of power.

According to witnesses, the southern press had striven to keep alive the fire of hate by urging Johnson to overturn the government by force of arms and to drive the true representatives from their seats in Congress. Universally, southerners had opposed the Freedmen's Bureau. Without the protection of the army, Union sympathizers would have been driven from their homes. Taxes were paid only on compulsion, and compensation for their slaves was generally expected. If they could, southerners would repudiate the national debt. They still upheld the legal right of secession. Men of the Union army who went South to engage in business were detested and persecuted.

With such evidence before them, the committee was of the opinion that Congress was not justified in recognizing the validity of recent southern elections. Conquered enemies should not be permitted at their own pleasure and on their own terms to participate in making laws for their conqueror. The issues before Congress were:

> Whether conquered rebels may change their theatre of operations from the battle-field, where they were defeated, to the halls of Congress, and through their representatives, seize upon the government they fought to destroy; whether the national treasury, the army of the nation, its navy, its forts and arsenals, its whole civil administration, its credit, its pensioners, the widows and orphans of those who perished in the war, the public honor, peace and safety, shall all be turned over to the keeping of its recent enemies without delay.

These were the issues, and the committee's answers—to borrow an earlier retort—was, "Gentlemen, you mistake us. You mistake us. We will not do it." [7]

[7] Senator Thomas A. Hendricks of Indiana had objected to the committee's meeting in the secret, free from public influence, as if with a sign over the door, "No admittance for the American people: this place is sacred to a political inquisition, whose will is law to the President and to Congress, and whose fiat binds the fortunes and determines the fate of eleven States and eight mil-

What are we to make of such a report? Its very temper justifies the earlier emphasis on the significance of the war as a civil war, where "forgiving and forgetting" were no simple matters. It breathes of fear and distrust. "Rebels" is a loaded word.

Beyond any question, the southern people had had their fill of fighting. The fear of a renewal, which the committee tried to arouse, was absurd, to say the least. Southern refusal to rejoice at military control and to embrace with sincere affection every northern visitor surprised no intelligent person. The suggestion that an imaginary southerner would join an imaginary foe in an imaginary war was a trick unworthy of a serious investigation.

Why did the committee go to such extremes? Most certainly because it believed that things of vital importance were at stake. Johnson's program was not producing the kind of South or the kind of future America that the Civil War justified. Sufficient punishment, too, was required. Conditions justified continued control by the Republican party because of all that it had stood for in the past and all to which it was pledged for the future. This included politics, economics, morals, and things social. For the attainment of its ends, any required means were justified.

The matter, however, ran even deeper. In a region where the late war had left political and economic chaos, where temporary governments were makeshift, where labor and race were united in one, where an army was in control and where a government bureau shaped much of human relationships, it was possible to find anything that anyone, for any purpose, desired. Johnson found what he

---

lion people. The Committee selects witnesses according to their own good will. . . . The representatives of eleven States stand suspended during their pleasure, while they may devise how the President of the United States shall be broken to their will or be degraded before the people." So one-fourth of the American people are arraigned before a tribunal of Fifteen, their fate determined "upon evidence of spies, informers, contractors, political agents and hostile officials." *Congressional Globe*, 39th Cong., 1st sess., pp. 867–885.

wanted for support of his program. Every traveler saw what he came to see. The Radical committee, looking for what would prove its point, found it, with supporting opinions. "Facts" could now justify a constitutional amendment.

This does not imply, as some historians have thought, that the whole plan of later reconstruction had now been conceived—that this was the first step in a well-organized plot. It only suggests that under the unique situation in which the committee, Johnson, and the South, as three separate factors, operated, a serious predicament was developing in which further action would gradually develop, not by plan but by circumstance. Yet many were aware that affairs were being allowed to degenerate into a conflict between two departments of the government and that no progress toward a final settlement was being made. Incrimination, not progress, was the rule. If an amendment meant settlement, it would be welcomed.[8]

[8] The comment of *The Nation* (May 22, 1866) on the committee's report is interesting. Its ideas, E. L. Godkin said, are "opposed to the genius of American Institutions and to the temper of the times. . . . Confiscation, disenfranchisement, retaliation, prescription of all kinds, as a means either of reconciling men to a new and distasteful order of things or of frightening them into obedience or acquiescence are expedients borrowed from mediaeval or pagan times."

CHAPTER

14

THE FOURTEENTH AMENDMENT

I

Newspaper editorials in this period reveal that a kind of restlessness had been developing throughout the nation—a weariness of the quarrel between the President and the Congress, which seemed at times to be largely personal.[1] People were demanding progress toward some

---

[1] As Charles Ray of the *Chicago Tribune* wrote, on February 8, 1866, to Lyman Trumbull, "You all in Washington must remember that the excitement of the great contest is dying out, and that commercial and industrial enterprises and pursuits are engaging a large share of public attention . . . people are more mindful of themselves than of any fine philanthropic scheme that looks to making Sambo a voter, a juror, and office-holder."—Illinois State Historical Society, Trumbull MSS. See also *The Nation*, April 20, 1866, which stated that Congress has done nothing but keep southern states out.

solution of the tragic situation into which the nation had drifted. Business was suffering; Congress was so occupied with Johnson and the South that serious economic problems were being neglected. Johnson had at least done something toward a final settlement, and Congress had evidently decided that this was unsatisfactory. But as yet, in its Freedmen's Bureau and Civil Rights bills, Congress had only dealt with certain specific items. It had not faced the larger problem of "resumption." Even here the result had been only to intensify the quarrel with the President. If the Joint Committee represented Congress at work on the larger problem, it was time for some indication of progress.

The basic issues to be settled were becoming quite clear to all. Even the points of difference were generally understood. They had been revealed in the Freedmen's Bureau debates, more clearly in the Civil Rights debates, and in the President's veto messages. Everyone understood that some decision had to be made regarding the Negro's rights, southern representation, the disenfranchisement of Confederate leaders, and the national and Confederate debts.[2] So insistent had become the demand for action that senators not on the Joint Committee and persons not even in Congress began offering suggestions for action.

On March 16, Senator William M. Stewart of Nevada introduced a series of resolutions that brought immediate response. He suggested that each southern state, as soon as it had amended its constitution ending all distinctions as to civil rights based on race or color, repudiated all debts incurred in the rebellion, yielded all claims for loss of slaves, and extended the franchise to all persons on the same terms and conditions, would be recognized as having fully resumed its relations to the government. Northern

[2] George W. Julian commented, "The political and social regeneration of the country made desolate by treason is the prime necessity of the hour, and is preliminary to any reconstruction of the States." He would return them to a territorial status and then retrain them under central government control. *Congressional Globe*, 39th Cong., 1st sess., p. 279.

states would also incorporate this same amendment into their constitutions. A general amnesty would then be declared for all who had taken part in the rebellion. Here was a specific proposal for ending the suspense and removing all the difficulties to resumption. Yet both Andrew Johnson and Thaddeus Stevens took a hand in bringing it to nothing.

Then Indiana reformer Robert Dale Owen, ever ready to save the nation, came to Washington to offer his program. He too would end discrimination, extend the right to vote to all, reduce representation for such discrimination before 1876, and void rebel debts and all claims for loss of slaves. He would give Congress the right to enforce these provisions. He too revealed the basic issues to be faced and offered a solution. His proposal met the same fate as had Stewart's, Congress could not agree on all its terms.

Yet these efforts had made action necessary and delay politically dangerous. Democratic approval of these efforts could not be ignored. The reason for the committee's hesitation and delay readily became apparent. It had been dominated from the beginning by the Radical element, with what has been called "social-revolutionary purposes" for reconstructing the South. However, in the debates on Trumbull's Civil Rights Bill, these Radicals had learned that reflection of such purposes in a report would meet strong opposition. They had to be constitutionally careful.

Both Thaddeus Stevens and John A. Bingham, who were to shape the report that was now being demanded from the committee, had been important figures in the prewar antislavery drive.[3] They had then argued that the Declaration of Independence conferred a national citizenship with a rather comprehensive body of natural rights and civil liberties. They had found additional support for

---

[3] Alfred H. Kelley, "The Fourteenth Amendment Reconsidered," *Michigan Law Review*, LIV (June 1956), 1049–1086.

this philosophy in an earlier decision by Justice Bushrod Washington. In the case of *Corfield* vs. *Coryell*, Washington had set forth in detail a long list of civil liberties guaranteed by the comity clause in Article IV of the Constitution. It stated clearly that citizens of each state were to be entitled to all privileges and immunities of citizens in the several states. From this comes the theory of "equal protection of the laws." Charles Sumner had argued this in the Roberts case; and in late 1850s Bingham himself had said in the House, "It must be apparent that the absolute equality of all, and the equal protection of each, are principles of our constitution . . . as universal and indestructible as the human race."

To this had gradually been added the "due process clause" of the Fifth Amendment, protecting persons from loss of life, liberty, or property without due process of law. Chief Justice Roger B. Taney had used this in the Dred Scott case, and Theodore Weld and James G. Birney had fought the "black laws" of Ohio with the same weapon. It appeared also in the Free-Soil platforms of 1848 and 1852.

These two constitutional doctrines now became the constitutional ideology of the Radical Republicans on the committee. They had been the legal weapons against class legislation by race offered by Lyman Trumbull in defending his Civil Rights Bill. They had on that occasion been attacked by the Democrats, who denied, as had Taney, that the Negro could be a citizen or that there was such a thing as national citizenship.

Trumbull, however, had argued that the Thirteenth Amendment endowed the Negro with citizenship "as a necessary incident of freedom" and that Congress had both the power and the duty to guarantee the rights that went with citizenship. Trumbull had then attacked the Black Codes, which of course did not make the Negro a slave but did deprive him of his rights as a free man. His bill was to end these discriminations and to give full meaning to the Thirteenth Amendment. Trumbull had cited as support Bushrod Washington's decision in the Corfield case. He was, he said, only protecting rights already existing.

Democrats and conservatives had seen in this, as they well might, the threat of social revolution. Senator Edgar Cowan of Connecticut, a Conservative Republican, was quick to comment, "Now as I understand the meaning and intent of this [civil rights] bill, it is that there shall be no discrimination between the inhabitants of the several states of this union, none in any way." He then called attention to the segregated schools of his state, and asked whether it was Trumbull's purpose to punish, for violation of a United States statute, the school directors who carried out this state law. He added, "To me it is monstrous."

Others noted the various state laws in the North prohibiting marriage between the races, and asked if the bill would invalidate them. A senator from Kentucky observed that in his state laws for certain crimes varied with the race. Would these be destroyed? Both Trumbull and Fessenden said no, and gave assurance that the bill would leave the two races in the same relationship as before. Yet doubts remained and the words "revolutionary" and "perfect equality" kept cropping up. The question of the constitutionality of such a sweeping act also began to be raised. One said, "It brings the two races upon the same great plane of perfect equality."

At that, Senator Bingham rose to state his belief that civil rights included the entire range of civil privileges and immunities within organized society, excepting only political rights. He accepted the conservatives' objections and interpretations, and agreed that Congress had no power to enact such legislation merely by right derived from the Thirteenth Amendment. The Civil Rights Bill, nevertheless, was aimed to strike down every state law that established any kind of discrimination against Negroes. It did have the revolutionary purpose; and since there was some doubt as to constitutionality and since all discriminatory legislation ought to be wiped out, Bingham thought the proper way would be by an amendment to the Constitution. Yet by eliminating the discrimination clause, the Civil Rights Bill was finally passed with the constitutional uncertainty remaining.

This was the situation that led to the framing of the Fourteenth Amendment. Agreement on the basic issues had not been reached but public pressure for a congressional program could no longer be resisted. The debates in Congress on the various proposals that had been made began to clear the air, and the Joint Committee set to work on the terms to be incorporated into a constitutional amendment. That was an important task and the time was too short to do a sound and enduring job. That would become clear in the years ahead.

II

The Joint Committee amendment, as presented to the Senate and House on April 30, 1865, by Fessenden and Stevens contained five sections.[4] The first proclaimed a national citizenship and stated that no state could abridge the privileges and immunities of citizens of the United States, or deprive them of life, liberty, or property without due process of law, or deprive them of equal protection of the laws.

The second apportioned representatives among the states according to the whole number of persons in each state, but added the provision that where the right to vote for federal and state officials was denied to any male inhabitant of twenty-one years of age and a citizen [except for participation in rebellion or other crimes], the

[4] For an excellent discussion of details, see Eric L. McKitrick, *Andrew Johnson and Reconstruction* (Chicago, 1960), pp. 326–363. The *New York Herald* editorialized on June 12, 1866, "The Congressional proposition for the amendment of the Constitution, as modified by the Senate, is an ingeniously contrived party platform for the coming fall elections."

basis of representation should be reduced in the proportion that the number of such males bear to the total number of eligible males in the state.

The third section barred from voting for representatives in Congress and electors for President and Vice-President, until July 4, 1870, any person connected in any way with the late rebellion. The fourth simply forbade the payment by the United States or by any state of the debts incurred in support of the rebellion or for loss of slaves. The fifth gave Congress the power to enforce the above articles.

As to the resumption of southern states in the Union, two bills followed. The first stated that when the above amendment became part of the Constitution, and when the southern states had modified their constitutions to conform, their representatives should be admitted to Congress. The only other condition was the payment of their share of the direct tax within a period not exceeding ten years.

The second bill barred from federal office most persons who had held high office in the Confederacy, or those who had left United States service of any kind for service in the Confederacy. This section, generally objectionable to all, was soon dropped.

Neither Johnson nor all of Congress accepted this program without debate and change. The disfranchisement section, especially, met sharp opposition. Some asked for more detailed statements of terms, and a few followed Johnson's attitude of rejecting the whole amendment.[5]

---

[5] Thomas A. Hendricks, Democrat from Indiana, noted that the first report from the Committee of Fifteen had been rejected, so "a second defeat of a party program could not be borne; its effects on the fall elections would be disastrous. A caucus was called and we witnessed the astonishing spectacle of the withdrawal for the time, of a great legislative measure, touching the Constitution itself, from the Senate, that it might be decided in secret councils of a party. . . ." Hendrick then charged that the new arrangement was one which allowed minorities to rule where they added to the political power of the Republican party, but not in places where the opposite was true. "Come now let candor and

At length, a five-man committee began work to make the desired revisions, and produced the final Fourteenth Amendment as it was to be submitted to the states for ratification. The main change from the original suggestion was to drop the punitive section and to add at the very beginning Bingham's definition of citizenship. The question here is whether the section was added merely to remove doubt as to the constitutional status of the Civil Rights Act, or whether the intent was to go beyond the scope of that act and put all civil rights as the Radicals saw them under the protection of the amendments.

Knowing the opinions Bingham had always held and the social revolutionary sweep of his purpose all along, many scholars believe that the purpose was to go well beyond the guarantees of the Civil Rights Act and to place all civil rights, in the expansive Bingham definition, under federal guarantees of equality against state law. They have noted that the very phrases used, by virtue of their history and derivation, are intentionally vague and not capable of precise legal description. The terms are those of prewar days and have a radical, humanitarian, equalitarian quality. They are not the terms of the Civil Rights Bill, which had, in the debate, permitted the states to retain segregation. "Privileges and immunities," "due process of law," and "equal protection" are not derived from the Civil Rights Act, but have a very familiar ring. Radicals were now amending the Constitution as the law of the land, not writing a statute.

Yet, in defending the amendment before the House, Stevens observed, "Some answer, 'Your civil rights bill secures the same things.' That is partly true, but a law is repealable by a majority. And I need hardly say that the first time that the South with their copperhead allies obtain command of the Congress it will be repealed. . . . This amendment once adopted cannot be amended without two-thirds of Congress. That they will hardly get." Others

---

truth have full sway and admit your party purpose."—*Congressional Globe*, 39th Cong., 1st sess., pp. 2938–2942.

echoed this idea. As James A. Garfield said, "The civil rights bill is now a part of the law of this land. But every gentleman knows it will cease to be a part of the law whenever the sad moment arrives when [the Democratic party] comes into power." Others supported the amendment because they thought the Civil Rights Bill was unconstitutional.

Opposition, however, talked of the revolutionary character of the first section. As one asked:

> What are privileges and immunities? Why, sir, all the rights we have under the laws of the country are embraced under the definition of privileges and immunities. The right to vote is a privilege. The right to marry is a privilege. The right to contract is a privilege. The right to be a juror is a privilege. The right to be a judge or President of the United States is a privilege. I hold if that ever becomes a part of the fundamental law of the land it will prevent any state from refusing to allow anything to anybody embraced under the terms of privileges and immunities. If the negro is refused the right to be a juror, that will take away from his privileges and immunities as a citizen of the United States, and the Federal Government will step in and interfere. It will result in a revolution worse than that through which we have just passed.

Bingham's reply to this is revealing:

> The necessity for the first section of this amendment to the constitution, Mr. Speaker, is one of the lessons that has been taught to your committee and taught to all the people of this country by the history of the past four years of terrible conflict . . . that history in which God is, and in which he teaches the profoundest lessons to men and nations . . . that is to protect by national law the privileges and immunities of all the citizens of the Republic and the inborn rights of every person within its jurisdiction whenever the same shall be abridged or denied by the unconstitutional acts of any State.

Then to get back to the Declaration of Independence, Bingham added:

> This amendment takes from no state any right that ever pertained to it. No state ever had the right, under the forms of law or otherwise, to deny to any freeman the equal pro-

tection of the laws or to abridge the privileges or immunities of any citizen of the Republic, although many of them have assumed and exercised the power, and that without remedy.

Here was both the lawyer and the old antislavery man talking.

The Fourteenth Amendment thus started on its troubled way. The American dream of possible social perfection had become part of the law of the land through those vague and elastic terms "privileges or immunities"—things which "no State shall abridge" in a land where all persons born there or naturalized are citizens.

III

The difficulties that beset the amendment in the days ahead were due in large part to the tangle of purposes that went into its making. Unquestionably the philanthropic motive was present, but the Negro's right to the ballot was not directly granted. The choice to grant or refuse was cleverly left in southern hands. For a price, they could deny the Negro the franchise. The reason for this was that something important even for the Negro's rights was involved—the continued dominance of the Republican party. The amendment had been framed in a way to make certain that if the Negro's vote were restricted or controlled, southern representation, now increased by the fact that the Negro was a citizen, would be reduced in proportion. That would accomplish two things. It would prevent the increase of Democratic power and also appease that large element in the Republican party which had a positive dislike for the Negro and was opposed to his enfranchisement. It was as important to protect the North from the Negro as to protect the Negro from the South.[6]

[6] Leon F. Litwack, *North of Slavery: The Negro in the Free States, 1790–1860* (Chicago, 1961). Litwack shows not only the intense dislike of the Negro, especially in the Northwest, but the discriminations of all kinds which he endured there. One of the chief reasons for seeking to secure him rights in the South was

An economic interest was also involved. Power in Democratic hands could threaten the Republican interest in public lands, the tariff, financial programs, railroad expansion, and other issues. It is therefore interesting that when southern and Democratic success proved less dangerous, the Fourteenth Amendment and its civil rights' purposes were largely ignored.

---

to keep him there, and even to drain the Negroes already in the North back to the South. See also Jacque Voegli, "The Northwest and the Race Issue," *Mississippi Valley Historical Review*, L (September, 1963), 235–251; and his *Free But Not Equal* (Chicago, 1967), *passim*. The charge of party purpose in the amendment had been made and admitted. Democrats charged that "stripped of all disguise, the measure is a mere scheme to deny representation to eleven states; to prevent indefinitely a complete restoration of the Union and perpetuate the power of a sectional party.—*Congressional Globe*, 39th Cong., 1st sess., pp. 2462–2464.

Thaddeus Stevens admitted the charge and remarked, "Give us the third section or give us nothing. Do not balk us with the pretense of an amendment which throws the Union into the hands of the enemy before it becomes consolidated. Gentlemen say I speak of party. Where party is necessary to sustain the Union, I say rally to your party and save the Union." He dismissed the charge that the third section was too strong, for southerners had neither confessed their sins nor humbled themselves.—*Congressional Globe*, 39th Cong., 1st sess., pp. 2533–2545.

THE FOURTEENTH AMENDMENT AND "THE CRITICAL YEAR"

I

The Fourteenth Amendment, shorn of its punitive section but strengthened and made deliberately vague in extent by a new first section proclaiming a national citizenship and protecting immunities and privileges, now went out to the states for ratification. Two things about the procedure need to be noted. Congress, by the Constitution, can choose only between legislature and convention ratification, and is given no right to dictate terms. Yet in the case of this amendment, in actual practice, the southern states not then in the Union were required to ratify as a condition for admittance. Furthermore, they were to be admitted only on the condition that they accepted whatever might be included in those vague terms, "immunities" and "privileges." This was, of course, before

the Fifteenth Amendment (which required Negro suffrage) had been passed.

Moreover, ratification had to be executed by a legislature from which most Confederates were excluded. In
other words, the effects of the amendment were to be
applied before the amendment was ratified, and acceptance of it was required as a prelude to accepting it.[1]

All the southern states except Tennessee (with Johnson's approval) refused to ratify. A period of "masterful
inactivity" followed, and further southern ratification
was delayed until admission on a better understanding
became a possibility. All that, however, lay ahead. Just
now, as *The Nation* observed:

> There are thousands upon thousands . . . who see behind
> the adoption of the Amendment such a time of peace and
> good will as this generation, at least, has never known. There
> is to be a grand revival of dry good and cheap carriage busi-
> ness at the South; the negroes are, somehow or other, to get
> into their proper place; the agitators are all to go home and
> raise cabbages or peddle popped-corn in the trains, and the
> Radical newspapers will have to offer free board and lodging
> to secure subscribers.

The editor, E. L. Godkin, was skeptical. An arrangement that allowed southern whites to deny Negroes political rights at only the cost of reduced representation
"really settled very little." That would not restore har-
mony between the sections, end agitation at the North
about the conditions of southern Negroes, silence Wendell

---

[1] President Johnson suggested that "the inference is plainly
deductible that while, in the opinion of Congress, the people of a
state may be too strongly disloyal to be entitled to representation,
they may nevertheless, during the suspension of their former,
proper, practical relations to the Union, have an equally potent
voice with other and loyal states in propositions to amend the
Constitution, upon which so essentially depend the stability,
prosperity, and very existence of the nation."—William A. Dunning, *Essays on the Civil War and Reconstruction and Related
Topics* (rev. ed., New York, 1931), p. 117. Senator Willard
Saulsbury suggested they were states if they were favorable to
the Negro, but for no other purpose.—*Congressional Globe*, 39th
Cong., 1st sess., pp. 39–43.

Phillips, or check northern attempts to interfere with southern institutions. And as to the constitutionality of it all, Godkin had only this to say, "You may talk as you please about 'the letter' or 'the spirit' of the Constitution, or the meaning of its framers; but if you talk too long the agitators will tell you they do not care a fig about your Constitution, and will have justice done."

As a matter of fact, neither Thaddeus Stevens nor Charles Sumner had thought an amendment necessary. Congress could take any action required to achieve justice. Only John A. Bingham's insistence that the Negro's rights would be permanently secure as part of the law of the land brought the Fourteenth Amendment.

The amendment represented not only a growing demand in the North for an end to reconstruction but also a grim determination to make the Negro's rights secure. The amendment was not a final answer. As the product of compromise, it was vague in meaning and intent. Its ultimate value would depend on the character of the decisions that courts in the future might hand down.

II

As it turned out in the years immediately ahead, this instrument framed to serve the Negro was primarily used to protect business organizations from state regulation. As the amendment stood, any individual regardless of color might seek its shelter. So when the courts held that a corporation was a person, the amendment became so much the weapon of such "individuals" that in the case of the *Missouri Pacific Railroad* vs. *Humes,* a judge declared that his court was not a harbor where refuge could be found from every act of ill-advised and oppressive state legislation.

In the next forty years, of the 604 cases before the courts under the amendment, only 28 (5 percent dealt with the Negro and his rights. The rest treated of matters of eminent domain, taxation, procedure, and especially police powers. They ranged from cases on the recovery of the value of a dog in Louisiana, the sale of cigarettes in Tennessee, the height of a building in Boston, the running of a barber shop on Sunday in Minnesota, to the regulation of graveyards in California. The emerging modern world, not the abstractions of the past, was having its way!

As far as the Negro was concerned, in the days ahead the courts upheld the existence of two kinds of citizenship, in which "state-citizenship" was a matter for the state to handle, and which meant that the Negro must look to the state for his protection. The Negro's right to a mixed jury was denied unless race reasons were proved, and segregated schools and separate coaches for travel were permitted if they were equal in quality. The Jim Crow era, and that of business corporation freedom, came to dominance. The United States had once again paid heavily for doing no more than providing "for each day as it came."

III

The amendment had indirectly served an immediate purpose. Northern acceptance, and southern rejection on Johnson's advice, had made crystal clear the vast gulf that separated the President from the Republicans in Congress. It was a conflict in many ways between the ideas and values of the past and those that four years of civil war had created. As such, it involved things economic, things social, things political, and things moral. The future character of the nation was at stake. It would go backward or it would sweep forward into the modern world.

Andrew Johnson, with his antiquated ideas regarding states' rights, had permitted the South to change its attitude from that of "a vanquished enemy into that of a power treating on equal terms." By his reverence for a strictly interpreted Constitution, he had turned what was primarily a political question into a legal one. He ignored the fact that reconstruction was "a question too momentous, too wide in its range, and affecting too vitally the destiny of the Nation to allow its being submitted to any court of law," or to be proscribed by constitutional forms. He had ignored another simple fact: in a democratic republic no agreement of any kind could be made based on the "outraged absurdity of making the color of a man's skin a reason for denying him anything which he and other men valued." Nor had Andrew Johnson learned that men with a conscience will "not cease to talk about and inveigh against such 'an absurdity' or to make its authors uncomfortable." Perhaps in the interest of peace they should do so, but they would not. "Therefore," stated *The Nation,* "if it be the talk of fanatics that shakes the republic to its centre, the only remedy is to leave the fanatics nothing to talk about." [2]

Then to make matters worse Johnson had allied himself with the Democratic party, and was using his office to build political power. It was time to call a halt.

IV

These were the circumstances that gave the 1866 congressional elections unprecedented importance.

Johnson started the campaign under serious handicaps. He had allowed southern reconstruction to monopolize his interests to the neglect of the great economic issues facing the nation. A firm stand on government expenditures, tax reduction, the quantity of greenbacks in circulation, and

[2] *The Nation,* Nov. 1, 1866; Jan. 17, 1867. It is interesting to note that rumors were circulating that Johnson was planning to use force against the Congress. In a speech, Montgomery Blair had said something about another Civil War whose "battlefields would be in the North"; and Blair, speaking for Johnson, was supposedly saying that "if the Radicals shall win the fall elections [the President] will not abide by the verdict of the ballot-box, but will rise in revolution." He would "disperse the Congress with the sword." *The Independent* took the matter seriously and, on July 26, 1866, charged Johnson as "daily directing the movement of the Confederate party from Abraham Lincoln's presidential chair." By August 9, it was viewing the Memphis and New Orleans riots as the first steps in Johnson's plans.

the excessive tariffs might have shifted public attention and won popular support. David A. Wells, a sound economist at the head of the Revenue Commission, had pointed the way and offered sound advice. Even the regulation of big business, which at this stage of growing strength and plunder offered a field of reform well fitted to Johnson's earlier attitudes, might also have won popular support. Johnson, however, was too bent on his reconstruction program to act. He would have thrust opposition to the Fourteenth Amendment into the campaign, had William H. Seward not opposed. He felt that nothing along these other lines could be done until the southern states were back in the Union.

Retaining Lincoln's cabinet had also proved to be a mistake. It early became clear that Edwin M. Stanton, James Harlan, James Speed, and William Dennison were not only out of sympathy with his program but were working with the Radicals and revealing administration secrets to them. Yet Johnson's bad habits of hesitation and indecision kept them long in office. Even when others resigned, Stanton—the most difficult of the lot—remained and much of the time acted in open defiance. His main purpose seemed to have been that of maintaining an effective army in the South, and the Supreme Court decision in the Milligan case, which held that a citizen could not be brought before a military court when civil courts were open, was to him as bad as Johnson's vetoes. It was his duty to remain in office.

These were indeed handicaps for an administration soon to be on trial in an election, and yet they were not the most serious. The party situation itself presented the greatest problem. The Civil War had played havoc with the old parties. Johnson owed his office to that fact. The Union party victory in 1864 had left the traditional groups in a queer position in which the Republican machinery had been used but the candidates and program had been national, not partisan, in character. The opposition, though labeled Democratic, had meanwhile attempted to bring into its ranks all those who were eager for peace, regardless of party. The result had been party chaos. Only now were men gradually beginning to think of themselves as Republicans and Democrats. The tendency was more and more to charge Johnson with being a Democrat, and all Democrats with being copperheads. Neither charge was true, but the sad fact was that Johnson was constantly being forced to rely on Democrats for support of his program, while the Republicans were coalescing in opposition.

This led Johnson's supporters to begin talking about a new Union third party. Harvey Watterson termed it "a national administration party," and thought of it as being made broad enough to attract both the old conservative Republicans and Democrats. Johnson again hesitated. But the Radical Republicans did not vacillate. With disloyal cabinet members leading, they allied their party with big business and went ahead with the claim of having always been the party of loyalty and the one that had saved the Union. It was once again its mission to rescue the nation from danger. As Republicans saw it, the war was not over; their mission was not ended. The Fourteenth Amendment was but a first step.

That was the situation when James R. Doolittle, John A. Dix, James G. Bennett, and others who supported Johnson made their call for a Union convention to meet in Philadelphia in August. Their basic problem was to prevent their efforts from appearing to be a Democratic movement and to hold conservative Republican support. This was no easy task. Radical Republicans were already claiming that Johnson, once a Democrat, had returned to the fold. The fact that Democrats widely supported his program seemed adequate proof. The struggle was still what the *Chicago Tribune* had called the civil war, a fight between the Republican party and the disloyal Democrats. Johnson's belated removal from office of a few Republicans who openly opposed him and his program was, therefore, denounced as an "unmitigated outrage" against good men whose only fault was "adhering to their party convictions."

So when the Union convention assembled, it was as notable for those who were not there as it was for those present. Republicans who earlier might have been classed as conservatives, such as John T. Sherman, Lyman Trumbull, and Oliver P. Morton were nowhere to be seen, while even Henry J. Raymond, William H. Seward, Fernando Wood, and Montgomery Blair (now clearly out of step with the Radical Republicans) seemed quite willing to play a secondary role. That opened the way for those usually associated with the Democrats to become most conspicuous. Raymond, who assumed the task of drafting the report of the Committee on Resolutions, found sharp reaction to his inclination to accept the Fourteenth Amendment, his use of the term "rebellion," and his reference to the ills of slavery. Then, most embarrassing, was the appearance of Clement Vallandigham in the Ohio delegation and Fernando Wood with the New Yorkers. Each had played a much too negative part in wartime matters even to be seated in the Convention. In fact, the only moment of enthusiasm seems to have occurred when Governor James L. Orr of South Carolina walked down the aisle arm in arm with General Darius N. Couch of Massachusetts. Even that gave evidence of having been prearranged.

Everywhere there seemed to be a studied effort to prevent an undercurrent of basic differences from rising to the surface. Delegates were given little chance to speak their minds or to engage in open debate. Speeches were confined largely to such generalizations as restoring the Constitution and defending the President's stand on the right of the restored southern states to representation in Congress. In their "Declaration of Principles," the delegates upheld the constitutional doctrine of the impossibility of secession, the right of a state to fix voting qualifications, the repudiation of Confederate debts, and the equal protection of person and property to all. They even suggested aid for federal soldiers and their families. Their appeal was for the election of congressmen who would uphold Johnson and these principles.

The Union convention is important more for what it revealed about the political situation than for its influence on the coming election. Clearly the delegates had not formed a new third party. Basic issues were still not clear. The old economic issues having to do with tariffs, lands, internal improvements, and finances were still there, in exaggerated form and calling for solution, but no one seemed inclined to face them. Big business needed regulation; there were basic factors in the emerging modern age with its new energy and its new technology presenting new social problems. Railroads and their control meant more for the future than the punishment of those who had taken a hand in rebellion. The public lands were being squandered as never before; financial policies were interest-involved to new degree. Yet in the confusion of reconstruction these issues had not reached the level of political party interest and expression. Immediate reactions to immediate situations were all that moved men.

Personalities were too much involved for a separation of Johnson the man from his program, or of the Radical Republicans from theirs. Even the significance of the conflict between the Executive and Congress was not understood. Everyone knew that the southern states would sooner or later be admitted back into the Union, but few were willing to face the fact that their admission involved political control, economic decisions, and the future of the Negro—to say nothing of the satisfaction that a victorious North still somehow had failed to gain. No one was as yet prepared to take definite and final steps. Hence the Convention had been composed of men who, for differing reasons, were dissatisfied with the existing confusion but who had nothing but dissatisfaction to offer. That exposed them to ridicule by the hostile press and even more to the vicious pen of the cartoonist.

Two outside events had already taken a hand in preventing the American people from forming and expressing objective opinions. On April 19, in the river town of Memphis, Tennessee, a riot involving a Negro regiment and the local police erupted. A Negro had apparently pushed a white man off the walk, a dangerous matter under any circumstance. A fight began and soon developed into a race riot that lasted two days. Some 46 Negroes were killed; 12 Negro schools and 4 Negro churches were burned.

Regardless of the local factors involved, Radical Republicans saw it all as evidence of basic southern attitudes toward the Negro and the failure and impossibility of Johnson's program. It seemed to prove the necessity for more troops throughout the South. Then, as if fate was against a rational formation of opinion, in July (a bad time for trouble anywhere) a riot broke out in New Orleans, another river town.[3] It grew out of the tangled condition of Louisiana politics in which a Radical group under the lead of Governor J. Madison Wells attempted to overthrow the newly established Johnson government by recalling the old 1864 Constitutional Convention. By use of the Negro vote, this group expected to control the state, disfranchise the ruling white element, and gain support from Congress.

Local officials appealed to Johnson for support and notified General Absalom Baird, the military commander, that they intended to arrest the delegates unless the meeting had his sanction. Baird replied that he had neither sanctioned nor forbidden the meeting, but that he would protect it from violence. He did later wire Secretary of War Stanton for immediate instructions. At the same time, the lieutenant-governor, working with the mayor, wired the President and asked whether the military was to interfere with the court now considering the case. Johnson immediately replied that the troops would sustain the court pro-

---

[3] Howard K. Beale (ed.), *The Diary of Gideon Welles* (New York, 1960), vol. 2, pp. 569–570; *New Orleans Times*, July 26, 28, Aug. 10; James M. Richardson, *A Compilation of the Messages and Papers of the Presidents*, (Washington, 1919) vol. 8, pp. 590–592, for Johnson's statement; George Fort Milton, *The Age of Hate: Andrew Johnson and the Radicals* (New York, 1930), pp. 345–349; John R. Ficklen, *History of Reconstruction in Louisiana* (Baltimore, 1910), pp. 146–179.

ceedings. He then asked Wells why the 1864 Convention had been recalled. Stanton, on the other hand, did not reply. He later gave the lame excuse that he did not consider it urgent. Meanwhile, General Baird, awaiting an answer from Stanton and instructions from the War Department, announced that if no word was received he would arrest any officer interfering with the delegates—this in spite of the President's telegram. The mayor then requested Baird to police the city and to protect the convention. It assembled without a quorum and adjourned until 1:30 P.M., but still no troops appeared.

Meanwhile, a large body of Negroes who had already rioted the night before, and who were armed with clubs and weapons of various kinds, started a march toward the Convention Hall. On the way they clashed with a group of whites. Police rushed to the scene, and soon the inevitable shots were fired. The police now arrived in force and the Negroes fled to the Convention Hall. A mob quickly gathered; a white flag from the Hall met no response as the mob surged forward. When the struggle ended, some 200 persons, mostly Negroes, were either dead or wounded. Whom to blame no one knew. General Philip H. Sheridan's report is probably the most reliable. He scattered the blame equally between the police and what he called "revolutionary men," but he bitterly condemned the brutality that had resulted.

This riot was, of course, exactly what the Radicals wanted.[4] In their hands, the New Orleans riot became a perfectly normal southern affair. Stanton, whose failure to instruct Baird made him as responsible as any other person, tried to place all the blame on Johnson. The Radical press rang with abuse. Said the *New York Tribune:* "The hands of the Rebels are again red with loyal blood; Rebel Armies have once more begun the work of massacre." It went on declare that "Johnson's statesmanship

---

[4] *The Independent* (Aug. 9, 1866) charged, "This man [Johnson] aided and abetted the New Orleans mob. He doubly inspired the murderers."

[has] again raised Rebel flags in New Orleans." To which Senator Zachariah Chandler added, "The same [rebels] are alive today . . . who have only changed their leaders, and their tactics. Then it was Jefferson Davis, now it is under Andrew Johnson.[5] They mean to overthrow the government."

The campaign of 1866 was getting under way.

[5] Unless the American people shall rebuke at the ballot-box the outrages which the President has abetted in New Orleans [said *The Independent*, on August 9, 1866], anarchy will become the common law of the South—nay of the North. . . . How long will the conservatives be blind to the mad career of Andrew Johnson? This man aided and abetted the New Orleans mob. He sent telegraphic messages which doubly inspired the murderers to their work. The President's policy is bloodshed. His instruments are fire and sword. His logic is threat and intimidation. He has turned treason into loyalty, and loyalty into treason. He seeks to invest the rebel states with the right of representation to which they are no better entitled than Indians on the frontier. He is the co-head of the rebellion.

16

THE CAMPAIGN
AND ELECTION OF 1866

I

The campaign of 1866 was exactly what one might have expected. The basic problem the nation faced, if it were to go ahead along a normal course into the modern world, was to bring the lingering Civil War to an end. Until the South was back in the Union and the Republican party satisfied, materially and spiritually, no progress was possible.

The actual fighting had now been over for a year and a half, and most Americans were settling down to a reasonably normal way of living and thinking. Emotions had cooled and most persons had accepted the idea that there would be no blood bath and that the southern states would soon be back in the Union. Different groups had different ideas as to what the government should be doing, but there was a growing feeling that Reconstruction was moving at too slow a pace, and that there was much else in American life that needed attention.

President Johnson had lost much public respect. Widespread feeling existed throughout the North that under his direction the southern states were too quickly having their own way and needed to be reminded of that fact. It was these attitudes that had forced the rather too hasty adoption of the Fourteenth Amendment, which, while not entirely satisfactory, did remove the lingering guilt over the wrong of slavery and the nation's obligations to the Negro. If given a chance freely to express their attitudes, the majority would at least give a vote for these ends, which at bottom would be a vote for peace. However, if Johnson would yield no ground, they would have no choice but to vote the Republican ticket.

A Radical minority, however, felt and thought differently. Those of this group in Congress were bitter both at Johnson, as a stubborn, bullheaded rival for power, and at the southern people, as proud aristocrats who, although badly defeated still insisted on assuming old attitudes toward both the Negro and the "Yankee North." Besides, both Johnson and the southerners had been, and still were, Democrats. That was why they were refusing to ratify the Fourteenth Amendment. To these Republicans, President Johnson was a constant reminder of the war and the uncertain future of their party. He had not only given back to "unrepentant rebels" the right of self-rule; he had attempted to prevent Congress from affording adequate protection and justice to the freedmen, for whom thousands of noble northern youth had given their lives. Johnson had, in fact, restored the Confederacy in all but name. The Old South was "resuming" its political privileges and its undemocratic ways with Johnson's blessing.

Johnson now assumed for Radicals the place once occupied by the Confederacy. He must be struck down as part of the victors' need for what they called "security and repentance." So far, they had achieved neither one. Johnson's policy had only produced a "defiant South" and increased the fear of returning Democratic control. Even a northern hold on the Negro was uncertain. These Republicans felt neither secure nor satisfied. They wanted something more in keeping with their ideals. Here was their opportunity to turn all the bitterness, all the frustration, and all the shattered hopes against a specific, tangible target: the person of Andrew Johnson.

II

If left as the clear-cut issue between two conflicting programs of Reconstruction, or even as a dispute between two departments of government, there might have been room for a third party and for a wide difference of opinion among the people. But if seen and understood as a continuation of the old struggle against the old foe, then complete victory was again possible. To achieve it, the end justified the use of any means.

That turned the campaign of 1866 into one of the most bitter in American history. It gave the Radical Republicans their chance at last to make clear to themselves what all along they had really wanted when they talked of "security and repentance," yet it also destroyed the last hope of the nation for gaining much of democratic value from the Civil War. The election would offer only a choice between Johnson and Congress. The Radicals would have their fling with victory, but in the end they would lose their dream and leave the Negro where they had found him—landless and voteless. The nation in turn would find its basic problems made only more difficult, with most of its efforts for the next half century spent in a futile effort to regain lost ground.

The campaign of 1866 opened with a definite effort to connect Johnson with the rebel South and the equally dangerous copperheads. As Henry Winter Davis wrote Sumner, the campaign must be based "not on the rights of the negro, nor on the general requirements of justice and humanity . . . they are vague generalities that solve nothing . . . but on the direct and practical consequences of allowing the rebel States to go into exclusive control of the men who led, or the men who followed in the rebellion." These ex-rebels must be kept out of Congress and the South shown to be "unsafe" in ex-rebel hands, where Johnson had placed it.

For these purposes, the New Orleans riot served almost perfectly, and Stevens quickly made the most of it to injure Johnson. He pictured a convention of highly respectable men, peacefully assembling, being massacred with Johnson's approval. Stanton, in turn, brazenly charged Johnson with being the "author" of the deeds perpetrated by his "pardoned rebels." The rebel and his rebellion would thus always be the target and the continuing danger. At length they even talked of Johnson leading a rebel army against the people's Congress!

The highlight of the campaign, and the only thing about which historians tell much, was the so-called "Swing around the circle." [1] The occasion for this was the dedication of a monument on the south side of Chicago to Stephen A. Douglas, who in 1847 had moved to that part of the city and had made a fortune of some two million dollars speculating in real estate. Douglas had also founded what he called Chicago University. The dedication was to be something of a national affair to honor a great Democrat, whose real merits had not as yet been completely overshadowed by the newly emerging mythical Abraham Lincoln.[2] The dedication could serve another

---

[1] "Andrew Johnson is making a tour among the people—showing them his face to divert them from looking at his heart. He has the face of a demagogue, the heart of a traitor. . . . Consumed with an egotism which he cloaks with humility, he makes a peacock's parade of his character, his career, his sacrifices, his policy, and his love of the people. In the midst of the spectacle thoughtful spectators give secret thanks to God that the basest citizen of the Republic, even though its chief magistrate, is unable to destroy but to disgrace it."—*The Independent*, Sept. 8, 1866.

[2] "Meanwhile, in the solemn hour when he stands by the monument of Douglas, let him forecast the epitaph on his own; Happy is he who after death, lives again in the Nation's grateful re-

purpose as well. A presidential trip to Chicago might bring the people to Johnson's side.

The President's party, which left Washington on August 28, contained such distinguished persons as General Ulysses S. Grant, Admiral David D. Farragut, Secretaries Welles and Seward, friendly congressmen, and a number of military personnel. Wives and even children, in some cases, were included. There were to be twenty-one stops, including one to view Niagara Falls and another to review the cadets at West Point. The trip to Chicago and the return by way of St. Louis was to take only about two weeks. From the start, it was an exhausting physical undertaking through a region that in late August and early September can be extremely hot. Travel in that day was both slow and uncomfortable; and with a crowd such as this, no one could have remained physically fit or mentally alert. Yet speeches would be demanded at all designated stops and even at unscheduled places. Much of the trip would be through Republican territory—through towns where returning soldiers had already begun to enlarge on their war experiences and to dream of pensions to be secured from Congress. If not hostile already, most of the people at least needed to be convinced; and the enemy had already been at work laying plans to make sure that convincing would be difficult. Hecklers had been prepared in most places.

Johnson, while an earnest speaker, was no spellbinding orator. He was essentially a stump speaker. One thing above all, as James R. Doolittle warned him, he must make no extemporaneous talks or remarks. Much of the press was already hostile and had shown a tendency to

---

memberance. Cruel is he who dying, is buried beneath the reproaches of the just and the accusations of the poor. Touched with insanity, corrupted with lust, stimulated with drink, let the President of the United States, standing for a half-hour by the grave's edge, calm his blood and chasten his thoughts, till he can reflect, for his warning, how a chief magistrate who betrays his country shall become a handful of dishonored dust."—*The Independent*, Sept. 8, 1866.

distort. "I would say nothing," Doolittle wrote Johnson, "which has not been carefully prefaced, beyond a simple acknowledgement for their cordial reception."

The day before Johnson left, both Hugh McCulloch and Orville Browning begged him to make no speeches. It was good advice that went astray. A listening crowd was too much for a man who felt himself misunderstood, misrepresented, mistreated, and insulted. It was the same old story of an acquired dignity and poise falling away and revealing the crude man from East Tennessee, explaining, fighting back, and completely off balance. Johnson had prepared only one speech for the entire trip. That had been enough in Tennessee politics, where he spoke only to each rural neighborhood. Now, as President of a nation, each speech was to a whole nation, as reporters spread whatever he said day by day throughout the land. One speech was not enough, and seemed to reveal an empty mind, a lack of understanding. When enlarged under heckling, it seemed to degenerate into a cheap harangue.

As a result, Johnson dropped from the dignity demanded of the nation's President to the level of an ordinary citizen engaged in a give-and-take verbal conflict on the level of speaker versus heckler. Back and forth it went.

"Why don't you hang Jeff Davis?"

"Why don't you?"

"You have the courts and the Attorney General."

"I'm not the Chief Justice."

"Congress is trying to destroy the government."

"It's a lie, a lie."

Calls for "Grant, Grant" and everywhere the chant of "veto, veto."

"They are ready to impeach me, just let them try," with the answer, "Too bad they don't."

And then the inevitable: "Though the powers of hell, death, and Stevens . . . combine, there is no power that can control me save you [the people] and God that spoke me into existence. . . ."

Worst of all was Johnson's final comparison of his persecution to that of Christ, his willingness to die for his country, coupled with constant reference to the Constitution, which he and the people must defend.[3]

III

The affairs were bad enough as they happened, but when they had passed through the hands of hostile reporters, sent along to distort, the whole nation saw it all in terms of the ridiculous, the undignified, the expression of passion and prejudice. Few said anything about the jeers, the taunts, and hisses, the planned riots, the charges of treason, and the openly dishonest newspaper reporting. The use of General Grant's absence, for a few days, to damage the President was typical.

Meanwhile Stevens, John A. Logan, Carl Schurz, Benjamin F. Wade, and Charles Sumner were making the most of Johnson's blunders. They compared him to Judas, Benedict Arnold, and Vallandigham. They called him "an imbecile," "a tyrant," and "an insolent drunken brute." Theirs was a war to complete the Civil War. "The rebellion" was still on, with slavery and the Union in the balance. Even Logan, whose early war record was none too admirable, was explaining: "There is but one way to treat with rebels. Take the torch in one hand and the sword in the other, and march to the music of the Union, with the flag unfurled, and sweep over their territory."

The leader of the continuing rebellion was Andrew Johnson, who had in war days risked his all for the preservation of the Union. He now took the place of the Confederacy, of the "slave power," of the hated Jefferson

---

[3] See George Fort Milton, *The Age of Hate: Andrew Johnson and the Radicals* (New York, 1930), pp. 296–344, for a favorable account. Walter L. Fleming (ed.), *Documentary History of Reconstruction . . . , 1865 to the Present Time* (Cleveland, 1906–1907), vol. 1, pp. 218–227, contains Johnson's Cleveland speech. The *New York Herald*, Aug. 31; Sept. 1, 4, 5, 10, 11, 30, gives reports of the trip.

Davis and all the rebels who would have destroyed God's experiment in democratic government and deprived the Negro of his just rights.

Here was American politics at its worst, and at a critical time in the nation's life. There were fundamental differences between Johnson's purposes and those of most Republicans, but not all Republicans were Radical nor were all Democrats in complete accord with Johnson's ways and programs. Most Americans, it seemed, wanted an end to Reconstruction. Regardless of party, they had accepted the Fourteenth Amendment, though without much enthusiasm. Yet as the campaign developed, and when the time came to vote, nothing was left but to fall back into the old party system. This did not represent a complete change of opinion, for none was required. Men would vote as they had in 1860 and for the same reasons. If there had been some reason for hesitating before the campaign had started, and certain vital matters seemed to require some thought, that was now ended. The voters were again either Republicans or Democrats. They, too, would start all over again at Appomattox. They had lost a lot of time.

The outcome of the election was a foregone conclusion before the voting began.[4] The wild rumors begun to inspire fear, and the actual cases of corruption employed, probably had little or no effect on the results. The newly organized Grand Army of the Republic may have. The really surprising thing was that while the Republicans swept the East with heavy majorities, the states of the Middle West were carried often by rather slim margins. The most significant factor seems to have been that the voter really had no choice except to vote the Republican or Democratic ticket. He may not have been a Radical

[4] The Republicans won every governorship that was involved, carried every state legislature, and dominated every northern delegation in Congress. Seldom has one party gained such complete control. Yet the reverses in the next election would indicate that the meaning of these victories was not as clear as it seemed.

Republican or a copperhead Democrat, but there was no way of voting that fact. So the total result was that the Radical Republicans gained complete control of Congress and the power to override any veto or opposition the President might offer. Johnson was now practically helpless, as far as influence on the reconstruction of the South was concerned. He was not even able to protect himself, the office he held, or the Constitution he had sworn to uphold.

The unfortunate thing was that few, when they voted, had any precise notion of what their vote implied. The real issues at stake, which had to do with adjustments required by a new age, played no part in the campaign or the election. No one knew what had been decided or what the consequences would be. The whole campaign centered around the man Johnson, who could not separate himself and his personal problems from those of the nation and the Constitution. He kept defending himself, thereby reducing the conflict to one between himself and any other individual in the audience who challenged. What was really at stake (if there was something important) was never revealed, and of course never decided. About all that became clear was that Johnson lacked a sense of humor to the point of self-pity, and that he was no practical politician who could yield when a position became hopeless, but only a poor symbol of an already lost cause.

Most voters may have thought that acceptance of the Fourteenth Amendment was the final step in reconstruction. They probably remembered that Senator Jacob M. Howard, in presenting the report of the Joint Committee on Reconstruction, had remarked:

> The Committee were of [the] opinion that the states are not yet prepared to sanction so fundamental a change as would be the concession of the right of suffrage to the colored race. We may as well state it plainly and fairly, so that there shall be no misunderstanding on the subject. It is our opinion that three-fourths of the states of the Union could not be induced to vote to grant the right of suffrage, even in any degree or under any restriction to the colored race.

Yet on the other hand, in September 1866, *The Independent* insisted that never before in our political history "had the majority of the people" shown such an "irresistable enthusiasm for Impartial Suffrage." The Republican party, it continued, "would accept nothing less. . . . Any meaner watchword is unworthy of so proud a campaign." It closed by observing that the attempt to concentrate "on the impending Constitutional Amendment" would "squander the sympathies of a million Northern and Southern loyalists." Following the election, it asserted that it could fill its columns with the names of men who now believed that the Republican party was uncommitted.

Nor should it be forgotten that Congressman George S. Boutwell had, in 1866, warned the "working people of the North" against the day when "the southern freedmen shall swarm over the borders in quest of the rights which should be secured to them in their native states," and that Roscoe Conkling, in his Utica speech of September before the election, had asserted that one part of the amendment was to give the Negro "liberty and rights at the South" so that he would "stay there and never come into the cold climate to die."

IV

With these things in mind, it is clear that acceptance of the Fourteenth Amendment was not all that was involved.[5] Yet underneath, and far more significant, was the fact that the outcome of the election could possibly change the whole course of Reconstruction. The real questions were: Had the voters intended to place unlimited power and permission to use it in the hands of a small committee of Congress, a majority of whom would go well beyond the amendment? Had the election endorsed the franchise for the Negro and the overthrow of

---

[5] Regardless of what had been decided, the southern states, with Johnson's approval, refused to ratify the amendment—a step which profited neither.

all that Johnson had done? Or was it only a decision against Johnson the man and his foolish talk? One thing it most certainly did not mean: It was no mandate to "the Republicans to try a reconstruction plan of their own." The debate in Congress had already proved that.

The Radicals, nevertheless, accepted the election as having given them the right to proceed as they pleased. Caution was abandoned; high moral purposes and political ends were tangled with revenge on one man, with the fate of a section as a by-product. Radicals assumed that reconstruction must be turned into revolution. A social and economic revolution had been sanctioned.[6]

In one sense they were right. As *The Nation* declared:

> The one thing which is now plain is that the Northern people are determined that there shall no longer be any such thing as political inequality on American soil, and that all men shall be equal before the law, and that no legal barrier shall stand between any man and any of the prizes of life. About the cause of this determination and about its wisdom and about the means used to carry it out, there may be a good deal of difference of opinion; about its existence we believe there is none.[7]

This much most Republicans accepted and had intended their votes to say. They had not, however, ordered a return to Appomattox.

[6] Speaking for the Radical Republicans, *The Independent* (Nov. 15, 1866) editorialized: "Andrew Johnson in the White House is now a child shut in a nursery. . . . The President and his premier [Seward] have had their Waterloo. . . . The chief lesson of the election is, that the Republican party everywhere, if it hopes to maintain its ascendancy must maintain its virtue. . . . We know the heart of the omnipotent North, and we know that it beats for justice to the Southern loyalists, whether white or black. To these men . . . the constitutional amendment, considered as a basis for reconstruction is worse than no reconstruction at all. . . . They rejected it before the election; they reject it now; they will reject it to the end."

[7] *The Nation*, Jan. 17, 1867. There was, in fact, in many quarters after the election a quiet reaction and a more kindly attitude toward Johnson until he encouraged the southern states to reject the Fourteenth Amendment.

CHAPTER

17

MILITARY RECONSTRUCTION PLANNED

I

The elections of 1866 meant little beyond the fact that the Republican party had scored an overwhelming victory. What that meant in terms of issues was not clear. No specific program on reconstruction had been offered in the campaign as future steps. Many, probably a majority, thought the Republican victory meant approval of the Fourteenth Amendment as the final statement of their party's demands. Most Americans were weary of the endless squabble: their vote was a vote for peace.[1] *The Nation*

[1] Benjamin B. Kendrick was probably correct when he said that the Republican speaker talked "finality" or "a mere step" according to the nature of the constituency he represented.—*The Journal of the Joint Committee of Fifteen on Reconstruction* (New York, 1941), p. 353; *Harper's Weekly,* Nov. 17, 1866; *The Nation,* Nov. 1, 1866. *The Independent* (Sept. 27, 1866) denied

stated bluntly its understanding "that when the amendment was proposed, its acceptance was the only necessary condition of readmission, and the elections were carried on with this understanding in all the Northern States." In debates following the elections, John A. Bingham, John Sherman, and even Benjamin F. Wade took this position. *Harper's Weekly* emphatically denied that it gave Congress *carte blanche*.

Others, however, thought differently. Stevens announced that he had been a Conservative in the last session, but that he intended to be a Radical in this one. The members laughed, but Stevens was not trying to be funny. He was just a man who knew that there had been a civil war and a victor. He believed, as did Sumner and other Radicals, that real reconstruction had not yet begun. Confiscation of lands for the Negro, the vote in his hands, and a thorough disfranchisement of ex-Confederates were now both necessary and possible. For Stevens, the issues in dispute were now settled. The southern states were definitely conquered territories; reconstruction belonged entirely to Congress; social and political reform in the interests of the Negro was to be a part of reconstruction.[2]

---

that "finality" was ever intended: "The Radical party, North and South regards the pending amendment as a proper measure . . . but it regards it as no more adopted to be a basis of reconstruction than would be a tariff bill . . . or a neutrality law. . . . It will not alter one whit the present relations of the white rebel or the black loyalist." Howard K. Beale charged that "the Radicals forced their program upon the South by an evasion of issues and the clever use of propaganda."—*The Critical Year: A Study of Andrew Johnson and Reconstruction* (New York, 1930), p. 406.

[2] Charles Sumner wrote on December 16, to W. W. Story, "Congress is doing pretty well; every step is forward. The next Congress, which will probably meet on the 4th of March, will be still better inspired. All that is possible will be done to limit the Executive power. It is possible that the President may be impeached."—Edward L. Pierce (ed.), *Memoir and Letters of Charles Sumner* (Boston, 1877–1893), vol. 4, p. 307. Thaddeus Stevens meanwhile insisted that "the foundations of their institutions—political, municipal, and social—must be broken-up and

On the very day that Congress resumed, Congressman John M. Broomall of Pennsylvania introduced a bill providing territorial governments for what had formerly been the southern states, and granting full and equal political rights to all male inhabitants who had not taken part in the late rebellion. The inferences were clear: There were at present no governments in the South, and the interest of the Negro was to dominate its future. Wendell Phillips put it even more bluntly: "Reconstruction begins when the South yields up her ideas of civilization and allows the North to permeate her channels and to make her over . . . until that process commences, reconstruction has not commenced." The South must cease to be southern.

With these things in mind, it seems rather futile to speculate on the alternatives President Johnson might have chosen. Compromise for him was not possible. He had taken a stubborn stand on what he considered principle and the Constitution. What the Radicals were demanding was an admission that he had been wrong, that it was all a failure. Johnson did prepare for Congress a message that simply stated the facts regarding the South, admitted the right of each house to decide on the eligibility of its membership, took notice of the Fourteenth Amendment, and suggested that he was willing to cooperate on the pressing economic problems then facing the nation. The hopelessness of the situation, however, evidently changed his mind; the message that Johnson finally sent was the same old rejection of congressional demands.[3]

Whether Congress now did what its more radical element had intended to do anyway (with or without Johnson), or whether his attitude had something to do with the next step, cannot be answered with any degree of certainty. We only know what was done, not why. At any

_____

relaid or all our blood and treasure have been spent in vain."— *New York Herald*, Dec. 13, 1865.

[3] "We are inclined to believe . . . that the effect of the late vote of the North on Mr. Johnson has been chastening, and that he is now in . . . a subdued frame of mind."—*The Nation*, Oct. 25, 1866.

rate, the course followed was in the main that which Stanton's American Freedmen's Inquiry Commission and Sumner's Senate Committee on Emancipation had earlier demanded for the Negro.[4]

The program that Congress now developed, with disagreement only on details, had a twofold objective: to destroy the man Andrew Johnson and to deal at last with the South in such a way as to realize those two rather vague things called "security and repentance." The Negro and his welfare, in terms of land and education, were in the background of each; but somehow he seemed more and more to lose his top priority. Revenge, not humanity; power, not reform, seemed to be, with a few at least, the stakes most in mind.

False rumors were started and given wide publicity to the effect that Johnson planned to use the army against Congress and had even asked the attorney general about the constitutional status of the House and Senate. Stanton went so far as to dictate an amendment to the Army Appropriation Act that would require the President to issue army orders only through the Secretary of War or General Grant. Fears thus aroused led to talk of impeachment. *The Nation*, in an editorial, spoke of the President "reduced to a cipher" and of the need to make him understand his "future insignificance." How far things had drifted is seen in a resolution for impeachment which was offered by a congressman from Ohio when Johnson vetoed Sumner's bill for granting the vote to all Negroes in the District of Columbia. Sumner's own comment was that "our only purpose for retaining him a day longer is simply to compel him to fill the measure of shame by

[4] John G. Sproat, "Blue Print for Radical Reconstruction," *Journal of Southern History*, XXIII (1957), 25–44. Even E. L. Godkin in *The Nation* (Jan. 18, 1866) was saying, "The South will never be really in the Union until Henry Ward Beecher can read an article from the *New York Tribune* on the steps of the principal hotel in Jackson, Mississippi, and 'peddle' the paper afterward . . . without fear of other harm than may come from a scathing editorial."

draining to the very dregs the cup of bitter-blasting humiliation that shall be held remorselessly to his lips." The first sip was the passage of the District bill over his veto, followed by a like procedure over the admission of Nebraska.

II

Meanwhile Congress had been busy framing the bills that were to inaugurate the second reconstruction. Thaddeus Stevens took the lead in an effort to make sure that the Negro was provided with both land and education. He insisted that it was

> ... due to justice, as an example to future times, that some proper pain should be inflicted on the people who constituted the "Confederate States of America," both because they declared an unjust war against the United States for the purpose of destroying republican liberty and permanently establishing slavery, as well as for the cruel and barbarous manner in which they conducted said war, in violation of all rules of civilized warfare, and also to compel them to make compensation for damage and expense caused by said war, therefore: Be it enacted that all public lands belonging to the ten states that formed the so-called "Confederate States of America," shall be forfeited ... and that the lands so seized and condemned be distributed among the slaves who had been made free by the war.

"The pain of traitors," Sumner added, "has been wholly ignored by a treacherous executive and a sluggish Congress." They had indulged a murderous enemy and ignored its loyal Negroes. His program for dealing with the southern states themselves was to place them under military rule; Confederate officers of all ranks were to forfeit citizenship for at least five years; and new constitutions incorporating Negro suffrage were to be required of each state. Here was both "revenge and security."

Confiscation was a bit too extreme for property-minded Republicans, but the "revenge and security" were more acceptable. Even Bingham, who had angrily opposed Stevens in the effort to deprive Southerners of citizenship and to impose perpetual conditions for membership in the Union, now yielded. So the Reconstruction Acts that ultimately emerged avoided confiscation, but the remainder, as Eric L. McKitrick has observed, bore the stamp of "Old Thaddeus Stevens." [5]

The first section of the new Reconstruction Acts announced that "no legal State Governments or adequate protection for life and property" now existed in the southern states. To remedy this situation, the "rebel states" were divided into five military districts, over each of which was to be placed a commanding officer not below the rank of brigadier general, with sufficient troops to enforce his authority.

This military commander and his "army of occupation" were to protect persons in their rights and property, maintain order, and punish all disturbers of the peace and all criminals. They could, if they chose, allow local civil officials to hear cases; but if they did not so choose, they could set up military commissions or tribunals to try cases. State authority could not in any way interfere. Where life and liberty were involved, final approval of the commanding officer was required. In other words, all civil and judicial power was invested in the army.

III

The South was indeed a conquered people who could escape only when, under military supervision, they would begin all over again to form a government. This time their conventions would be made up of all males, twenty-one or over, regardless of race, color, or previous servitude, who had been residents for one year and who had not been disfranchised because of crime or participation in the

---

[5] Eric L. McKitrick, *Andrew Johnson and Reconstruction* (Chicago, 1960), p. 484. When the Reconstruction Acts passed, Stevens arose and said, "I wish to enquire, Mr. Speaker, if it is in order for me now to say that we endorse the language of good Laertes, that Heaven rules as yet and there are Gods above."— *Congressional Globe*, 39th Cong., 2nd sess., p. 1215.

rebellion. Such a convention could frame a constitution, submit it to the qualified voters and to the Congress for approval, elect a legislature which would adopt the Fourteenth Amendment, and this time elect to their conventions, to their legislatures, or to Congress no person excluded from office by the Fourteenth Amendment. Furthermore, until Congress had admitted those elected, their governments would still be considered as merely provisional governments which could be altered or rejected at will.

Reduced to practice, this meant that only three groups could qualify to take part in the formation and control of the new governments: practically all the Negroes in these states, northerners who had come South and remained a year, and native southerners who could prove that they had taken no official part in the war. In all, out of a population of about 4,000,000, only 700,000 could qualify as voters. The majority of these, of course, had few if any qualifications for the difficult work to be done.

Since supervision and control were to be in the hands of the army, Congress by a series of acts quickly moved to check the power of the President as commander in chief. It fixed the headquarters of the general of the army in Washington, where Congress could at all times keep in touch, and then required that all orders and instructions relating to military operations issued by the President or the Secretary of War should, as Stanton wished, be issued through the general of the army. Furthermore, the general could not be removed, suspended, or relieved of command or assigned elsewhere except at his own request and by the previous consent of the Senate. Anything done contrary to these regulations would be null and void. Any officer of the army who should transmit or obey any order not so issued would be imprisoned. All state militias were to be disbanded immediately and any further organizing prohibited. Both the army and the Freedmen's Bureau were to prohibit whipping or maiming of a person by any pretended civil or military authority in any state lately in rebellion. By this act the command of the army was practically taken from the President and given to General Grant, and the army's civil authority was greatly increased.

The next important step in the second reconstruction, passed over the President's veto, was the Tenure of Office Act. Having clipped the President's military powers, Congress now aimed to destroy his rights of appointment —even his control over his own cabinet. It provided that any officer (including cabinet members) appointed by and with the advice and consent of the Senate would hold office for the term of the President by whom he had been appointed and for one month thereafter, subject to removal by and with the advice and consent of the Senate. If the President should remove any such official when Congress was not in session, he should report such removal with reasons within twenty days to the new Congress, which could approve or repudiate the President's action. Any person accepting an office and attempting to hold it contrary to this act would be subject to a fine not exceeding $10,000 or imprisonment not exceeding five years, or both.

For the practical purpose of reconstruction, these acts reduced the President to a mere figurehead and instituted a near parliamentarian form of government. Johnson could no longer play any effective part in the system. Congress was in control, and the South was at its mercy unless the Supreme Court should interfere.

IV

The part that the Court was to play in the new order was somewhat confused.[6] A series of court reforms that had only an indirect relation to Reconstruction were al-

---

[6] See Stanley Kutler, "Reconstruction and the Supreme Court: The Numbers Game Reconsidered," *Journal of Southern History*, XXXII (1966), 42–58. Also his *"Ex Parte McCardle:* Judicial Impotency? The Supreme Court and Reconstruction Reconsidered," *American Historical Review*, LXXII (1967), 835–851. Kutler seems to admit that the Court bowed to Congress until it

ready under way before the struggle between Johnson and Congress had developed. Many, including even a few judges, had reached the conclusion that the Court, raised to ten in number in 1863, was entirely too large and unwieldy. Consequently, in 1866, bills to reduce its size ultimately to seven members were passed without prolonged opposition by both the House and the Senate. Johnson, long an advocate of the election of judges, approved.

It seems clear that these moves did not represent either fear of, or hostility to, the Court. Yet as applied, they did reveal an intention to reduce the South's overrepresentation on the Court. It should be noted that it was the southern judicial circuits that were eliminated.

But the Court was not to escape the efforts of the Radicals to make certain of congressional control of Reconstruction. On April 3, 1866, Justice David Davis, speaking for the Court, had held the conviction of a civilian, L. P. Milligan, by a military commission to be illegal. In a ringing opinion that would become "one of the bulwarks of American civil liberty," Davis declared that "martial rule can never exist where the courts are open and in proper and unobstructed exercise of their jurisdiction." It can rule only in "the locality of actual war."

This brought a storm of protest and abuse from the Radicals. John A. Bingham and Wendell Phillips went so far as to threaten the abolition of the Court. Stanton was furious, and issued secret instructions to military leaders in the South to go ahead keeping "the mantle of military tribunals" around both Negroes and military personnel.

The Milligan decision would have made impossible the trials of the so-called Lincoln conspirators and that of Henry Wirtz. It might even suggest that the Court would subject all Reconstruction Acts to judicial review. In alarm, some talked of packing the Court or reducing its

---

became clear that there was no intention to upset the reconstruction program. He insists, however, that the Court kept busy through the period with legitimate business.

membership. A bill actually passed the House requiring the agreement of two-thirds of the justices for any decision. Fortunately, it did not come to a vote in the Senate.

The Court took the hint. In the cases of *Mississippi* vs. *Johnson* and *Georgia* vs. *Stanton,* where efforts were made to enjoin the President and military officers from executing the Reconstruction Acts, the Court declined to assume jurisdiction. By so doing it wisely refused to go out of its way to pass judgment upon these acts. More important was the *Ex parte McCardle* case, involving a Mississippi editor arrested and tried before a military commission for publishing criticisms of Radical Reconstruction, and in which the officer in charge refused to produce the prisoner on presentation of a writ of habeas corpus from the civil court. This action, upheld by the Federal District Court of Mississippi, then went to the Supreme Court. Threatened with a possible decision on its reconstruction program, Congress hastily passed an act depriving the Court of jurisdiction in this case and all similar cases. The Court meekly bowed to Congress and, as James G. Randall says, by an "acquiescence of silence," lost "a dignity hard to recover."

Stanley Kutler's comment on an earlier situation sums the matter up even more soundly: "So Congress tailored the judicial system to better suit the demands and needs of the dominant section and, of course, the dominant party." Not until it was quite safe to do so did the Court, in *Ex parte Yerger,* again assert its complete independence. This time Congress yielded for, after all, most congressmen were lawyers, and lawyers, where interests are not too keenly involved, do respect the courts.

V

Now in control, Congress passed two supplementary acts outlining the steps by which military reconstruction was to be administered. The job would be done over again under new supervision and with a new group of so-called "Southerners" in charge. They would have behind them a military force sufficient to insure control. The army was being rapidly mustered out, which in practice meant that an increasing percent of the army in the South tended more and more to be Negro in character. In numbers this military force was not large, but in a region primarily rural, a small body of troops strategically placed in urban centers was sufficient. More would have been of little use. The degree of military control in the South cannot be measured by the number of soldiers employed. It can only be measured by the fact that it proved entirely adequate to control the situation at all times. Later the Radical governors were allowed to create largely Negro militias for their use.[7] In this period, the South was in the power of "an army of occupation."

VI

In spite of its drastic character, the new reconstruction program had literally been rushed through Congress in the final weeks of the session without adequate debate. It was a case of taking this or getting nothing. There had been some heated discussion and a few compromises on details but no radical change in the character of the measures. This program represented either what Republicans as a whole demanded in terms of "security" and "Southern punishment," or their reactions to the person of Andrew Johnson and a fear and hatred of the "Southern rebels," who must be rendered helpless to damage either the Negro or the party. Perhaps it was a bit of both. It must have satisfied some deep need, for, as ill-advised as it proved to be, Republicans of all shades voted for it almost as a solid unit.

[7] Otis A. Singletary, *Negro Militia and Reconstruction* (Austin, 1957), pp. 9–16.

18

THE SECOND RECONSTRUCTION BEGINS: IMPEACHMENTS

I

The passage of the new congressional Reconstruction Acts left the southern people in utter confusion. They, too, were back where they had started at the end of the fighting. They had no idea as to whether they had any rights or whether their existing governments had any authority. They had little idea of what the future held in store. Was this the end of change or was this just another phase with more to come? If they had been stunned and helpless with defeat, they were even more so now by the action of Congress.

Southerners had accepted defeat, laid down their arms, and "cooperated" with Lincoln and Johnson in setting up local and state governments to take the place of those that had existed under the Confederacy. Now the northern victors, two years after the war had ended, were still not satisfied. Stability was as far off as it had ever been. The threat of social revolution in addition to political chaos hung over their heads. Confusion and helpless indignation ruled. Southerners had made serious mistakes. They had taken too much for granted, and they had not revealed enough of humility and regret for their past. They had not ceased to be southerners in dealing with the Negro.

An interesting thing about this new reconstruction program is that Congress had added to its interest in the Negro a bit of "punishment and humiliation" for Johnson and for the South. In the haste to express their feelings, congressmen had passed the military and tenure acts without providing any practical means by which these acts were to be implemented and reconstruction ultimately brought to an end. That had to be done later by two supplementary acts that came as a kind of afterthought to the main business of punishment and humiliation. These acts described in detail the procedure by which the South was to be remade, and the important thing about them was the care taken to insure the absolute control of the army.[1]

The commander could suspend or remove any civil official at any time and appoint anyone he might choose in his place. In registering voters, the army boards were given absolute authority to go to any extreme in determining who should register or not register because of some civil or judicial service rendered to the Old South

[1] "The Army of the Republic must re-encamp in the Southern States . . . to reconstruct the American Union on the basis of Political Equality. No other than a military plan is adequate to the present emergency. Treason cannot govern—it must be governed. Every unreconstructed state must go without self government until its citizens become loyal. . . . Military government ought never to have been relaxed from the rebellious South." Nearly 3000 loyal people, it was charged, had been murdered in the South since Lee's surrender and "the basest of American Presidents" was alone responsible. "Let him be impeached forthwith."—*The Independent*, Feb. 28, 1867.

and then to the Confederacy. When Johnson, through Attorney General Henry Stanbery, attempted to gain an opinion as to the constitutionality of these acts, Congress immediately passed a statute stipulating that no military commander should be bound by the opinion of any civil officer of the United States, even its attorney general!

In this spirit, the new order began to take shape. It operated in two distinct fields: the one had to do with President Johnson, the other with the South. Attention, therefore, must shift back and forth between Washington and the southern states. Each party must now be forced to yield that satisfaction which the victor in the late civil war had from the very beginning needed and unconsciously had been seeking. This was simply to be the climax of their quest.

II

With the South safely in the hands of the army, Congress turned its attention to the President of the United States. The only possible object in this case was humiliation, for Johnson had already been stripped of all effective influence as far as reconstruction was concerned.[2] The procedure employed against him, therefore, need have no relationship to truth or justice. The purpose was conviction. Any means to that end was justified.

The move began with a resolution offered by Congressman James M. Ashley of Ohio declaring that he personally impeached Andrew Johnson, "acting President of the United States," of high crimes and misdemeanors, and asked that the Judiciary Committee of the House inquire into the conduct of the President. The Committee did conduct such an investigation, hearing any charge, however

[2] Some writers find a reason for impeachment in a desire on the part of Congress to remove the last obstacle in the way of complete domination of the South; "The most remarkable feature connected with the impeachment trial—a feature which completely overshadows all others—is the fact that it can take place at all."—*The Nation*, April 16, 1868.

absurd, that anyone could present. It even dealt with one individual who offered, for $25,000, to produce letters implicating Johnson in Lincoln's assassination. When all was finished, the committee at first decided that action was not justified. Later, however, one member under heavy pressure changed his vote, and impeachment was recommended. Yet when dissenters on the committee insisted that they had not found one particle of evidence which would be received by any court in the land, the House voted down the resolutions, 108 to 57. Thus failed the first effort at impeachment.

Then came the fiasco involving Stanton's removal from the cabinet. The simple facts were that Johnson had retained Lincoln's cabinet and that some of the members had early accepted the Radical Republican position against Johnson's program. All but Stanton ultimately had the good grace to resign. Only this strange, sometimes almost unbelievable man had remained, professing loyalty but secretly betraying the President at every turn. Secretary of the Navy Welles and others had repeatedly begged Johnson to remove him. Johnson, as usual, had hesitated. Now, when it was too late because of the Tenure of Office Act, which many believed had been passed primarily to protect Stanton, Johnson took the fatal step. He asked for Stanton's resignation and appointed General Grant as acting Secretary of War. Grant accepted, but Stanton refused to resign and kept possession of the Secretary's office.[3] Meanwhile, in open defiance of the recently passed army act, Johnson transferred General Philip Sheridan and General Daniel E. Sickles and later removed General John Pope from their posts in the South. Grant, already bitten by the presidential bug, hesitated, objected to the President's interference with army men, but stated clearly that Stanton must apply to the courts if he were to regain

[3] See the article by Harold M. Hyman, "Johnson, Stanton and Grant: A Reconsideration of the Army's Role in the Events Leading to Impeachment," *American Historical Review*, LXVI (1960), 85–100, which suggests a closer understanding between Stanton and Grant than has been thought.

his office. Grant later agreed to turn the office back to the President if the Senate disapproved of Stanton's removal. Yet when the Senate reinstated Stanton, Grant turned the keys over to the Attorney General, who immediately gave them to Stanton.

When called before the cabinet, Grant became confused. Under Johnson's questioning, he practically admitted that he had not carried out what Johnson considered an agreement. That made him hate the President, which, of course, made him immediately the Republican candidate for the Presidency. Later correspondence between Grant and Johnson did not alter the controversy or clear up the misunderstanding.[4]

Johnson now took the bull by the horns and issued an order removing Stanton. Failing to get General Sherman to accept the office, he appointed Major General Lorenzo Thomas, a stuffy old officer, as ad interim Secretary of War. Then for a time Thomas attended cabinet meetings, while Stanton and Grant took over the army for their own purposes. Thomas, after much talk and one blustering attempt to assert his right to the office, sat down with Stanton and enjoyed a round of drinks. That ended the affair which, in the impeachment charges, constituted violence.

III

On February 24, 1868, the House passed the Covode Resolution "that Andrew Johnson, President of the United States, be impeached of high crimes and misdemeanors in office." Specific grounds for such action were neither given nor asked for, but the bitter attacks on the President during the debate again showed that punishment for

---

[4] The whole affair was, in the end, a matter of whose word or interpretation was to be accepted. As one editor put it, "The first requisite of a gentleman is that he should tell the truth." Since this editor was friendly to Grant, he concluded, "It is a pity that the chief-magistrate of a great republic is not a gentleman."— *The Independent,* Feb. 3, 1867.

opposition to Congress in reconstruction was the real motive. That was Johnson's crime. Two days later, a committee was appointed to "exhibit particular articles of impeachment . . . *and make good the same.*"

Having already voted impeachment without charges, it was now necessary only to frame articles of impeachment in such a way as to attract the most votes. Justice to Johnson was not even considered; any charge that might influence a vote was included or rejected on that basis. An effort was made in some of the articles of impeachment to permit a senator to vote for conviction without personal embarrassment.

From the charges that the Committee of Seven, which was in charge of the prosecution, compiled, eleven were finally adopted under the title, "Articles exhibited by the House of Representatives of the United States, in the name of themselves and all the people of the United States, against Andrew Johnson, President of the United States, in maintenance and support of their impeachment against him for high crimes and misdemeanors in office." [5]

The first eight articles dealt with Johnson's removal of Edwin M. Stanton as Secretary of War and the appointment of Major General Lorenzo Thomas in his place. The crime involved was an intent to violate the Tenure of Office Act, in violation of the Constitution and the consent of the Senate. In eight different ways that border on the ridiculous, the accusers twisted this into an effort to "unlawfully seize, take and possess the property of the United States," then in the custody of the rightful Secretary of War, and to fill an office that was not vacant.

The ninth article charged Johnson, as Commander in Chief, with having communicated directly with an army officer instead of through the general of the army as the

---

[5] These articles must be read if they are to be properly evaluated. See Walter L. Fleming (ed.), *Documentary History of Reconstruction . . . , 1865 to the Present Time* (Cleveland, 1906–1907), vol. 1, pp. 458–470. The best account of impeachment is still D. M. De Witt, *The Impeachment and Trial of Andrew Johnson* (New York, 1903). See also *The Nation*, May 14, 1868.

recent act of Congress required. The tenth and eleventh articles accused Johnson of "high misdemeanor in office" for having on various occasions criticized Congress and having used "utterances, declarations, threats, and harangues, highly censurable . . . and unbecoming in the Chief Magistrate of the United States." As James G. Randall stated, "Ultimately the House adopted eleven verbose articles whose sentences are so stilted and so tautological that the mind balks at reading them through." [6]

The trial began on March 5 and lasted until May 26. Since they had found nothing in Johnson's actions that even suggested corruption, Congressman Benjamin F. Butler insisted in the opening statement that the Senate was not a court in any sense but was acting in its political capacity and dealing with a strictly political problem: "the fitness of Johnson to retain the office of President." That permitted personal abuse and an appeal to emotion. It raised no bar against those acting as judges having preconceived notions of guilt. It permitted the public to bring pressure upon the judges. It allowed the matter of admission of testimony, questions of procedure, even of intent, to be decided by party vote. Party loyalty alone should determine the verdict. Butler went so far as to assert that to be judged guilty, Johnson need not have committed any real crime.[7]

Having pushed aside any restraints that a "judicial Court" might impose, Butler questioned Johnson's right of removal in Stanton's case and charged deceit in the

---

[6] James G. Randall and David Donald, *The Civil War and Reconstruction* (Boston, 1961), p. 607.

[7] "We claim and respectfully insist that this Tribunal has none of the attributes of a judicial court as they are commonly received and understood. . . . We suggest, therefore, that we are in the presence of the Senate of the United States convened as a constitutional tribunal to enquire into and determine whether Andrew Johnson, because of malversation in office, is longer fit to retain the office of President." *Proceedings in the Trial of Andrew Johnson . . . Before the Senate for High Crimes and Misdemeanors* (Washington, 1868), vol. 1, p. 90.

President's claim of intent to test the constitutionality of the Tenure of Office Act. He then turned to what he considered "the graver matter" of Johnson's attacks on the Congress. After a long parade of examples that indicated an effort "at stirring up a rebellion," Butler insisted that the right of freedom of speech was not involved, only that "of propriety and decency of speech and conduct in a high official of the government." Johnson like "a common scold" had "slandered Congress." He closed with Johnson's encouragement of the southern states to reject the amendments, all of which added up to "the intent" to usurp "the powers of Congress." Johnson had failed to overthrow Congress only "because of the want of ability and power, not of malignity and will."

William M. Evarts and Attorney General Henry Stanbery headed Johnson's defense. Even though given but ten days in which to prepare their case, the defense was conducted on a rather high level. The strategy was to force the prosecution to provide facts, not simply an appeal to emotions. Had Johnson actually removed Stanton? Was he not still acting as Secretary of War? Had Johnson's intention not been that of procuring a test case to be brought before the courts for final decision? And after all, was not Stanton a Lincoln appointee and, therefore, even under the Tenure of Office Act, removable by Johnson? (Even John T. Sherman agreed that he was.) If the House really had a case in which serious crimes and misdemeanors were involved, why did they insist that the Senate was not acting as a jury? Then, rising above party interests and personalities, defense attorneys called attention to the serious damage that would threaten the whole structure of American government if an executive could be convicted for purely political reasons. As Lyman Trumbull remarked, "No future President will be safe who happens to differ with a majority of the House and three-fifths of the Senate." [8]

---

[8] One of the most interesting things about this trial is the strained effort on the part of the prosecution to turn what

Such arguments combined with the efforts of Chief Justice Salmon P. Chase to give the trial a courtroom quality, and his insistence that "intent" must be considered sobered Conservative Republicans. Even though the matter of intent was defeated, some twenty Republicans broke ranks. William P. Fessenden, James W. Grimes, Lyman Trumbull, and a few others showed signs of voting their consciences instead of their party. For the first time, it became apparent that the vote might be close and conviction uncertain.

With that realization, the pressure on hesitating senators became unbelievably bitter and unreasonable. Bishop Matthew Simpson of the Methodist Church was called on to bring Senator W. T. Willey into line, and he later attempted to have the annual Conference of his Church set aside an hour of prayer for the President's conviction. Senator Joseph S. Fowler was threatened with blackmail because he insisted that "I cannot become a fugitive from myself through time and eternity."

Fessenden read in his mail, "Is it possible that you have turned traitor, and that your name will be handed down with that of Benedict Arnold?" [9] Edmond G. Ross of

---

William P. Fessenden saw as foolish acts, words and "Cussedness," into serious crimes. That permitted the defense to stress the ridiculous and to bring a bit of relieving humor, which was as effective as serious argument. See Thomas Nelson's magnificent description of General Thomas' use of force in "the attempted seizure" of Stanton's office: *Proceedings in the Trial of Andrew Johnson*, vol. 1, pp. 170–171; or William M. Evart's biting humor in this same volume, pp. 297, 326–327. The effort to convict because outside opinion demanded it seems to have had considerable effect on senators, vol. 2, p. 137.

[9] Fessenden's reply was, "Everybody, too, seems to forget that Senators have taken their oath to try the man impartially, and if anyone avows his determination to keep his oath, villains and fools set him down as a friend of the President. If he were impeached for general cussedness, there would be no difficulty in the case. That, however, is not the question to be tried. . . . I cannot and will not violate my oath. I would rather be confined to planting cabbages for the remainder of my days." Again he said the difficulty was that "Johnson was a fool."—Francis Fessenden,

Kansas was told that his state "had heard the evidence and demands the conviction of the President." If he failed, he would be found guilty of accepting a bribe and political death would follow. It was the same with John B. Henderson and Peter G. Van Winkle, while Grimes, assailed as "a traitor and a Judas," became so distraught under the pressure that he suffered a stroke. Trumbull had to face the threat of being hanged "to the most convenient lamppost" if he again showed his face on the streets of Chicago.

How desperate the Radicals had become was revealed in Butler's blunt comment regarding one senator: "Tell the damn scoundrel that if he wants money there is a bushel of it to be had." Why the more sincere were so deadly in earnest was revealed in Charles Sumner's words:

> This is one of the last great battles with slavery. Driven from these legislative chambers, driven from the field of war, this monstrous power has found a refuge in the Executive Mansion, where in utter disregard of the Constitution and laws, it seeks to exercise its ancient far-reaching sway. Andrew Johnson is the impersonation of the tyrannical slave power. He is the lineal successor of John C. Calhoun and Jefferson Davis; and he gathers about him the same supporters.

To Sumner and his followers the Civil War had never ended.

It was in such an atmosphere that the final vote on Johnson's guilt took place. Knowing that widest agreement was possible on the vague and emotion-laden eleventh article, the Radicals forced that to the first vote. One by one the ballots were recorded until one last vote of "not guilty" would decide the issue. That vote fell to the quiet, unpretentious Senator Edmond G. Ross of Kansas. Amid deathlike silence, he faced Chief Justice Chase's question, and answered in a quiet, conversational

---

Life and Public Services of William Pitt Fessenden (Boston, 1907), vol. 2, p. 184.

tone, "Not guilty." [10] In the confusion, efforts at adjournment failed until the roll was finished. Attempts to reverse the balance on other articles failed after two adjournments; the result remained the same.

IV

Those Republicans who had voted their consciences paid a heavy price in subsequent days.[11] They were literally crucified. When it was too late, in most cases, a grateful nation realized that they had revealed not only courage of the rarest kind but wisdom as well. Even Sumner was later driven to comment, "You were right and I was wrong," but he was too cowardly to allow it to be reported until after his death. It must also be noted that the better element in the nation later tried to make amends.

So the first step in the second reconstruction had miserably failed—failed because it deserved to fail, as do all such drives born of passion and with no sound national purpose behind them. The most alarming fact about it all was that Congress was only revealing a widespread national attitude. The determination to convict the President at any cost, which began with the assertion that the Senate was not a court bound by any laws, rules, or

[10] The hostile *Independent* (May 21, 1868) described Ross's face as "ghastly white" as he stood up and "to his own ineffaceable dishonor uttered a response which flagrantly betrayed his colleagues and scandalously acquitted the President." The paper repeated charges of "downright corruption for money."

[11] For a differing opinion, see "The Seven Martyrs?" *American Historical Review*, LXIV (1959), 323–330. The senators who voted against impeachment were: James A. Bayard, Charles R. Buckalew, Garret Davis, James Dixon, James R. Doolittle, William P. Fessenden, Joseph S. Fowler, James W. Grimes, John B. Henderson, Thomas A. Hendricks, Herschel V. Johnson, Thomas C. McCreery, David S. Norton, David J. Patterson, Edmund G. Ross, Willard Saulsbury, Lyman Trumbull, Peter G. Van Winkle, and George Vickers—19 as against 35.

precedents, had reached a climax in the firm denial of the Senate's right to acquit even before it had heard the evidence or the respondent's case. Moreover, Republican members were threatened with infamy if they acquitted, and one of the managers for the prosecution openly "dared" them to acquit. Meanwhile the *New York Tribune* boldly announced that this was "altogether a party proceeding—the mere execution of a determination to which the party had already come, and that any senator who refused to carry out this determination would be expelled from the party, and that all talk about the sanctity of their oaths was 'cant'." [12]

Impeachment had indeed exposed the strange tangle of values and interests that Reconstruction had wrought in the American mind.

[12] *The Independent* (April 30, 1868) had declared, "The importance of convicting the President is incalculable. His acquittal would be a national calamity. Not to speak of party necessity . . . the public safety required the removal of the public enemy. . . ." It even suggested that if there were no other way, the people had the right of revolution. On May 14, 1868, *The Nation* answered, "The Managers of the Impeachment rested their case on Saturday . . . the President's conviction is a foregone conclusion." A week later (May 21, 1868) it added, "On the announcement of the result, a suspicion pervaded the Senate Chamber of fraud and corruption." It then spoke of "the double handful of perverted brains which filled Fessenden's hat," and of "the treachery" of Ross, Fessenden, and Trumbull. Chase "inclined toward the enemy."

MILITARY RULE
AND REVISION

I

President Johnson took impeachment in stride. He had chosen his course and had convinced himself that he was defending the Constitution. He did not react sharply to the abuse heaped upon him, and he accepted the outcome of the impeachment trial "without arrogance, or an appearance of unseemly joy." Not until more abuse followed his vindication did Johnson seem to take notice and to think for a time of seeking renomination. Even then he said little and soon forgot it. His term ended in comparative quiet.[1]

[1] "When in a few weeks, his term shall end, and he shall go back to lead in person the Klu Klux Klan in Tennessee, he will be found by his old neighbors to be a more rusted, corroded, and mildewed thing than the ancient sign in Greeneville which still

As to the Radicals, it had already become apparent that they had overplayed their hand. The extreme lengths to which they had gone to intimidate and pressure those trying to act as honest jurors in a trial backfired and brought reaction against the Republican party itself. As *The Nation* asked, "Can any party afford to treat its leading men as a part of the Republican press has been treating leading Republicans during the past few weeks? . . . We have . . . heard language applied to Mr. Fessenden and Mr. Trumbull . . . which was fit only for a compound of Benedict Arnold and John Morrissey." [2]

For party reasons if for no other, it was best now to leave Johnson alone, to make sure of his successor, and to give attention to the South. Satisfaction might be salvaged there.

II

The steps to be taken in the military reconstruction of the southern states had been clearly stated in the various acts of Congress on the subject. In practice, the procedure varied somewhat in the different states, but the larger pattern was the same. The outcome, however, depended on local conditions. As a result, the period required for readmittance ranged from two to ten years.

The first step toward the new order was for the army to screen and register the voters. Since anyone who had held civil or military office in the Confederacy was barred, the eligible voters were reduced to three groups—any Negroes who might apply, all northerners ("carpetbaggers") who had been in the South for one year, and all white southerners ("scalawags") who could prove that

---

says 'A. Johnson, Tailor'! The sight of that rusty sign will perhaps make him wish that he had never laid aside his needle and thread, and he will then, for the first time in three years, be of the same opinion with his fellow countrymen."—*The Independent*, Dec. 17, 1868.

[2] *The Nation*, May 14, 1868.

they had been loyal to the Union or at least had not held Confederate office.

The terms "carpetbagger" and "scalawag" have lost much of their meaning in recent years.[3] Many Negroes who were to play a prominent part in the new governments were from the North and were as much "carpetbaggers" as were the white imports. The term "scalawag" once suggested a low class of white; but if used to include native whites who saw the necessity of accepting the inevitable and getting over with the unpleasantness as quickly as possible, it included all kinds of people—especially a group of oldtime Whig planters and professional men. Yet the labels "carpetbagger" and "scalawag" carried heavy emotional charges and played an important part in Reconstruction days, as they have since in the writing of history. Like most labels, they badly distorted the facts and need to be used in quotation marks.

III

To make certain that all Negroes registered and voted correctly, two outside agents took an important role. The first of these, the Union League, was organized in Philadelphia in 1862 to combat disloyalty and to win support for the wavering Lincoln administration. It had spread from city to city, had added something of a social-club quality, and had, more and more, formed centers for Republican party effort. It had followed the Union army into the South, provided teachers for Negro schools, and zealously advocated Negro suffrage. It now dedicated itself to the building of a dominant Republican party in the South.[4]

[3] See David Donald, "The Scalawag in Mississippi Reconstruction," *Journal of Southern History,* X (1944), 447–460; Bernard A. Weisberger, "Dark and Bloody Ground of Reconstruction," *Journal of Southern History,* XII (November, 1946), 469–486; *The Nation,* July 6, 1871.

[4] Walter L. Fleming (ed.), *Documentary History of Reconstruction . . . , 1865 to the Present Time* (Cleveland, 1906–1907), vol. 2, pp. 7–19.

Adapting its club idea to the situation, the Union League organized secret lodges, with elaborate initiation ceremonies, oaths and pledges, songs and speeches, nocturnal meetings, high-sounding titles, prayers and passwords—all of which bound the Negro hand and foot to the Republican party. Negroes were, as one reporter observed, lined up, given ballots, and marched past ballot boxes "voting once for me, once for Jim who couldn't come." The Union League spread rapidly and for two years controlled the political situation in nearly all the southern states. It then gave way to the militia, largely Negro, now being organized in most of the states.

The Freedmen's Bureau, already exercising an important economic and social influence, in many places took a hand in politics. Many of its officers sought political office.[5] Never as effective politically as the Union League, the Bureau nevertheless added its part in arousing Negro interest in politics and in building Republican strength. The point is that the Negro himself had a larger stake in the ultimate outcome than did any other. He needed guidance, not stimulation to political participation. His problem was whether he should turn to the old white planter class for leadership, or rely on his new-found northern friends. As a rule, he chose the latter, for they promised greater immediate returns. Perhaps in the long run, when reconstruction came to an end, the Negro would have found himself better off had he become a permanent political part of a native southern party. His present decision, as Vernon L. Wharton states, took "from his side the very men who could best have guided his steps in the new path." Set free by forces "despised by his [former] masters, and [now] used as a pawn in political war, the freedman was the symbol of the South's defeat, and the scapegoat of the Lost Cause." This, of course, is

[5] LaWanda and John H. Cox, "General O. O. Howard and the 'Misrepresented Bureau,'" *Journal of Southern History*, XIX (November, 1953), 427–447.

merely guessing. All that is certain is that the Negro did pay heavily for his decision when reconstruction ended.

Be that as it may, the army did a thorough job of registering voters. For once the Negro was treated as a citizen, even though, as John Hope Franklin has remarked, he was largely without the qualifications to participate effectively in a democracy. Negro registration outnumbered the white in South Carolina, Mississippi, Louisiana, Alabama, and Florida—a fact that led early historians mistakenly to assume complete Negro domination throughout this phase of reconstruction.

For this reason, much of the work of the so-called revisionists in recent years has consisted of a re-evaluation of the part played by the "scalawag," the Negro, and the "carpetbagger" in the conventions, the legislatures, and the era that followed. Scholars have gone back to the pre-Civil War period in the South to note the growing class consciousness among the nonplanter element, the dissatisfaction with the rule of the few, the widespread Union sentiment before the outbreak of war, and the fact that common men such as Governors Joseph E. Brown and Zebulon B. Vance had already achieved political success.

Revision has also taken note of sharp and continuing division between Whigs and Democrats, which may have been submerged in the secession crises but which never completely disappeared. Basic differences in economic interests ran too deeply to be wiped out. Most so-called "scalawags" had once been Whigs; many had been planters or professional men.[6]

The so-called "scalawag" has been, to a large degree, rehabilitated in spite of the disgraceful conduct of a Franklin J. Moses, the financial escapades of a Joe Brown or a James L. Alcorn, and the marital and weird political

[6] Richard N. Current, "Carpetbaggers Reconsidered" in *A Festschrift for Frederick B. Artz* (Durham, N.C., 1964), p. 144.

difficulties of an Albert Morgan.[7] The Whig element in the Republican ranks deserves recognition, but it is also well to remember that the *New York Times,* commenting on the South Carolina Convention, stated, "There is scarcely a Southern white man in the body whose character would keep him out of the penitentiary."

Revision has also taken a new look at the Negro and his part in this phase of reconstruction. It has begun to understand that, in spite of a bondage that robbed him of so much, many a Negro under slavery had "absorbed the basic materials of the western culture." He had acquired the English language and a surprising number of Negroes had learned to read and write. Even as slaves, some had learned the essentials of good farming, the use of farm machinery, and the proper care of the soils. The Negro had, in the older parts of the South, proved as capable in restoring a tumble-down agriculture as he had in producing the ruin.

A few Negroes had gained skill in most of the trades and in domestic manufactures. Blacksmiths, carpenters, and masons with competent skills were found on most large plantations. Women who could spin and weave, who were excellent cooks, and who knew how to run a household—children and all—were to be found everywhere. Some Negroes had become factory hands and worked in tobacco, iron, sugar, and other types of industry.

In many lines, Negroes all over the South were as skilled and capable of assuming the responsibilities of everyday living as were those they had served, and far more competent than many of the lesser whites. This is not to say that the Negro did not resent his bondage, nor even an effort to treat slavery as a training school. Yet the Negro on his own lands quickly proved that he did not lack skills.

[7] See Hodding Carter, *The Angry Scar: The Story of Reconstruction, 1865–1890* (New York, 1959), pp. 288–310; *Proceedings of the Constitutional Convention of South Carolina, 1868* (Columbia, S.C., 1868), pp. 685–873.

In such a situation, a Negro endowed with ability could hardly have failed to become familiar with the larger social order of which his race was a part, and now to be able to play more than "a clown's role" in a free society. With the assistance of such educated Negroes from the North as Francis L. Cardozo, Robert B. Elliott, J. J. Wright, Jonathan Gibbs, and others, Hiram Revels, Beverly Nash, and their fellow ex-slaves, were in a position to assume political responsibility. Yet it cannot be ignored that the northern Negro, however well educated, did not represent the South. He, too, was an outsider. The unforgivable thing about Reconstruction and the Negro was the failure to provide the land and the education that went with freedom. Thaddeus Stevens was right when he insisted on this as basic. He was wrong only when "he would strip a proud nobility of their estates for the purpose" of humbling "proud traitors." [8]

IV

The conventions now elected were, with only one and possibly two exceptions, predominantly white. Generalizations are difficult, but one fact seems clear: the new governments, as now formed, were never Negro-dominated, as was once thought. Only in South Carolina, and at times in Louisiana, was the Negro in a majority in any branch of government, and then it was in the lower house. Two Negroes, both from Mississippi, reached the United States Senate, while fifteen were elected to the House. A few served in important state offices, but not

[8] W. E. B. Du Bois pointed out all this in 1910 in his "revisionist" article. He reprinted the speech of the Negro Thomas E. Miller, once a member of the South Carolina legislature, who stood on the side of honesty and reform under Governor Wade Hampton, while whites opposed. He rightly credited the Negro with giving the South more of democracy, free public schools, and much social legislation.—"Reconstruction and Its Benefits," *American Historical Review*, XV (July, 1910), 781–799.

one was chosen to the governorship. Most, but not all, who did reach high office were from the North. Native Negroes played a minority part in the legislatures, seldom dictating policies but regular in attendance. They held office in town and county, but never to the extent that their numbers justified. In office, Vernon Lane Wharton [9] insists, they did as well and as badly as the whites. Some were honest, some corrupt. Some were ignorant, some capable.

Revisionists have also attempted to rescue the carpetbagger from the shadows into which earlier historians cast him. Here they have had less success. It is indeed stretching history a bit too far to compare the thin migration of northern men into the prewar South or the heavier movement in Reconstruction days with the westward movement that pushed the frontier across the continent and transformed the wilderness into the complexities of an urban, industrial society. These differ entirely in both motivation and characteristics. The carpetbagger had nothing to do with the southern westward movement that built the cotton kingdom. He came to the South, as a rule, for political reasons and long after the southern West was completely settled.

V

It is possible to accept as worthy those northern visitors with troubled spirits who sincerely believed that the South needed considerable making over, without ascribing all wisdom and virtue to ordinary men, white and black, who seized the chance to gain place and power in a captive South which they could never have got in their own native Massachusetts, New York, Pennsylvania, New Hampshire, or Illinois.[10]

---

[9] Vernon Lane Wharton, *The Negro in Mississippi, 1865–1890* (Chapel Hill, N.C., 1947), pp. 157–180.

[10] *The Nation* (Dec. 7, 1871) commented, "The carpet-bagger is not a politician; he has no aims, opinions, ideas, passions, or prejudices; he is simply a man who has not succeeded in any of

Nor does it make sense to explain the waste and corruption in reconstruction governments as the southern expression of what was going on in the North. The men who now ruled the South were neither all saint nor all sinner. Southern waste and corruption grew out of the inexperience, the lack of political skill, and the attitude of viewing office as a sinecure which these men held toward the job they were doing. It was a thing in itself.[11]

The rulers of the Old South might have turned their attention away from planting long enough to vote a few bonds for railroads and harbors, but the job of local recovery would have fallen upon men who themselves would have had to bear the burden of heavy taxes for any extravagance undertaken. Nor is it mere speculation to suggest that much of the northern corruption of the day was possible because the national government was so occupied with reconstructing the South and so willing to use any means toward this end that business was allowed to go its own way and to apply Southern reconstruction values to its conduct. Perhaps in reconstructing the South, the North was reconstructing itself and encouraging waste and corruption at home. If the Constitution and the courts and the Presidency were to be sacrificed in order to punish the South, why should not any business man do the same in their relation to the public lands and the public treasury if "progress" required it? The spirit of the age and the men who applied it were created, in part at least, by the war and Reconstruction; the new Republican party sprang from them, as did many of the

---

the ordinary walks of industry, and who, in travelling in quest of better luck, has got employment from the Southern Negroes in managing the machine which the war threw into their hands, and with the nature of which they are not themselves familiar; and he does this with the firm determination of making all he can out of the job, and with no other determination whatever."

[11] The determination not to accept Negro political control and the ultimate reduction of the conflict to "black versus white" in every state are the important facts.

politicians of the time. Reconstruction had a national price and, as the main political business of the day, created the atmosphere in which all else developed.

VI

The Ku Klux Klan, which now appeared in the South, was an immediate and direct answer to Negro prominence in politics. It would match the Union League's appeal to superstition and greed, with intimidation. It began as a secret protective society, suggested perhaps by the night patrols of slavery days, and was approved by a general southern inclination to resort to the use of force in order to counter insult or injustice. On a more substantial level, it represented a reaction to the whole reconstruction program and the military force on which it relied. It was at first only one of many such local protective groups organized to check Negro theft, barn-burning, and general disorders. Soon, however, it spread throughout the South as its white-robed, masked horsemen began their nighttime visits to "offensive" Negroes and whites. Methods ranged from fear inspired by ghostly talk and appearance to whippings and other personal violence. Members fell upon Union League councils, dispersed Negro militiamen, and saw to it that Negroes did not vote. They were effective enough to cause Congress to pass a new force bill against their activities and in some cases to suspend the right of habeas corpus. They caused Grant to restore a degree of martial law in two southern states.

Walter L. Fleming believed that the first part of the movement was good in resisting disorder and making property and persons more secure. The invasion of a lawless element which used the organization as a cloak for misdeeds, however, soon destroyed whatever constructive value it once had.[12] Its appearance showed at least that southerners had begun to react to the new situation they faced. Some were beginning to find a way out by working

[12] Walter L. Fleming (ed.), *op. cit.*, vol. 2, pp. 327–375.

with the carpetbagger and the Negro; some were ready for resistance, even with force where necessary. Reconstruction was beginning to take a new turn. Home rule under Radical Republican control would have its inning, but underneath was developing a new more native impulse to "redeem" the states from outside rule. Already race attitudes were taking the place of reconstruction motives. The nation, North and South, was turning toward a new future.

CHAPTER

20

RECONSTRUCTION
IN ACTION

I

The constitutional conventions that army registration produced were made up of "carpetbaggers," "scalawags," and Negroes. In spite of the heavy Negro registration, white men greatly outnumbered the Negroes in all conventions except those in South Carolina and Louisiana. At no time were their efforts directed to the establishment of permanent Negro rule in the South. They proclaimed the equality of all persons before the law in terms of civil and political rights, and in few, but in only a few, cases was there pressure for social equality between the races. Even integrated schools were seldom demanded, and the providing of lands for the Negro was never pressed to the point of an economic revolution. Details of how reconstruction proceeded in two typical states will be sufficient to illustrate the situation.

The Mississippi convention and the constitution that it created reveal this phase of Reconstruction at its best.[1] Here military commanders and native whites seemingly got along reasonably well; and the troops were, if anything, more inclined to repress the Negro than to push him forward. Yet the Union League was at work in Mississippi. As the Negro began to show an interest in politics, white leaders launched a desperate but tardy effort to bring the Negro voter under their control. The more realistic, however, realized that with existing attitudes this was impossible. It might be better for the white men to join the Republican drive and in alliance with the Negro avoid what one old Whig called "the jaws of inevitable ruin." "The Loyal League is upon you," wrote James L. Alcorn, "and the influence of the 'old master' on the freedman is neither more nor less than nonsense. . . . The 'old master,' gentlemen, has passed from fact to poetry!" He, Alcorn, would "sit in council with the Negro, vote with him, and join him on a platform acceptable to him as well as to the whites." [2]

Such a solution, however, was not satisfactory either to the Negro or to a large majority of the whites. The Negro would join the Republican party, and most of the whites, after playing with the idea of a new "Constitutional Union Party," would remain in the Democratic fold. A few at the top would temporarily turn "scalawag."

---

[1] Vernon Lane Wharton, *The Negro in Mississippi, 1865–1890* (Chapel Hill, N.C., 1947), *passim;* James W. Garner, *Reconstruction in Mississippi* (New York, 1901), *passim.* The best studies of land adjustment are: Willie Lee Rose, *Rehearsal for Reconstruction: The Port Royal Experiment* (Indianapolis, 1964) and John G. Sproat, "Blue Print for Radical Reconstruction," *Journal of Southern History,* XXIII (1957). Much of value can also be gained from *Autobiography of Oliver Otis Howard* (2 vols.; New York, 1907), *passim.*

[2] Vernon Lane Wharton, *op. cit.,* pp. 173–176; James W. Garner, *op. cit.,* pp. 62, 63, 88, 90. Judge William Yerger stated, "As men of sense let us endeavor to remedy what we cannot alter and gather together whatever may tend to palliate our misfortunes."

But that term in Mississippi did not imply a low-class white man bent only on obtaining office. Most were Old Whigs who found it easier and far more sensible to work with the Negro than to "aid in the reorganization of the Democratic party." In other words, as one of them explained, "Men who think that 'the war' knocked all the Old Whig spirit out of the Whigs are just . . . fatally mistaken." Throughout reconstruction, they attempted to draw conservatives together. David Donald estimates that within two years after readmission from 25 to 30 percent of the white voters in the state had joined the Republican party.[3]

Meanwhile, the registering of voters, often with Negroes as clerks and judges, showed 60,167 Negroes and 46,636 whites eligible to vote—with 76,016 in favor of the convention and only 6277 opposed. As a result, the convention as chosen contained 67 native southerners, 24 northern-born (mostly ex-Union soldiers), and 9 foreign-born or of unknown origin. Of the 67 openly avowed Republicans, only 33 were resident whites. In all, 84 of the delegates were white and 16 were Negroes. The so-called "scalawags" and "carpetbaggers" would therefore dominate the convention. Nevertheless, a half dozen capable Negroes, such names as Hiram Revels and Blanche Bruce, played a valuable part—that of T. W. Stringer, formerly of Ohio, being as important as that of any other man in the convention. The others as a rule sat silent and voted as directed.

The convention opened with an address by the chairman, who announced that "this hour brings to a close a period in Mississippi history." The members then began the new era by voting themselves a salary of ten dollars a day with forty cents a mile for travel. The next step was

[3] David Donald, "The Scalawag in Mississippi Reconstruction," *Journal of Southern History*, X (1944), 447–460. Praise for Alcorn's cooperation with Negroes is expressed in *Harper's Weekly*, January 1, 1870. James Orr's work in South Carolina is praised in *Harper's Weekly*, September 10, 1870.

to purchase stationery to the total cost of $1,927.27. Then followed weeks spent in an effort to seize control of all offices in the state for their friends and in the appropriation of funds for relief of the unemployed, in a situation where there was a decided labor shortage! At this point the military commander, who had ignored most of their extravagant efforts, reminded members that the convention had been called for the sole purpose of framing a constitution. That brought a frantic effort to lay taxes for the payment of convention expenses, and, at last, just 111 days after convening, the convention began the task of framing a constitution.

Most of the ideas incorporated into the constitution were supplied by Republicans who came from the North and West, and were borrowed from state constitutions in those sections. The first step, which took the most time, was the framing of a new franchise provision. It removed all property and educational qualifications for voting and required an oath so sweeping in character as to bar anyone who had been connected in any way with secession and the Confederacy. The abridgment of the right to travel in public conveyances and the making of distinctions between citizens in reference to property rights of any kind were prohibited. A move to require school attendance and to enforce separate schools for the races was checked and the matter left to the legislature. The obligation to education, however, was made clear. Needed judicial reforms were left for the legislature to inaugurate. Then for the first time in the state's history, the apportionment of the legislature was to be made on the basis of the total population regardless of race and the constitution itself was to be submitted to the people for ratification.

The right to pass on the constitution made resistance on the part of Democrats and conservatives possible. To them the franchise provision was especially offensive, and many openly declared that continuance of military rule was preferable to that which the constitution promised.

To the Negro went the warning: "If you abandon the people with whom you have ever lived and who now invite you to their protection in the future, you cast your destiny with an enemy between whom and us there is eternal war." Where such appeal failed, intimidation and force were applied if necessary. By such efforts, the constitution was rejected by some 7500 votes.

The rejection of the constitution had a salutary effect on both parties. The opposition now formed a new party under the name of the national Union Republican party. They named Louis Dent, a northerner and son-in-law of General Grant, as their candidate for governor and a Negro as their candidate for secretary of state. The Radical Republicans, in turn, relying more and more on the Old Whig element, chose as their candidate for governor James L. Alcorn, one of the state's largest and most important prewar planters. They too offered a Negro for the office of secretary of state. The constitution, with the franchise section to be voted on separately, was again presented for adoption. Alcorn swept into office with a heavy majority; the constitution was adopted by an even heavier vote, and the franchise provision was defeated in like fashion. Congress was satisfied and Mississippi re-entered the Union.

The legislature of the new government was heavily Republican in both houses, yet it contained only 35 Negroes in a total membership of 140. In a state where the Negroes formed a majority of the population, they comprised only 35 percent of the House and 13 percent of the Senate. It was due largely to the pressure of the governor that a Negro, the capable John R. Lynch, was chosen speaker.

Governor Alcorn set the pattern for his administration (and the ultimate destruction of the whole Republican regime) by announcing his purpose to make the colored man the legal equal of any other man. In the next four years, starting with a nearly empty treasury, he organized and maintained at state expense a biracial system of common schools, gave state aid to normal schools, and established a Negro state university. He reorganized the state judiciary and gave it a new code of laws. He renovated, rebuilt, or built new public buildings, established two state hospitals, and developed and expanded asylums for the blind, the deaf and dumb, and the insane. He eliminated from the laws all racial discrimination, and in 1873 persuaded the legislature to pass a civil rights bill that in theory gave Negroes equal access to all places of public entertainment. A Negro, Hiram Revels, had already been elected to the United States Senate.

Such a progressive program weakened Democratic opposition and brought a sweeping victory for the Republicans in 1873. But it contained two fatal weaknesses. First, it was expensive. Taxes, which had been shifted to real and personal property, increased too rapidly. Government cost, which before the war averaged something less than $750,000, now ran well over $1,500,000. Property holders, as a result, were soon in rebellion. Moreover, the program had been carried by Negro support but it did not grant the Negro politician his proportionate share of the spoils. His growing demand for office involved a political equality few whites would grant. Gradually the line in politics now ran between the races, not between the old parties.

Soon Alcorn himself and other white Republicans began to join the Democrats. They called the new alliance the "Republican Party of Mississippi." The Negro vote, however, was still the deciding factor; and in the state election of 1873, with the color line rather sharply drawn, Adelbert Ames, an army man and provisional governor, defeated Alcorn for the governorship. Ames pledged his administration to economy and wider political opportunity for the Negro. The two, however, did not go together. More political jobs for the Negro pushed the load of state services higher, while the move toward economy by cutting political salaries and having the legislature meet only every other year met solid Negro opposition. The shifting of court expenses from the state to the counties merely shifted the dissatisfaction, forced the cutting of school funds and university appropriations, and eliminated useful state reports.

Taxes were then placed on railroads and an effort was made at some tax relief, but changes came too late to save Ames and his party. His administration had been remarkably honest and, for the social benefits given, not unreasonably expensive. Mississippi, however, was not ready for the growing threat of Negro political equality, if not dominance, which Ames had accepted. By 1875, white Mississippi was ready for a revolution. Too much, too fast, had brought its reaction. The race question had been allowed to take over, and with it the doctrine that "ends justify means" changed hands. In bloody violence and brutal, unreasoning intimidation, the Negro was pushed out of politics and reduced to social Jim Crow inferiority.[4]

II

The reconstruction story in South Carolina, which probably shows this phase at its worst, started out somewhat differently from that in Mississippi, but it ended in much the same way. With the passage of the new reconstruction acts, "no legal government or no adequate protection of life or property" existed in the state. What remained of government from the past now was subject to military control, to be abolished or modified at will.[5] The

---

[4] See James W. Garner, *op. cit.,,;* this is the best of the "Dunning" studies. William C. Harris, *Presidential Reconstruction in Mississippi* (Baton Rouge, 1967), reveals the story from the inside and gives a balance that is not possible where only the national approach is taken.

[5] "The life, liberty, and property of every individual are placed at the mercy of military satraps. Military commissions and drumhead court martials have been everywhere substituted for trial by jury. Worse than all this, the people are menaced with Negro rule and supremacy at the point of the sword and bayonet."—*Charleston Daily Courier*, April 9, 1868.

army now in control seems to have been moderate and orderly in conduct. Its officers were cooperative and kept the public welfare always in mind. There were some clashes and some ill feeling, but these were not the rule. Registration for voting resulted in the acceptance of 80,832 Negroes and 46,929 whites. In the constitutional convention then elected, 76 of the 124 delegates were Negroes, of whom two-thirds had only recently been slaves. Yet the consensus of opinion seems to be that they were in character and conduct quite superior to the 27 native whites who had been elected. Only two such whites, Albert Mackey and Thomas Robertson, played a constructive part in the work of the convention. Aside from these two and Francis L. Cardozo, a highly capable native-born but Glasgow-educated Negro, the leading spirits of the convention were "non-Southern adventurers of both races." [6]

The constitution produced was " 'in letter' as good or better than any other constitution the state has ever had." It provided for universal manhood suffrage and for the popular election of presidential electors and all state and local officials, including judges. It put an end to imprisonment for debt, outlawed dueling, opened public schools to all regardless of race, desegregated the militia, petitioned Congress for money to provide land for the Negro, and put an end to discrimination of all kinds in property rights, education, and legal matters. It even protected homesteads up to a certain value against the process serving of creditors. It enlarged the rights of women and gave the state its first divorce law. Then, most important perhaps, came the reform of local and judicial administration and revised taxation. It was all done in fifty-three days.

From an abstract point of view, the constitution was a remarkable document, far in advance of anything the South had ever known. Yet the difficulty was that it had

[6] Francis B. Simkins and Robert H. Woody, *South Carolina During Reconstruction* (Chapel Hill, N.C., 1932), pp. 37–43.

no relationship to the traditions and realities of South Carolina. Francis B. Simkins and Robert H. Woody have remarked that it "might have been copied from some manual or improvised by a board of experts sitting in some distant city. . . . It had the earmarks of theoretical perfection" [7] but, it was not native; it was not practical. It involved heavy expenditures and required an administrative ability not available. Yet much would be permanent.

With a constitution framed and adopted, the Fourteenth Amendment ratified, and a legislature and officials elected, South Carolina had met all the requirements of the Reconstruction Acts. Late in July 1868, Congress admitted the South Carolina delegation to both houses. Military rule ended, and South Carolina resumed its place in the Union. Then began nine years of Radical Republican government and the bitter struggle for "home rule," against what South Carolinians considered "the most infamous revolution in history."

The Radical government which now assumed control under that surprisingly modern constitution suffered heavily from the character of its personnel. Its first governor, Robert K. Scott, from Ohio, was impeached for corrupt inefficiency. His successor, F. J. Moses, a native white, was far worse. Fraud, bribery, extravagance, and personal immorality reached new levels even by reconstruction standards and opened the way for reform. That came in the person of Daniel H. Chamberlain, a native of Massachusetts, well-educated, honest, and capable enough to remain in power to the end of reconstruction. It was "carpetbag" rule at its best.

With the heavy Negro majority in the state, the Negro played a more important part here than elsewhere. He "outnumbered and in many cases outshone" his "carpetbagger" and "scalawag" contemporaries. Seven Negroes went to Congress; two became lieutenant-governors and

---

[7] Francis B. Simkins and Robert H. Woody, *op. cit.*, pp. 37–43.

two were speakers of the House. Francis L. Cardozo served as both secretary of state and state treasurer; Alonzo Ransier became chairman of the state Republican executive committee and went on to Congress; Robert B. Elliott was twice elected to Congress, as was Robert Smalls. In each and every case, they did exceptionally well and won the respect of their colleagues.[8]

The Negro dominated the general assembly, in which much of the extravagance and corruption in reconstruction developed. Bribery was the rule; foolish expenditures for wine, cigars, furniture, and even clothing were a regular practice; and in the end bonds and grants to railroads pushed expenses and indebtedness beyond reason.

Gradually, as in Mississippi, the political division began to form along racial lines. The Democratic party under the leadership of Wade Hampton and Martin Gary entered the campaign of 1876 both to establish white rule in South Carolina and to support the National Democratic ticket. By intimidation, violence, and some honest efforts to bring the Negro to their side, they engaged Governor Daniel H. Chamberlain in a life-and-death struggle for control. In the end, both Hampton and Chamberlain claimed victory; each was inaugurated with his own legislature, speaker and all. Fortunately, much of this later stage of conflict was conducted in the courts, and the final outcome was decided in Washington. Chamberlain was victor, yet it was always understood that without federal support he could not have remained in power at any time. He was often in trouble, and even Grant did not always respond to his call. Soon, with Rutherford B.

---

[8] "Specific testimony as to the abiilties of the local Negro officeholders is not available but in the absence of any severe attack in the Democratic press, it can be assumed that the Negro officeholder measured up to the average of the local officeholder of the day." They seemingly operated without "serious friction with the whites."—George Brown Tindall, *South Carolina Negroes, 1877–1900* (Columbia, S.C., 1952), p. 64.

Hayes in office by Democratic acquiescence, the game was up. Chamberlain reluctantly stepped aside, and white rule and Negro submergence began in South Carolina.[9]

III

It is unnecessary to follow in detail the course of reconstruction in each of the other southern states. They differed widely according to local conditions and leadership. Economic factors probably played a larger part in Alabama than elsewhere because of its great natural resources in timber, coal, and iron ore, plus the rivalry of railroad interests to give access to them. Railroad interests were equally important in Virginia, and the exploitation of convict labor had a part in several states. Louisiana, owing to its unique physical and social background and the fact that it fell under Union control early in the war, experienced more of class and political corruption than any other state.[10] Arkansas required an oath of its citizens to accept the political and civil equality of all men regardless of color, and thus gained early readmission to the Union. Georgia, troubled by old political and economic rivalries, was ultimately returned to military control for seating ex-Confederates and refusing to seat Negroes elected to its legislature. Florida and Texas, both under Conservative control, early complied with the congressional provisions and were back in the Union by July 1868. North Carolina's story belongs largely to Johnson's first efforts at "resumption," and Tennessee's to the unique situation that it occupied politically during the war —and as Johnson's home state.

What does need to be noted more than the details of reconstruction in the individual states is the fact that revision has drastically altered the old myth of a South as a whole turned over to "Negro-carpetbag-scalawag" rule

[9] See Francis B. Simkins and Robert H. Woody, *op. cit.*, pp. 474–539.

[10] For the unique story in Virginia, see A. A. Taylor, *The Negro in the Reconstruction of Virginia* (Washington, 1926).

with only waste and corruption resulting.[11] There was, unfortunately, plenty of each of these in all the states. Yet more recent studies have shown that this side of Reconstruction has been both exaggerated and misunderstood. Debts accumulated were sometimes for things that the past had failed to provide—for example, schools and public improvements. Sometimes, as in Alabama, a state debt "was not, at any time, an actual 'debt,' but always a potential one," which, as Horace Bond has shown, could be reduced from $25 million or $30 million to less than $10 million to the satisfaction of both debtor and creditor.[12] The extent to which southerners themselves were involved has also become clear, and the number who were guilty of embezzlement of public funds matches that in the North.

The most important revisions, however, have been those touching the Negro in Reconstruction. Here the few detailed studies tell quite a different story from the one that pictured a broken South helpless under Negro rule and forced to wage a noble fight for freedom. These studies nowhere find the Negro using his numbers to submerge the whites or to force extreme measures upon them. Even in state offices, the Negro never occupied the proportion due him; and in the counties where a few Negroes became justices of the peace or even sheriffs, as in Mississippi, Vernon Lane Wharton has found little difference in administration from those counties under white Democratic control.

As to Negro morals, Simkins and Woody suggest, that "the tendency of the Negro to work less and frolic more had its compensations. Perhaps he was fulfilling the legiti-

---

[11] While the writers of the so-called Dunning School of Reconstruction have been criticized for their point of view and interpretation, their works constitute a valuable source for factual material on the state level. They should still be consulted for details on each state.

[12] Horace Mann Bond, "Social and Economic Forces in Alabama Reconstruction," *Journal of Negro History*, XXIII (1938), 290–348.

mate craving of every free man for recreation; perhaps his wife deserted the field work because she was busy with the task of setting up a home. To censure the Negro . . . for moral delinquencies involves the creation of arbitrary standards." [13]

[13] Francis B. Simkins and Robert H. Woody, *op. cit.*, p. 338. For a revisionist summary of Reconstruction in South Carolina, see A. A. Taylor, *The Negro in South Carolina During Reconstruction* (Washington, 1924), pp. 564–569; William C. Harris, *op. cit.*, pp. 246–250.

21

ECONOMICS
AND POLITICS

I

The Civil War and Reconstruction forced an agrarian revolution on the South. The great majority of its people had always been connected in some way with agriculture and had lived in rural areas. With peace they expected to continue, economically speaking, as they had done since colonial days. The plantation with its broad acres and slave labor had represented the large-scale agricultural effort and had furnished most of the section's export, but the small farmers had been more numerous and their production more varied. Since this had been the long-established pattern, it was generally assumed that with peace it would be resumed but with paid labor substituted for slavery.

To resume such a program would have been exceedingly

difficult. In the end, it proved impossible. The capital for
beginning again did not exist. The lands, always subject
to erosion and other harmful factors, had run down badly
under neglect and the ravages of the armies. Fences were
down; tools were worn out; seed was difficult to obtain;
and farm buildings were in disrepair. Most important of
all, the labor force had escaped from bondage, and was, in
most cases, rather intoxicated with its freedom. Furthermore, the Freedmen's Bureau and the army represented
outside factors that had to be dealt with in all labor
relationships.[1]

How to secure a permanent labor force to be kept in the
country, and one that could be made responsible and kept
efficient under supervision, was the problem. The so-called
Black Codes had been the southern answer. They had not

[1] The Freedmen's Bureau, spread like a protective umbrella
over the Negro, acted as a kind of government within a government. As General Otis O. Howard, Commissioner of the Freedmen's Bureau, said, "Scarcely any subject that has to be legis-
lated upon in civil society failed, at one time or another, to
demand the action by this singular Bureau." With its broad
powers to protect the Negro's rights, to supervise his labor relations, and to deal with "abandoned" lands, the Bureau and the
army stood squarely between the southern white man and the
Negro, and between President Johnson's reconstruction program
and that of Congress.

Much of the Bureau's problem in the South had to do with securing a foothold for the Negro farmer on "abandoned" and
confiscated lands, while President Johnson's problem had to do
with the return of such lands to their former owners. A conflict
was inevitable both in purpose and in accomplishment. Howard's
assurances to the Negro as to his rights on the land had to be
withdrawn on Johnson's orders and new conditions imposed.
"Why did I not resign?" Howard asked. "Because I even yet
strongly hoped in some way to befriend the freed people." In the
end, of course, he turned to Congress, which had already begun a
struggle with the President. Perhaps it was also Howard's loyalty to the devoted women and men who were doing such remarkable work in founding schools and forwarding Negro education
that held him to his job. *Autobiography of Oliver Otis Howard*
(New York, 1907), vol. 2, pp. 235–244; Henry Lee Swint, *The
Northern Teacher in the South, 1862–1870* (Nashville, 1947).

been aimed at a return to slavery, but the effort to check the Negro's wanderings and force him to become a permanent agricultural worker under strict supervision, appeared that way to a suspicious North.

As a speaker in the South Carolina House explained, "To make the disorganized labor available—or, indeed, to make it work at all, is the most difficult and delicate question which has ever been presented to a people." To which a newspaper editor added, "Something must be done to enforce and secure regular labor or this fine country will become a wilderness." That was just assuming that the plantation system must be resumed or starvation threatened. It required what all large-scale economic effort requires: division of labor, supervision of labor, and a permanent labor force.

To the Negro, the plantation system represented slavery. He could see little difference except that wages, at some uncertain time ahead, were supposed to be paid. As one planter described his procedure, the Negro's attitude is understandable.

> I have 21 hands all told. I get up at three o'clock, think over my day's business, . . . ring the bell twenty minutes before day for all hands to rise, the women to go to cooking for breakfast and dinner, the men to get off to work before sunrise, every set of hands having their work for the day told them. I have quite early breakfast, saddle and mount my little mule and am with my hands or going from one set to another until the middle of the day, come home, get dinner and go off again frequently in less than an hour.

To the Negro this was merely going ahead with the old life. Freedom meant little.

In many cases the planter's lack of confidence in the freedmen added to the difficulties. A Charleston planter insisted that the Negroes were always a nuisance. "You'll find that so in less than a year—they'll all be idle before winter. I would not give ten cents apiece for them." A Virginia planter declared that if he had to depend on free Negro labor, he would not take the best estate in his section as a gift, while a Georgia planter rejoiced when his "lawless gang" and their insolence wandered off.

The heavy migration of Negroes to the cities and to the West soon brought official state efforts to attract "industrious immigrants" from northern Europe. Some even proposed the importation of Chinese coolies. Such efforts, however, brought light response, and the majority soon agreed that the Negro was in the South to stay and to furnish the bulk of the labor. "He is familiar with our habits and customs," one editor commented, "and when the political swell has subsided he will be as docile and industrious a laborer as we could desire."

Yet as things stood labor was needed immediately, and the Negro could have his say to a large degree as to the conditions under which he worked. One condition was that it would not include the gang and the plantation. The Negro was determined to have a piece of land on which he could work as he pleased and profit in proportion. In the face of protests and prophecies of failure, planters began to break up their lands and rent to the Negro. The trend once begun, most had to follow, for as Freedmen's Bureau officials stated, "There was a desire, amounting to a passion, on the part . . . of the more enterprising blacks, to obtain land by lease." They would no longer work under an overseer.

At first the planter furnished the tools, the seed, and the year's supplies. He dealt with the local storekeeper, who became the nucleus of crossroads towns that began springing up all over the South and took a share of the crop when harvested. Soon, however, the Negro, having tasted independence, established his own contacts with the merchant, and the notorious lien system came into being. Tenant houses on small one- or two-horse farms appeared all over what had once been a plantation. As one planter wrote, "I moved my family to town to educate my children and practically abandoned my plantation to renters. I still retained some share hands . . . but it didn't work well, so had to drop the share plan."

Even renting did not satisfy the Negro. Here and there some more enterprising Negro wanted to own his land, and some new "town dweller," interested in a cotton gin, a bank, or a business of some kind—even a small local cotton factory—was willing to sell. The storekeeper was equally willing to assume the risk with mortgage or a lien. The process was complete. The plantation was coming to an end; the southern small town had been born; and a whole new set of land and labor relationships, uniquely southern, had evolved. It constituted a revolution.

II

A second phase of reconstruction economic developments had to do with the railroads. Before the war, in spite of magnificent waterways, the railroad had quite sharply altered the means and direction of transportation. The war had been fought largely along waterways and railroads. It had both built and destroyed. The southern system had been in all essentials blocked out before the fighting began and with war the gaps were quickly filled. Northern and southern lines in the East were completed, as was the central line through the Deep South. The Georgia and Tennessee lines were already the best in the section, and both the New Orleans and the Mobile lines were well along to the Ohio River.

The Union armies had destroyed bridges and tracks as they advanced, and Sherman's army made a specialty of making corkscrews out of rails. Lines in Virginia, Tennessee, Georgia, and the Carolinas suffered most, but the grades and often the ties still remained. On the other hand, in order to keep supply lines open, many roads behind the advancing Union army had been rebuilt with better rails, warehouses, and machine shops. Some northern regiments became famous for this work, and nearly one-third of the southern railroad mileage was again in use by 1865.

The Union policy regarding railroads after the war was one of peace without victory. The general rule was to return the lines to their former owners. The roads were to be transferred as they stood. Owners could take whatever United States equipment they wished at appraised value on short-term credit—later to be scaled down about 25 percent. In some cases the debt was simply written off, and the lines restored could charge the federal government for the services they performed. By July 1866, the United States was out of the southern railroad business, and southerners were in it.[2]

Southern railroad presidents, with their northern allies, were thus in an excellent position to prosper. They could also fish in the troubled waters of southern state and military district politics. Almost alone among southerners, they were in a position to share in and be a part of the new economic day. With the breakup of the plantation as almost the only large-scale capitalistic effort the antebellum South had known, and with the resulting rise of the small local towns with their lawyers, merchants, and bankers, a turning to the development of the region's great natural resources was inevitable. Northern bankers and even English capitalists had long known of the rich coal, iron ore, and vast timber resources awaiting exploitation in the section. Transportation to carry these out was all that was lacking.

Horace Mann Bond and C. Vann Woodward have each told the economic and political story of what now happened.[3] They have stressed the fact that most of the men who had, before the Civil War, been interested in a diversification of southern economy, the building of railroads, and the development of industry had been Whigs in politics. In the shifting political developments of Reconstruction, they had taken whatever side promised the quickest recovery and the restoration of a normal southern life as part of an expanding nation. They had assumed the role of "redeemers" in the final restoration of home rule throughout the South and had begun the alliance that

[2] C. Vann Woodward, *Reunion and Reaction: The Compromise of 1877 and the End of Reconstruction* (Boston, 1951), pp. 113–142.

[3] Horace Mann Bond, "Social and Economic Forces in Alabama Reconstruction," *Journal of Negro History*, XXIII (1938), 290–348.

would bring the much needed northern capital southward. As a result, the men who now became governors or held important state offices were, in spite of wearing the Democratic party label, largely supporters of Republican economic policies.

They were linked with the railroad interests, the iron and coal developments, and the real estate schemes for the building of industrial centers. This was noticeably true in the border states, where business and railroads, usually with northern financial backing but with a southern front, took control. Virginia early "bowed to the money interests." Its holdings in the stock of its own railroads were sold at a sacrifice to private interests, and its debts were funded to the benefit of the bankers, landholders, and railroads. In Kentucky, with powerful newspaper support, the liquor and tobacco interests, together with the Louisville and Nashville Railroad (L & N), dominated the state. Tennessee's first "home rule" governor was president of powerful coal and iron companies and closely allied with Thomas A. Scott's Texas and Pacific Railroad schemes.

More important were the economic and political connections of the Redeemer group in Alabama, where the L & N was building its empire. The existence of coal, limestone, and iron ore all together in one area foretold the rise of a great new industrial area in the center of that state. Almost as soon as the war ended, Albert Fink, superintendent of the L & N, began making investments for his road in that region. He projected new towns and industries of various kinds, and was a leader in the formation of the Southern Railway and Steamship Association for the pooling of freight and the checking of cutthroat competition.

Back in the 1850s, as a part of Stephen A. Douglas' Illinois Central plans, lands in Alabama had been granted for the building of railroads running northward to meet his line at Cairo. Young men in the legislature, such as J. L. M. Curry and Luke Pryor, had been urging funds for what was called the Tennessee and Alabama Central.

The man who stood behind these legislators was James W. Sloss, who seems to have been in some way connected with almost every industrial and commercial enterprise in the state. As early as 1855, he was president of the Tennessee and Alabama Central and in politics was an ardent Democrat. Somehow Sloss and his friends seem to have retained some of their wealth through the war. Their railroad interests had become closely bound with the L & N, which had begun pushing southward toward Alabama's rich coal and iron deposits.

Meanwhile, a rival for control had appeared in the Nashville and Chattanooga Railroad, which soon had a working agreement with the Alabama and Chattanooga, backed by Russell Sage and a group of Boston financiers. The struggle between these two railroad groups became so tangled with reconstruction that it is difficult to tell where economic interests end and political efforts begin. The endorsement of railroad bonds to the extent of $12,000 per mile for the Sloss roads was the work of the Provisional Assembly, hurriedly enacted before the Radical Republicans took control. When they did, the bonds of the rival Alabama and Chattanooga were endorsed up to $16,000 to the mile. Then followed a wasteful scramble in which bribery became the weapon on each side. In the end they apparently joined in securing loans. Debts piled up; and when the Radical regime fell, Alabama was sadly in debt—to what extent no one was certain.

Actually, most of the debt consisted of bonds issued to aid railroad construction, and it would become a tangible debt only if the state foreclosed its mortgages on railroad property. That would, of course, leave the state in debt to the bondholders in the amount of the endorsements and loans, but in possession of increasingly valuable railroad property. That would reduce the debt drastically and leave the historians to puzzle over the degree of guilt to assign to each regime.[4]

But the size of the debt Reconstruction bequeathed to

[4] See page 245.

Alabama is not the important point. The more significant thing is that what was once viewed as simply a struggle between a carpetbag-scalawag-Negro government, with its plunder and corruption, has been shown to have been largely a conflict between economic interests, heavily but not entirely local, for the transportation benefits of the great natural resources of Alabama. The panic of 1873 did more to destroy this local control than did the Radical Republicans, and with the elections of 1874, in which local government was restored and white supremacy established, economic independence was lost. Northern capital and capitalists took command.

In Virginia as well, railroads had much to do with the course reconstruction took. Rivalry between one group representing the interests of Baltimore and another those of Norfolk carried their struggle for control of the profitable Virginia and Tennessee line into politics. Under the skillful political manipulations of William Mahone, who shifted parties and backed anyone who favored Norfolk, a combination of Democrats and dissatisfied Republicans achieved both "home rule" for Virginia and victory for Mahone's Southside Railroad.

The Louisiana story, with its fantastic Lottery group whose economic power overshadowed that of the politicians and included many of them, and that of the Georgia railroad group, which led in the work of redeeming Georgia from the rule of carpetbagger Rufus B. Bullock, provide further convincing evidence of the fact that economic interests played no small part in the reconstruction story.

The quick revival of business interests in the South is, after all, not surprising. From its beginning, the Whig party was a national body with its southern wing, under Henry Clay's leadership, as strong and loyal, if not more so, than the northern wing, under Daniel Webster. Southerns Whigs had opposed secession because they held the same business philosophy and represented the same business interests as did the old northern Whigs. The Sloss group was conscious well back in the late 1840s of Alabama's great natural resources. Efforts had been made well before the war to secure northern capital and organization. It should also be remembered that the plantation, with its large-scale capitalistic production and its division and supervision of labor, was just as much big business in its own unique way as was the New England textile industry or the activities of the great New York business houses.

These northern and southern interests, regardless of the part they played in producing the war, were the first to want peace. Northern business, with much support from Horace Greeley's *New York Tribune*, "preferred the economic to the political exploitation of the South." Investments required southern stability. From the ranks of the old southern Whigs came the men who, in Reconstruction, joined the Republican party in the South as the shortest step by which to achieve the return to a normal southern life. They understood that capital and economic improvement were the first steps upward. Nor did they desert with the rest when the issue became one of Negro political equality. It was these same Whigs, though elected as Democrats, who relied on Republicans in Congress for material aid in Reconstruction.

So it is not surprising that, with the panic of 1873, these businessmen played the major role in bringing Radical reconstruction to an end and establishing white dominance. And the business element in the Republican party, on its side, shortened and smoothed the road to reunion by economic aid to recovery.[5]

[5] William B. Hesseltine, "Economic Factors in the Abandonment of Reconstruction," *Mississippi Valley Historical Review*, XXII (September, 1935), 191–210.

22

THE REPUBLICAN PARTY AND REFORM

I

A tangling of morals and politics characterized the Republican party from the beginning—a resort to politics in order to force Americans to live up to their ideals and commitments. For practical political purposes, the party had at times drifted away, but there had always been a goodly element insisting that the Declaration of Independence was a fundamental part of the Republican creed.

In a real sense, the birth of the Republican party was part and parcel of the great reform movements that in the Middle Period of American life kept alive the idea of possible social perfection. It was the final political expression of opposition to the greatest of the evils threatening the American dream. It was created to oppose an aggressive "slave power."

Most of the reform efforts in the beginning were directed against some larger abstract evil and were carried forward by local groups through lectures, tracts, petitions, and so forth. They relied heavily upon the evangelical churches for support and held largely to the idea that a good society was possible only to the extent that men themselves were good. The techniques for producing such a society were those of the revival meeting—conviction of sin, repentance and abandonment by the sinner himself. The appeal to conscience was the way to reform.

The movement against the sin of slaveholding was in the beginning one among the varied movements sweeping the Northeast and spreading across upper New York and on into the farther West. Most of its adherents were interested also in other reform movements. Only gradually did antislavery become the dominant reform effort of the day. Like most of the other movements, it was at first more or less abstract in character, opposing slavery as a sin. The appeal was to the slaveholder and to his conscience as a Christian. Only gradually did it assume crusading proportions, become sectional in its membership, and achieve a leadership and organization all its own.

The movement into politics was also gradual and produced something of a split among antislavery groups. One faction, discouraged by the progress of reform, individual by individual, insisted that the road to change in the United States was through politics. The common expression regarding any wrong was: "There ought to be a law agin it." So the early decision to vote only for men who were known to oppose slavery led to the formation of the Liberty and Free-Soil parties, bringing men who were "in morals" also into politics. Charles Sumner and Garrett Smith entered by that route. Fighting sin, once considered primarily the church's business, now became the task also of the political party.

The rise of the Republican party in opposition to the supposed threat to the extension of slavery into the territories marked the climax of this movement. The character of its membership and the reason for its organization placed heavy emphasis on a moral purpose, and its first national platform emphasized that fact. This remained a kind of undercurrent as the party matured in the next few years under more politically minded leadership. William H. Seward talked of a "higher law" and Abraham Lincoln chided Stephen A. Douglas for not caring whether slavery was voted up or down. It reappeared in the Republican Convention of 1860, when the interest in homesteads, internal improvements, finances, and the prospect of success caused the Declaration of Independence to be nearly forgotten. Good old Joshua Giddings, however, brought it back with a threat to withdraw if it did not become an essential part of the Republican creed. The party was not to be allowed to forget its obligation to all mankind—particularly the downtrodden portion.

II

The profound significance of this Giddings episode must be understood if the Republican party and its motivation in Reconstruction is to make sense. It so well illustrates that mixture of conscience and expediency always present in Republican action that it cannot be forgotten. No political party is willing to destroy itself for the sake of conscience if there is a way out. The maintainence of party solidarity is too important, and conscience without efficient political backing is noble but not practical. The problem faced by Republicans in Reconstruction was always one of achieving a noble end without taking too great a risk of losing to the "ignoble" Democrats. The day of pure abstract reform, as it existed in the 1830s and 1840s, was over. The high emotional temper and the complete abandonment of self for the sake of reform were no longer there. The Garrisons had cooled off. Their place was now occupied by such shrewd idealists, playing with political tools, as Thaddeus Stevens, John A. Bingham, and William P. Fessenden. Hard-headed, pragmatic politics was the price of survival. Yet these men were in morals as truly as was the unchanging Charles Sumner.

III

The Radical Republicans had in part misunderstood the deeper meaning of the sweeping Republican congressional victories in 1866. They had assumed more than many of those who cast the vote had intended, and more than the future would grant. The first Reconstruction Act, passed March 2, 1867, ignored the profound American distrust of the military arm in civil affairs and the more important fact "that the constituency on which Republican Congressmen relied in the North, lived in a race-conscious, segregated society devoted to the doctrine of white supremacy and Negro inferiority." The Radical Republicans had taken a serious risk for the sake of conscience.[1]

In the first place the establishment of military rule in the South by the Reconstruction Act intensified the quarrel with the Supreme Court, which, already in the *ex parte* Milligan case, had struck a serious blow at the whole concept of military rule as it had been exercised both during and after the war. Congress reacted sharply to this decision and on two recent occasions the Court seemingly "admitted an unwillingness, or, more properly, a lack of power, to interfere with the Congressional program." Then, only a week after its last admission of restraint, the Court announced that it would take jurisdiction in a more serious case involving military control, that of *ex parte* McCardle. The announcement aroused again the fear that the next step would be a move to test the constitutionality of the whole Reconstruction program.[2] In near panic, the Congress answered with proposals that, if passed, would have weakened the Court almost as much as their acts had already weakened the President. Fortunately, the more conservative checked extremes. Yet the

---

[1] C. Vann Woodward, "Seeds of Failure in Radical Race Policy" in Harold M. Hyman (ed.), *New Frontiers of the American Reconstruction* (Urbana, Ill., 1966), pp. 125–126.

[2] Stanley I. Kutler, "*Ex parte McCardle:* Judicial Impotency? The Supreme Court and Reconstruction Reconsidered," *American Historical Review*, LXXII (1967), 835–851.

wisdom of military control, even in the South, had been questioned. "The Court," as *The Nation* observed, "is made the object of abuse, and the agreement of the judges on a point of law of unusual clearness is denounced unsparingly as a judicial conspiracy." Reaction had already set in.

IV

In granting the Negro the franchise, the Congress had taken a still greater risk. Such a step had been carefully avoided in all earlier action. The Civil Rights Act had given the Negro ample legal protection for personal and property rights, but it had not bestowed the franchise. The Fourteenth Amendment had straddled the issue and left the matter indirectly in the hands of the South. Now, by the Reconstruction Act, the Negro was not only a citizen; he was a voter in a situation where his white neighbors were heavily restricted. Yet even here it is clearly apparent that this "hastily-thrown-together act" was not primarily designed for the protection of Negro rights and the establishment of equality. It was shaped, as C. Vann Woodward states, to place the control of the southern states in hands friendly to the Republican party.[3] Nothing was done in this act for Negro education or landholding. Proposals for these ends had been voted down. Nor was any provision made to check Negro disqualification for voting by educational or property-holding requirements. Moreover, the whole program could be rejected by any southern state that might prefer to remain under military rule.[4]

[3] Leon F. Litwack, *North of Slavery: The Negro in the Free States, 1790–1860* (Chicago, 1961), pp. 75, 263.

[4] C. Vann Woodward, *Reunion and Reaction: The Compromise of 1877 and the End of Reconstruction* (Boston, 1951), pp. 125–247. Thaddeus Stevens commented, "If it be just, it should not be denied; if it be necessary, it should be adopted; if it be punishment to traitors, they deserve it." *Congressional Globe*, 39th Cong., 2d sess., p. 252.

The reason for avoiding a clearcut program for Negro equality lay not in the South but in the racial attitudes of Republican-dominated northern states, where discrimination was the rule. Everywhere except in five New England states (where only 6 percent of the northern Negroes lived), the Negro was denied equal voting rights. Discrimination extended also to the courtroom, the schoolhouse, and even the church. Some advances had been made during the war, but in the main northern Negroes remained pretty much as Leon F. Litwack described them in 1860. The northern Negro, he said, "remained largely disenfranchised, segregated, and economically oppressed." He was barred from juries, schools, workshops, libraries, theaters, public conveyances, museums, and literary societies. Although the white man was responsible for the Negro's plight, he turned it all against the Negro:

> Having excluded the Negro from profitable employments, the whites scorned his idleness and poverty; having taxed him in some states for the support of public education, they excluded his children from the schools or placed them in separate and inferior institutions and then deplored the ignorance of his race; having excluded him from various lecture halls and libraries, they pointed to his lack of culture and refinement; and, finally, having stripped him of his claims to citizenship and having deprived him of opportunities for political and economic advancement, the whites concluded that the Negro had demonstrated an incapacity for improvement in this country and should be colonized in Africa.[5]

In the Old Northwest, where the Republican party was born, an Ohioan averred that not one man in a thousand favored social and political rights for the Negro. Lyman Trumbull of Illinois, who fathered the Civil Rights Bill, frankly admitted that "there is a very great aversion in the West—I know it is so in my state—against having free negroes come among us. Our people want nothing to do with the negro." As to his own feelings, Trumbull confessed, "We, the Republican party, are the white

[5] Leon F. Litwack, *op. cit.*, p. 279.

man's party. We are for making white labor respectable and honorable, which it can never be when negro slave labor is brought into competition with it." Representative William Richardson, from the same state, insisted that "God made the white man superior to the black, and no legislation will undo or change the decrees of Heaven."

Senator Thomas A. Hendricks, a Democrat from the neighboring state of Indiana, declared that "we are not of the same race; we are so different that we ought not to compose one political community . . . I say . . . this is a white man's Government, made by the white man for the white man. . . ." Senator Samuel S. Cox of Ohio, was of the same opinion; and even Senator James W. Grimes of Iowa, who was to vote against impeachment, wrote in 1865:

> As to the Negro I have not changed my opinion from the beginning. I think I shall come pretty nearly to the measure of my duty when I secure him his rights as a party in the courts, as a witness on the stand, as a scholar in the school, and as a christian in the church . . . but I am under the impression that he can live some years and so can we, without bestowing on him the elective franchise.

The *Chicago Tribune* agreed with Grimes and asserted that the Negro was more ignorant and more servile to the demagogues than were the foreign immigrants of any nation.

That these men expressed the attitudes of the people in their home states cannot be doubted. In the seven states of the Northwest at the outset of the civil war, service in the militia was limited to male whites and the Negro was denied the right to vote. Neither Illinois nor Indiana provided for the education of Negro children or accepted Negroes as witnesses in court trials where whites were involved. Four states forbade interracial marriages. Three even prohibited Negroes from settling within their borders. George W. Julian of Indiana gave the reason: "The real trouble is that we hate the negro. It is not his ignorance that offends us but his color."

V

One of the main reasons why northern men were anxious for the Negro to have rights and privileges in the South which they were unwilling to grant to him in their own states was the firm belief that when slavery was ended "the Negro would flee Northern race prejudices and return to his natural environment and the congenial climate of the South." [6] Republicans all along had argued that slavery alone caused the Negro to escape to the North. Free the slaves, they said, and the warm climate, abundant lands, familiar labor, and a sentimental attachment to the South would hold the freedmen there and lure the northern Negro back. That would "drain away all the race problems which now vexed the North." The Negro was a creature of the tropics. That was his natural habitat. As Secretary of the Treasury Salmon P. Chase wrote to the Union commander of the Department of the Gulf, "Let, therefore, this South be opened to Negro emigration . . . and it is easy to see that the blacks of the North will slide southward, and leave behind them no question to quarrel about as far as they are concerned." [7]

The great spokesman for this myth and for outside colonization of northern Negroes was Abraham Lincoln. In August 1862, he told a delegation of Negroes that

> . . . we have between us a broader difference than exists between almost any other two races. This physical difference is a disadvantage to us both and I think your race suffers very greatly, many of them by living among us, while ours suffer from your presence. In a word we suffer on each side. If this be admitted, it offers a reason at least why we should

[6] V. Jacque Voegeli, "The Northwest and the Race Issue," *Mississippi Valley Historical Review*, L (1963), 235–251. See also Voegeli, *Free But Not Equal: The Midwest and the Negro During the Civil War* (Chicago, 1967) and William Gillette, *The Right to Vote: Politics and the Passage of the Fifteenth Amendment* (Baltimore, 1965).

[7] V. Jacque Voegeli, "The Northwest and the Race Issue," *Mississippi Valley Historical Review*, L (1963), 242.

be separated. . . . It is better for us both, therefore, to be separated.[8]

His remedy was colonization in some favorable clime.

In his annual message, December 1, 1862, Lincoln discussed the problem of the free Negro and northern prejudices. He noted the widespread fear that the Negro, set free, would swarm forth and cover the whole land. He then asked:

> But why should emancipation south, send free people north? People of any color, seldom run, unless there be something to run from. *Heretofore* colored people, to some extent, have fled north from bondage; and *now*, perhaps, from both bondage and destitution. But if gradual emancipation and deportation be adopted, they will have neither to flee from. Their old masters will give them wages at least until new laborers can be procured; and the freed men, in turn, will gladly give their labor for the wages, till new homes can be found for them, in congenial climes, and with people of their own blood and race. This proposition can be trusted on the mutual interests involved.

Here was consolation for his own people by assurance of the ultimate removal of free Negroes from the North. Here was colonization satisfactory in environment for the dislodged Negro. Even the South would have dependable labor until something better came along. Each and all were thus taken care of on the basis of mutual interests, but with no consideration of the human and moral values involved![9] Lincoln's message ignored the fact that the northern Negro was not willing to be colonized. As Frederick Douglass observed, "We are Americans by birth and education, and have a preference for American institutions as against those of any other country. . . . I see no necessity for the separation."[10] Nor had Lincoln taken into consideration the feelings of the abolitionists, who

[8] Roy P. Basler (ed.), *Abraham Lincoln, Collected Works* (New Brunswick, N.J. 1953–1955), vol. 5, p. 372.

[9] *Ibid.*, pp. 518, 536–537.

[10] Philip S. Foner, *The Life and Works of Frederick Douglass* (New York, 1965), vol. 3, p. 286.

had long since abandoned colonization and who were now expecting the war to do more than to preserve the Union as it once had been.

VI

The fall elections following passage of the 1867 Reconstruction Acts, as had been the case following the Emancipation Proclamation, went sharply against the Republicans. Their vote was heavily reduced in the New England states, Nebraska, and Iowa. Democrats won in Connecticut, New York, New Jersey, and Maryland, and gained individual victories in Pennsylvania and Ohio. In every state where the voters had a chance to express themselves on Negro suffrage, they rejected it.

The Republican press frankly attributed the reverses to the Negro question. Some saw in it a repudiation of Radical Republican moves to enfranchise the Negro. Radicals, in turn, shamed their fellow members by pointing out that while Negro suffrage existed throughout the South, the Negro could vote in only six northern states. The *Independent* charged that

> ... the Republican party notwithstanding high mettle and its still more boasted high principles—even yet quakes at meeting a negro by day as at seeing a ghost by night. . . . When Negro Suffrage is proposed for South Carolina—a Southern State—the Republican party uplifts a lion's paw, and magnificently enforces obedience; but when Negro Suffrage is at issue in Ohio—a Northern State—the Republican party borrows a hare's legs and runs from its own principles. . . . The plain deduction is, the Republican party—though it has shown much friendliness to the Negro . . . cannot yet look him in the face without remembering his color and forgetting his rights . . . a sufficient mass of the Republican party to hold the balance of power . . . not only dislikes the Negro, but are more willing to tread him under foot than to give him a helping hand. Both in and out of Ohio, by such Republicans, a Negro is less respected than a rebel. . . . [The editorial ended by observing that] the states that now need reconstruction are the Northern. . . . Fellow-countrymen it ought to bring a blush to every white cheek in the loyal North to reflect that the political equality of American citi-

zens is likely to be sooner achieved in Mississippi than in Illinois—sooner on the plantation of Jefferson Davis than around the grave of Abraham Lincoln.[11]

Until this time surprisingly little open opposition to the Reconstruction Acts existed in the South. Submission to the inevitable seemed to be the general rule. The fact that socio-political demands had been made in the South which northerners had been unwilling to accept for themselves may have induced a calm in anticipation of a northern reaction against extremes. At any rate, with Republican reverses, the southern temper changed rapidly. The first reaction was to point out the hypocrisy implied in the existence of one policy for the South and a different one for the North. Then gradually the pattern of acceptance began to alter. Cooperation with the Negro to achieve stability, which had produced Republican governments in some states, slowly gave way to a drive for white supremacy and the "redemption" of southern society.

This drift toward self-rule was not checked by what occurred in Republican ranks in the campaign of 1868. The platform drawn up at Chicago in May of that year congratulated "the country on the assured success of the reconstruction policy of Congress, as evidenced by the adoption, in a majority of the States lately in rebellion, of constitutions securing equal civil and political rights to all . . . [and] the guarantee by Congress of equal suffrage to all loyal men at the South," as "demanded by every consideration of public safety, of gratitude, and of justice." It then added the significant statement that "the question of suffrage in all loyal States properly belongs to the people of those States." The dominance of the Republican party in the South was thus assured through a combination of "loyal" white and Negro voters, while the matter of Negro suffrage in the North was left to each state.

On this basis, seven southern states were admitted back into the Union in time to vote the ticket in 1868. So with

[11] *The Independent*, April 18 and Oct. 17, 1867.

General Grant safely in the presidential chair, the final step in Reconstruction could be taken—passage of the Fifteenth Amendment. Outwardly this amendment seems to assure the Negro the right to vote, yet it merely outlawed the use of race as a test for voting. It was clearly the work of moderate men. It left, as a possibility, the disfranchisement of the Negro by the poll tax, the grandfather clause, the literacy test, and such other tests as an ingenious southern legislature might devise. The state, North and South, was still in control; and since the Negro was already enfranchised in the South, there is considerable reason to think that the amendment was designed more to serve the interests of local northern political groups than to further benefit the Negro.[12] At least the amendment did not represent a bold move toward Negro rights, and it did not preclude the adoption of "property or educational tests."

Meanwhile, President Johnson's amnesty proclamations of September and December 1868, which restored the voting rights to most former Confederates and played a part in Democratic victories in Virginia, Georgia, and North Carolina in 1869 and 1870, indicated further southern reaction. The rise and spread of the Ku Klux Klan as an agent of intimidation and organized violence was an even greater threat to the existing southern Republican governments.

VII

The necessity for giving some meaning to the Fifteenth Amendment and for checking the sweep of reaction led Congress in 1870–1871 to pass three enforcement acts. The First Enforcement Act forbade state officials to discriminate on the basis of race or color, and it outlawed

---

[12] William Gillette, *op. cit.*, pp. 46, 50. Charles Sumner reminded colleagues, "You need votes in Connecticut. . . . You need them also in Pennsylvania. . . . They [Negroes] will vote for those who stand by them in the assertion of Equal Rights."— *Congressional Record*, 51st Cong., 2d sess., p. 904.

any attempt to control the vote of a citizen by force or threat of any kind. The Second extended federal control over elections and provided for supervision of elections. The third, aimed at the Ku Klux Klan, made it a federal offense to conspire to overthrow the United States Government or to conspire to prevent persons from holding office, serving on juries, or exercising equal voting rights.

These laws appeared on the surface to be thorough and even harsh. Some persons condemned them as infringing on individual and state constitutional rights.[13] Yet in application this display of federal power proved decidedly ineffective as far as the Negro was concerned. "Between 1870 and 1896, when the bulk of this legislation was repealed, 7372 cases were tried and hundreds of offenders who were never brought to trial, were arrested." In spite of this the steady disfranchisment of the Negro continued. By 1877 the Negro vote had been largely neutralized and a solid Democratic South assured. The government won some three-fourths of its early cases, then yielded to public pressure, and as state and local officials refused to cooperate and intimidation increased, "the Acts were virtually dead letters." "Southern intransigence and Northern apathy" allowed "white supremacy" to become "a more vital principle than Republican supremacy." [14]

The Republican party was caught in a strange situation. It could muster the vote to pass sharp federal legislation for the benefit of the southern Negro, but it could not support the abstract principles behind that legislation. Its strength as a party lay in the North, yet the margin of victory in race-conscious Connecticut, Indiana, New

---

[13] The question of constitutionality has, of course, been clearly settled by the Supreme Court in our own day. In fact one scholar has insisted that Reconstruction failed because the Radical Republicans were too constitutionally minded. See Alfred H. Kelley, "Comment on Harold M. Hyman's Paper" in Harold M. Hyman (ed.), *op. cit.*, pp. 40–58.

[14] Everett E. Swinney, "Enforcing the Fifteenth Amendment, 1870–1877," *Journal of Southern History*, XXVIII (1962), 202–218.

York, and often in Ohio was narrow. Where the question of Negro emigration or Negro franchise was involved, the balance could be easily shifted. It was the same old Republican problem of choosing between its conscience and political expediency. Regard for the possible political effects in these states had been largely responsible for the failure of the Republican party to come forward at any time with a clear-cut, bold stand on Negro suffrage. On the other hand, when immediate political danger was not involved, the party closed ranks; and it could honestly claim credit for the justice and equality so far achieved. Reform and party interests had to go together if abstract values were to be preserved. As long as the Democratic party stood for race prejudice and discrimination, the Negro's interests could best be served by such measures as preserved Republican party unity.[15]

VIII

If Reconstruction had been carried on in a vacuum and if the only determining factor had been the Negro's place in American life, this explanation of Republican motives might be sufficient. Unfortunately, neither condition existed. Reconstruction ran its course at a time when the United States was rapidly leaving one age in the history of the Western world and entering a strangely different one. The magnifying force of a civil war, making use of modern technology and organization, had hurried developments forward, and peace had revealed a business order already vastly altered. To its leaders, the South with its rich undeveloped resources and its economic potential soon ceased to be just a place where ex-Confederates and

[15] Since this chapter was written, a significant study on the problem of "motivation in Reconstruction historiography," by those brilliant young scholars, LaWanda and John H. Cox, appeared in the August 1967 issue of *Journal of Southern History*. I have not been able to take advantage of it. They insist that the Republicans followed conscience in spite of the political risks.

ex-slaves lived. Northern states, in turn, were not inhabited only by individuals whose sole concern was with Negro migrations. For business reasons, it was time to get on with something other than the political and social interests of reformers and their Negroes.

It should be remembered that by 1860 the Republican party had an economic program as well as antislavery extension principles. The southern threat to the nation's future had not been confined to slavery in the territories; southern attitudes toward the public lands, internal improvements, protective tariffs, and finances stood directly across the path of national economic progress. It was holding back the modern world.

With secession and the withdrawal of southern representatives from Congress, changes began at once. In rapid fashion came a homestead act, a new national banking system, higher tariff laws, and federal aid in different forms for the building of railroads. War needs pushed economic developments further and faster toward a new national social and economic way of life. Peace found the need for economic reform, not in terms of aid but in terms of restraint. The Republican party had already reconstructed the economic order, and the demand for restraint would soon come from the farmers of "the race-conscious" old Northwest and, a little later, from the Republican-voting dwellers of the smaller urban centers.[16]

While economic influences had been quite apparent in cotton seizures and in the confiscation of abandoned lands, the larger economic facts in Reconstruction had to do with the dismal failure to provide the Negro with any sound economic base from which to rise and the immediate interest of northern investors in southern opportunities. Soon the southerners elected to Congress as Democrats were depending on Republican votes to help restore their broken-down physical structure, and north-

[16] See John D. Hicks, *The Populist Revolt* (Minneapolis, 1931) and Richard Hofstadter, *The Age of Reform* (New York, 1955).

ern business men were demanding an end to Radical reconstruction.[17] An alliance between northern business men and southern conservatives was inevitable. Restored order and political stability alone could create a field in the South for safe investments and bring that section back into the currents of a prosperous national life.

By the 1870s, aided by a growing business depression, Conservative Republicans began to talk of Negro enfranchisement as a serious mistake. "Let the South alone," was a much-heard remark. Evidently speaking for an element in the party which had once supported Reconstruction but which had now changed its mind, *The Nation* editorialized:

> We do not need to tell any of our readers what the state of things in that region is. It is not simply that men suddenly raised from a condition of bestial servitude, inheriting the weaknesses of barbarism, aggravated by the weaknesses of slavery, have been admitted to participation in the rights and responsibilities of society; it is that they have been put in full and exclusive control of that most delicate and complicated piece of mechanism known as the government of a civilized State, with its debts, its credit, its system of taxes, its system of jurisprudence, its history, its traditions, its thousand knotty social and political problems. . . . We do not hesitate to say that a better mode of debauching the freedmen, and making them permanently unfit for civil government, could hardly have been hit upon had the North had such an object deliberately in view. . . . It were better that all the blacks and whites now living south of Mason and Dixon's line were sunk in the sea than go on as we are going.[18]

Radical Reconstruction had failed. Some persons were of the opinion that failure also awaited "the devoted Northern woman who toils her life away under the delusion that she can fight all Africa with a spelling-book and multiplication table."

But was Republican reform all a failure? Under exist-

---

[17] Kenneth M. Stampp, *The Era of Reconstruction, 1865–1867* (New York, 1965), p. 207.

[18] *The Nation*, Dec. 7, 1871.

ing conditions it is only possible to say that the Radicals did about as well as could have been expected. Armed only with the Declaration of Independence (which many considered to be but a bundle of "glittering generalities") and an American dream of possible social perfection, they had faced the restrictions of a revered Constitution, the open hostility of a President, the racial prejudices in their own party, a stubborn South that everyone knew must be "restored," and a dangerous political rival in the Democratic party. They had kept control of Congress and added to "the law of the land" three amendments ambiguous enough in other hands and at another time to have great meaning. That was something.

CHAPTER

23

THE ELECTION OF 1868
AND THE NEW DAY

I

The election of 1868 marks the beginning of the final phase of Reconstruction—the passing of one set of men and interests and the beginning of a new age. With Grant's election, the nation began to turn away from the South and to center its interest on the more important things taking place in national life. Reconstruction had largely run its course; the feeling that it had failed was becoming widespread.

Stevens, Sumner, Fessenden, Trumbull, and Johnson now stepped aside and gave place to the ruthless exploiters of a new era. Even Grant appeared to be something of a survival from an earlier time—a President chosen for his past rather than his present. Grant never quite knew what was taking place around him or what it all meant. He became a pathetic, bewildered, shuffling figure whom others used for ends he never understood. He was Reconstruction's final tragedy.

In the South, the carpetbagger was being told to pack his bag, the Negro to go back to his menial tasks, white men to adjust their differences and decide whether to go forward or to settle back into the old ways. The social revolution was over.

Democrats began to stir and to find new hope. Republicans dropped their Lincoln image and began to take a hard, cold look at reality and political necessity. Everybody grabbed and pushed and hurried to be there first and to get the most. Strong men took control, and the weaker were trod underfoot as they protested again with words from the nearly forgotten Declaration of Independence. Greenbackers, antimonopolists, and Populists took up where the abolitionists left off. Steam and the machine came into their own to cut space, create a new interdependence, and put the living of the many into the hands of the few. Meanwhile the American farmer with his abundance was ruining himself and his fellow farmers throughout the Western world. They, like the Negro, were not to be allowed to preside over their own revolution.

II

The political order had already reached bottom with the fumbling over reconstruction. It had lost all sense of responsibility or control over the new age that was emerging. Corruption, born of the reconstruction creed that ends justify means, ran riot, and the Republican party (with its halo for saving the Union) and the Democrats (in disgrace for their part in rebellion) offered little hope for political progress. Yet the national problems demanding solution were never greater. The war debts, the war tariffs, the extravagent disposal of the public lands, and especially the control of the giant corporations often closely linked with government policies—all were allowed to grow more complex and more difficult while the Republican Congress punished Johnson and the South.[1]

The Republicans early decided on General Grant as their 1868 candidate, for no reason that had anything to do with his fitness for public office. He was a hero and he had broken with Johnson. That was enough. Following the Lincoln tradition, Grant was nominated in Chicago, at a convention which Bishop Matthew Simpson [2] opened with a prayer and which spent most of its time damning Johnson and groaning at mention of the men who had checked impeachment. The party pledged payment of the war debt and pensions for the soldiers, and, of course, it took credit for saving the Union. Grant responded by stating, "I shall have no policy to enforce against the will of the people. . . . Let us have peace."

Just what this meant no one knew, least of all Grant. Benjamin F. Wade, who had visited him earlier, reported that he could not discover "what the devil he was for. I could get nothing out of him. As quick as I would talk politics, he'd talk horses. Well in these times a man may be all right on horses and all wrong on politics."

Even in the war, Adam Badeau felt that "neither he nor the rest of the staff knew why Grant succeeded; they believed in him because of his success. For stretches of time his mind seemed torpid. . . . They could never follow a mental process in his thought. They were not sure that he did think." Grant and his administrations would be the price the nation would pay for Reconstruction.

The Democratic party started the new era under a

[1] "The great need of the country now is the appearance in the Executive Chair of somebody to give weight and dignity to, or in short, to make an issue of one of the great reforms now awaiting popular attention. Parties are evidently getting into a state of disorganization, and need remarshalling on new lines. . . . It is melancholy, but true . . . that the national legislature shows itself incapable or unwilling to deal thoroughly with a single evil except slavery."—*The Nation*, March 9, 1871.

[2] Simpson had even tried to get the Methodist Conference in Chicago to set aside a day of prayer for the impeachment of President Johnson.

cloud. In spite of the fact that war Democrats had supported Lincoln and the war to an extent that produced the Union party of 1864, the term copperhead was now being widely applied to the whole party. The *Cincinnati Commercial* insisted that the South was again "seeking domination of the United States through the machinery of the Democratic Party," which was "the same in character and spirit as when it sympathized with treason." *The Nation* charged it with no motive save returning to power, and declared that if the nation remembered the 600,000 soldiers who had perished in the war, it could never consent to letting those who had "dabbled and hindered" while these men were fighting return to power.

Not only this, but the party's old leaders were gone. Douglass was dead. Johnson had been ruined by Reconstruction. Vallandigham had shot himself while attempting to show a jury that a client could not possible have shot himself in such and such a position. Its southern leaders were either dead or discredited. What the Democratic party's course for the future would be was a question.

Two different plans had gradually emerged. A Western group in Ohio thought the party should go back to its old Jacksonian position and oppose the growing Republican trend toward a Hamiltonian approach to the tariff, finance, and neglect of the common man. The Ohioans had succeeded in sending Allen G. Thurman to the Senate and electing William (Fog Horn) Allen, who had a long Jacksonian record, to the governorship of the state. They had launched what became known as "the Ohio idea." They called attention to the huge profits made by manufacturers under the existing tariff and by bondholders who had bought their bonds with depreciated greenbacks and were now receiving as much as 20 percent on the capital invested. The Ohioans contrasted these gains with the plight of the poor Western farmer whose debts, contracted in cheap money, had now to be paid at increased rates. They would keep the greenbacks in circulation and use them to pay all debts. "One currency for the bond holder and for the plow holder" was their cry. They would reduce the tariff and destroy monopolies everywhere.

Such a program for Democratic party recovery did not suit the Eastern wing. It would accept the new business age and seek success by following the Republicans in paying the debt in gold, reducing the tariff moderately, accepting Reconstruction as finished, and spending their efforts on Republican corruption.

At their convention in New York in 1868, where many old Confederate leaders were to be seen, the Western Democrats pushed for their greenback and tariff programs and offered George H. Pendleton as the party candidate. For a time Pendleton led the voting, but in the end the East had its way and Horatio Seymour, New York war governor and sound-money advocate, was nominated. The vice presidential candidate was young Francis Preston Blair, a former supporter of Lincoln, who now declared that the only way to restore the government and the Constitution "was to choose a president who would declare radical reconstruction null and void . . . disperse the carpetbag governments and supersede them with white governments." The Democrats had failed to take a stand for reform, yet it was quite clear that they were gathering considerable support from a growing liberal element, even in the Republican party itself.

The campaign, more than the candidates, showed the profound changes taking place in national life. The Republicans turned to the bankers and railroads for funds. Jay Cooke donated $1500, on condition that the bonds he had marketed be paid in gold. Edward Pierpont, who had made a fortune out of government legal business, contributed $20,000. In all, business gave the Republicans more than $200,000. Zachariah Chandler was able to spend $50,000 in Indiana, $40,000 in Pennsylvania, and like amounts in other doubtful places. He organized the "Boys in Blue," talked pensions, and waved the bloody shirt for all it was worth. "Scratch a Democrat and you find a rebel under his skin," was the cry.

Yet with a soldier's reputation, the Grand Army of the

Republic emerging, and the copperhead appeal still good against the Democrats, Grant won by only 300,000 votes. The 400,000 Negro votes in the South had, in fact, given the Republicans victory. North and South Carolina, Tennessee, Alabama, Arkansas, and Florida had all gone for Grant. Ohio and Indiana were close, and New York, New Jersey, and Oregon went Democratic. The political order was beginning to adjust itself to the realities of the day.

III

The nation as a whole wanted and half hoped for a moderate administration. Henry Adams asserted that the newspaper men hailed Grant as a reformer. And why not? He had been a good soldier and soldiers represented order. Any man who had commanded a million men in the field must know how to administer. And had he not said, "Let us have peace"?

What party leaders failed to recognize was that Grant was something left over from an age rapidly fading into history. More than any other American, Grant suggested the continuing Civil War. He represented the moral creed of Reconstruction—that the ends justify the means. He accepted the drift in government that dealt in personalities, when statesmanship was demanded to face the problems of the emerging industrial revolution. He certainly knew much about horses; he knew nothing about politics as they applied to the modern world.

The first shock came when Grant announced his cabinet. Most people thought the telegraph company which carried the news was just playing a joke on the public. A Galena neighbor, Elihu B. Washburne, was made Secretary of State as a compliment and was expected to resign at once; another Galena neighbor was made Secretary of the Navy, to be followed by a landlubber who when he visited his first ship and saw the hatch exclaimed, "Why the damn thing's got a bung-hole"; as Secretary of the Treasury, a department store head was named—a man who, with friends, had just presented Grant with a purse of $65,000 with which to buy a house. Mediocre men filled the other places, and constant shifting was required in the years ahead. Only Hamilton Fish, who succeeded Washburne, did credit to his office. Minor appointments were even worse—evangelists and cranks at home and abroad. At one time, forty-two of Grant's relatives were on the federal pay roll.

In office, the orgy began. Since he had no program and since he remembered that expansion had once been a popular issue, Grant began trying to annex San Domingo and perhaps Cuba. Only with difficulty were the few intelligent people about him able to wean him away from such a program.

With the only idea he had ever had for a national policy rejected, Grant accepted the Presidency as a kind of reward for past services and a chance to pay personal bills by appointments to office. He had the military idea of delegating authority to subordinates and expecting loyalty from them. He accepted opposition as disloyalty to the nation, and he soon began to gather about him an administration following of "regulars" as against critics. In this way, he became the victim of those he thought were his friends—men who seemed to have the qualities he admired but lacked. Benjamin F. Butler, Roscoe Conkling, and their kind soon had his ear, and honest officials began to lose their jobs. Officeholders became mere office workers. The country, as one man wrote, was at the mercy of an oligarchy of stipendaries. From the smallest post office to the richest customhouse "graft and corruption ran riot." The nation sank to what William A. Dunning has called "the nadir of national disgrace."

Judges and governors were bought and sold. Jay Gould and Jim Fisk manipulated the Erie Railroad to its ruin and their enrichment. Gould even attempted to corner the nation's gold supply behind Grant's back, but with his unintentional aid. The Crédit Mobilier, a joint stock company formed to build the Union Pacific Railroad, turned itself into a share-holding corporation, squeezing millions out of contracts and corrupting congressmen by selling

stock below value "where it would do the most good."
Even James A. Garfield, president-to-be, and Vice-President Schuyler Colfax were involved and were subsequently forced to lie themselves out of it.

Then came what was known as the "salary grab," where a corrupt Congress raised all House and Senate salaries by a third and doubled that of the President. Congressional salaries were then made retroactive for two years. That was too much for an indignant public, which a year later forced a return to the old salaries.

Meanwhile, in New York City William M. (Boss) Tweed was carrying graft and corruption to new levels and extending his power to Albany, where votes were bought and sold at fixed prices. Judges and governors accepted bribes for favors, and public offices were taken over by fraudulent means. Soon New York City was at the mercy of the gang, and the plunder taken is estimated at from $45 million to over $200 million. Yet in Robin Hood fashion, business (legitimate and illegitimate) paid the bills, while the poor received something of food and shelter and their drab lives were lightened by picnics and Christmas presents. As Gustavus Meyers remarked, Tweed "had a great good heart."

But Tweed and plunder, while most extravagant, were not confined to New York. Pennsylvania, with its Quays, Camerons, and Gas House Gang, did quite well, as did those who practiced open bribery in far-off Kansas, Iowa, and Wisconsin.

What is most interesting about all this is the almost total lack of any feeling of guilt. Morals had become largely a matter of personal conduct, and were quite separate from what a man might do in public life. Morality and public service had become two different things. Those who plundered and corrupted were as a rule "God-fearing" men, good church members, loyal husbands, fine neighbors—models to be held up to youth. Daniel Drew, who not only rigged the stock market to his own enrichment but also plundered railroads and corrupted legislatures and the courts, was so loud in his religious demonstrations that the neighbors complained. He climaxed a long career of cutthroat competition by endowing a theological seminary but never donating the funds.

Jay Cooke, who helped to finance Grant's campaigns as a way of making sure that bonds bought with cheap money would be paid in gold, was wont to observe that "we must get down at the feet of Jesus and be taught by no one but himself." Yet when the Crédit Mobilier scandal broke and Attorney General George H. Williams started legal action, Cooke wrote to an agent:

> Now I want you to go to the Attorney General at once and tell him how wrong this whole procedure is. This whole persecution of the Union Pacific is nonsense, and is damaging our credit abroad. If the government sets the example of enjoining the payment of interest coupons, who will buy our bonds abroad. The whole thing is wrong, ill advised and scandalous.
> Williams ought to make a public apology for such an attack and instruct the lawyer to desist from anything of the kind. . . . It will damage us hundreds of millions unless withdrawn at once. No man of sense would buy a railroad bond or anything else in this country if such legal proceedings are permitted under the sanction of the highest office of the government.

The inference clearly is that corruption must be accepted where prevention or punishment might hurt business. This does not mean that such men as Jay Gould and Jim Fisk, who made their millions by methods fair or foul, were held in high esteem. Nor does it mean that their notorious personal conduct was excused because they became rich. It only implies that "credit is a tender plant" and that in this era only personal morals were accorded the same care. It does, however, help to explain Conkling's political statement that "those who hold the securities of the country, the property holders in general, dare not risk a Democratic president now." It also explains why another wrote:

> Let us confess it with shame, President Grant has dropped us by easy stages to these depths of shame . . . selfishness and shamelessness . . . low aims and base purposes . . . and such

degradation of all things which the nation had held to be
high and holy . . . that today the country hangs its head and
holds its nose and waits for this administration to pass.

IV

The facts are there, but why such a period? Was it the
result of a civil war fought for the highest ideals and
purposes for which any people ever waged war and which
gave them an Abraham Lincoln? Was it the letdown and
relaxation from high purpose and intense effort? Or must
we charge it largely to Reconstruction as the last dark
and bloody phase of that bitter struggle?

The situation is too complex for a simple answer, but it
is perfectly clear that Grant was not nominated, elected,
and re-elected on the strength of his personal qualifications or his political accomplishments. He had been put
forward only because he, better than any other candidate,
could ensure continued Republican party control. That
control had been necessary for winning both the Civil
War and Reconstruction. Many believed that it was still
necessary to preserve the fruits of those two struggles.
For them the Civil War had not ended. The Democratic
party stood for the treason which precipitated civil war
and which refused to accept its results in terms of Negro
rights. Thus, regardless of what went on in the first
Grant administration, many who had been most ardent
in reforming the South still stood firmly by Grant in 1872.
The necessity for Republican control, even though it
brought national disgrace, justified their vote. It was com-
pleting a job.

Furthermore, the bitter struggle against Johnson had
seriously damaged the executive department itself. The
balance between the legislative, judicial, and executive
departments had been badly upset. Congress had gained at
the expense of the others. The political party situation
was even worse. Even before the war, no party could
nominate its real leaders or offer men of real ability and
experience. "Dark horses" or "doughface" candidates

such as Zachary Taylor, Franklin Pierce, and James Buchanan were placed in the nation's highest office. Now Grant was added to the list. Both our boasted system of checks and balance and our equally praised two-party system had broken down. War and Reconstruction had proved too much for them. "Reform" and "progress" had not worked together. Perhaps, after all, it was time to put that troublesome old Declaration of Independence aside for a while, come down from that "city as on a Hill" and catch up with the modern world. The last political drive would come in 1872 and clearly reveal the tragedy of it all.

24

THE DEMOCRATIC PARTY AND REFORM

I

With the Republicans in complete control, the Democrats in the Reconstruction period could do little other than criticize and oppose. Yet they were still a *potential* threat, and, with Southern support, a *real* one. Nevertheless, they were highly vulnerable to charges of continued indifference to the moral side of slavery and to the Negro's rights. Too many of them still felt kindly toward the South, a fact that soon led to the assumption that Democrats who had supported Lincoln and the war were, in truth, no longer Democrats, while the residue was strictly copperhead.

Republicans based this charge on the Democrats' wide hostility to emancipation and their constant demands for peace. Prominent Democratic newspapers had called Lincoln's Emancipation Proclamation "unconstitutional, dictatorial, and ruinous." They had waged the congressional campaign of 1862 on an appeal to racial prejudice and to the fears of white workingmen that the free Negro might be a competitor.[1] These appeals were effective enough in that election to cause the loss to Republicans of Pennsylvania, New York, Ohio, Indiana, and Illinois and to cut the Republican vote drastically in five other states.

This resurgence of Democratic strength continued throughout the next two years and reached a climax in the national election of 1864. Military reverses and war weariness as victory seemingly faded from sight gave the Democrats new hope and Lincoln new reason to fear defeat. "Earnest Union editors such as William Cullen Bryant, Theodore Tilden and Horace Greeley had reached . . . a deep seated conviction that the Lincoln administration was largely a failure."

A group under B. Gratz Brown and Wendell Phillips when so far as to nominate John C. Frémont as a candidate for the Presidency, while Lincoln's supporters were forced to fuse into a Union party of faithful Republicans and war Democrats and to accept Andrew Johnson—Southerner and Democrat—as his running mate. Then, almost on the heels of Lincoln's nomination, came the Wade-Davis Bill as a congressional rejection of his announced Reconstruction plan. Following this, a strange backstairs effort to supplant Lincoln and to offer a more vigorous candidate was secretly launched. While this move failed, talk of a new candidate continued. At one time Lincoln was prepared to step aside. Only the fear of party damage prevented drastic steps.

This situation naturally opened the door for Democrats, in 1864, to gather up all the war-weariness, the dissatisfaction with the war's conduct, and its seeming unwillingness to reach an end. Their convention, meeting in Chi-

[1] See James M. McPherson, *The Struggle for Equality: Abolitionists and the Negro in the Civil War and Reconstruction* (Princeton, N.J., 1964), p. 109.

cago, nominated General George B. McClellan, disgruntled soldier, on a platform demanding that hostilities cease so that peace could be restored "at the earliest possible moment" on the "basis of the Federal Union of the States." It was not a demand for "peace at any price" such as its radical element favored; and McClellan in his acceptance statement quickly rejected such an idea. He stressed, as had Lincoln, the restoration of the Union. The chances for victory were too good to be jeopardized by radical positions.

A Democratic victory did indeed seem possible until early September, when the fall of Atlanta started Sherman on his march across Georgia to the sea and made sense out of the bloody advances that Grant was making around Richmond. The army thus made Lincoln's election possible. Democratic talk of peace and national restoration were empty echoes of Lincoln's own words. The Democrats entered Reconstruction with far less prestige than they had held in war days.

II

In their role as critics, Democrats had provided most of the opposition to passage of the Thirteenth Amendment. Only William H. Seward's well-organized and well-financed lobby, along with hints of conservative policies toward the South, had won over the sixteen Democrat votes necessary for the two-thirds majority. Even at that, only two of these votes came from Democrats who had recently won re-election to the succeeding Congress. It was a break, however, and it opened the way for Democrats to play a part in efforts that both Seward and the Blairs were making to create a new conservative party to support Johnson and to check the "radical" Republicans. Both of these moves failed, in part because of Johnson's lack of cooperation; but they did serve to keep alive Democratic hopes of reuniting the party. In fact, what most hindered conservative Republican efforts to check radical moves was the danger "that the anticipated great Conservative party of the future would be [only] a thinly disguised resurrection of the Democracy."

For the present, therefore, Democrats could only join with the more conservative Republicans in opposing extreme demands. They could encourage the southern states to reject the amendments and to await the inevitable reaction. They would aid John A. Bingham and his followers in modifying the reconstruction measures of Thaddeus Stevens, and they would vote with Conservatives in the impeachment trial. Georges Clemenceau, then correspondent in the United States for a Paris newspaper, noted that "any Democrat who did not manage to hint in his speech that the Negro is a degenerate gorilla, would be considered lacking in enthusiasm." That was exaggeration, but E. L. Godkin was nearer the truth when he wrote, "the Democratic Party is essentially now, whatever it may once have been, a party of habit, prejudices, and traditions." It was not a serious threat to Republican control.

III

By 1872, however, it was becoming increasingly apparent that Reconstruction was failing and that the American people had grown weary of the unending turmoil.[2] It had even become respectable for a Republican to criticize and openly oppose the renomination of President Grant. Some were even hinting that Democratic critics had in many ways been right. Republican dominance had not produced a final and satisfactory solution to the problems left by the Civil War. In their struggle with President Johnson and in their overzealous dealing with the Negro, Republicans had neglected the emerging modern world. Grant as President had provided the final evidence. Corruption must be ended and a new look taken not only at past

[2] An editorial in *The Nation* on March 11, 1875, admitted that Reconstruction was "an absolute failure."

policies but at those needed for a new day. Not only was reform and a turning about to face the future in order; it could not much longer be delayed.

Yet under the existing party situation in which Democrats had been the ones most critical of conditions and most insistent on reform, a recognition of evils and moves toward changes by Republicans were difficult. Regardless of how right Democratic leaders had proved to be in their economic and political demands for peace, free trade, and a quick return of the southern states, these things could not possibly be accepted as sound. They came from the so-called "party of treason." Liberal and intelligent Republicans thus faced a serious dilemma. Grant's apparent blindness to corruption and his popularity in spite of it offered little hope for a new kind of crusade against a new set of evils. Republican faces were largely toward the past. Since Republican glory and strength came from that source, few could see the need for reform. Yet out in Missouri, under the lead of B. Gratz Brown and Carl Schurz, a revolt was under way. It had not started as a party revolt, but as opposition developed it became one. Other liberal Republicans could not long ignore that fact.

For the present, few Republicans, however much disturbed by corruption and a growing dissatisfaction with Reconstruction, were willing to take part. It would mean nothing less than abandoning a sacred party and a sacred heritage. It would cost something that had to do with credit for saving the Union and freeing the slaves. It would be turning away from what had become soundness and respectability. No! Reform, if it came, must be Republican reform. If the party as a whole would not join in, then the better element—the real Republicans upholding true Republican principles—must take the lead. There was no other way, for Grant had refused to take his critics seriously. He called them "sore-heads." He went on his way little moved, confident that party loyalty, fear and contempt for Democrats, and the "bloody shirt" were still enough.

Under these circumstances, reform-minded Republicans needed more than a just cause and a moral appeal. They needed votes. It was becoming perfectly clear that not enough Republicans would accept even a slight variation from the regular organization to supply these votes. Only Democrats could supply them, and this might require tariff reform and a more lenient southern attitude. That was too high a price. One might tolerate some splintering of the "Grand Old Party" in order to draw it back to true principles, but there would be no union with the hated Democrats! Men could break with Grant, but not with the party. This was the situation in late 1871 and early 1872.[3]

The ingenious and crooked course that now led to the formation and revolt of the Liberal Republicans had to begin with a frank statement that any move was only against Grant and his betrayal of Republican principles in office. The object was simply a return to old Republican principles within the party by good and loyal Republicans. This position would keep the Liberal Republican movement sound, and clear it of any connection with the Democratic party!

In line with this approach, Horace Greeley, editor of the liberal *New York Tribune* and chairman of the Union General Republican Committee of New York City, hater and critic of old Democrats, wrote as late as May 1871:

> The feuds which temporarily weakened us are superficial. They grow out of mistakes in appointments, with a few grave errors in the removal of true and worthy Republicans by the same hand that appointed them. These errors have alienated some support from the administration, but not from the party which called it into being.

Out in the West, meanwhile, Horace White, editor of the powerful *Chicago Tribune,* was caught in the same tangle. He had been even more critical of Grant than had Greeley, and he seldom had a good word for the Demo-

---

[3] James M. McPherson, "Grant or Greeley? The Abolitionist Dilemma in the Election of 1872," *American Historical Review,* LXXI (1965), 43–61.

crats. Of late, however, he had favored an end to Reconstruction and peace for the nation. Yet when Ku Klux
Klan violence broke out in the South, he praised Grant's
interference: "The further continuance of these barbarities should not be tolerated, even if it be necessary to
place a soldier in South Carolina for every Ku Klux in
the State." Then, for a time, White's antisouthern feelings
tempered his criticisms of Grant. He was still a good
Republican.

Yet the change was only temporary. When the Missouri
group held a convention, adopted a national platform, and
called on all liberals to meet in convention at Cincinnati
in May, White began to waver. When Ohio free traders
seconded the call and Lyman Trumbull, Gustave Koerner
and David Davis (old Lincoln men) joined the revolt,
hesitation and talk about favoring reform without openly
breaking with the party regulars was no longer possible.
But, like Greeley, White was "embarrassed by Democratic complications and endorsements." He feared, he
said, that the liberal movement was already too identified
with Democrats. Carl Schurz, however, had suggested a
clever way out by reversing the facts in the situation. "If
the Democrats support us," he asserted, "we have abandoned no principles to gain their support."

The point is that the Liberal Republicans could still
think of themselves as the best of Republicans even while
breaking with the Grant administration. They lost none
of the glory and pride that now clustered about the party.
The *real* problem was to convince themselves and others
that they were not drifting toward the hated Democrats
by demanding the very things the Democrats had long
advocated. There was only one way out: to continue denouncing the Democratic party as an obsolete affair
whose *unprincipled* members could now vote *their principles* honestly and honorably by joining the Liberal
Republicans.

Early in September 1871, Horace Greeley led off with
a harsh editorial blast at the Democrats. "It does not seem
in reason," he wrote, "that a party so organized and con-

ducted should long exist. But it needs all the blows that the Republicans can deliver upon it to bring down to the dust of defeat this preposterous sham, which has no longer any excuse for being."

Horace White went even further. In March 1872, he wrote his friend Lyman Trumbull, "The continued existence of the Democratic party is a menace of evils more important even than those which the Liberal Republicans seek to remedy." White was certain that association with Democrats had destroyed Andrew Johnson, and that it would in like fashion destroy the Liberal Republicans. In a later editorial he announced: "All that Liberal Republicans ask of the Democratic leaders is to disband their party organization. Shortly after this modest request, he performed the miracle: "The result of the election in Connecticut confirms the suspicion that the Democratic party . . . is no longer capable of sustaining a platform strong enough for candidates to stand upon—in other words it is dead."

With the Democratic party now out of the way, White hurried off to Springfield to take command of Lyman Trumbull's efforts to become the Liberal Republican candidate for President in 1872. Into the ranks of the Liberal Republicans he could now welcome those he had just reduced to ex-Democrats.

Greeley, now finding the regular Republicans of New York state unwilling to accept his lead, began to mute his strong tariff views, to speak kindly of the South, and to say little about Democrats. He was also making himself available to the Liberal Republicans for high office. Meanwhile, David Davis had accepted the nomination by the National Labor Reform Convention and was openly competing with Trumbull for the support of Illinois. In the East, serious liberals were talking of Charles Francis Adams as the best possible candidate, while Charles Sumner, willing to allow Preston S. Brooks to rest in peace, joined with George W. Julian, Jefferson Davis' bitter enemy, in bolting the regular Republican party.

The stage was thus set for the weirdest political convention ever held on the American continent. It resembled earlier third-party conventions only in rebellious emotions. It lacked something. Men were really doing what, down deep in their hearts, they had no wish to do. It was larger in numbers and therefore in factions. It never achieved unity, and it lacked that spontaneity which comes from emotions suddenly released. It permitted a small group of newspaper men, sophisticated and worldly wise, to shape its course and to create a situation in which things were ultimately done that no one on sober reflection wanted done. They nominated Horace Greeley as their candidate to oppose Ulysses S. Grant. Just why, no one could say. Greeley was a kind of American institution, an idealist, an impractical critic, a man who had been on all sides of too many issues to win votes.

The Democratic Convention accepted the realities that the Liberal Republicans had refused to acknowledge: that the opponents of Grant had in fact come completely over to the principles and policies of the Democratic party. They, too, nominated Greeley as their candidate. They did it as reluctantly as most of the Republicans had done so. As a result the potential Democratic vote, North and South, was never realized. Grant, with the support even of most of the old abolitionists, was given a second term.

Historians have been inclined to view it all as a kind of comic tragedy. Greeley was a mistake and the blame rests there. Yet the larger truth seems to be that in the atmosphere left by war and Reconstruction, the nation was not ready for either reform or a political party change. Anything savoring of Democratic influence or possible southern resurgence simply could not succeed. Greeley may have been a political mistake, but there was no other public figure of the day who could have done for the nation what Greeley did. Thrust forward for high public office, he forced thinking Americans to see the confusion and unreality into which the country had drifted—the desperate need for shaking off the past and the impossibility of doing so under present conditions. Greeley represented a move against the inevitable corruption associated with political factors that had made Grant possible. Even his shift on the tariff had its influence. He had cleared the air regarding the misgovernment of the South and blunders in Reconstruction. His speech at Pittsburgh is an appeal to the American conscience yet unheeded:

> Fellow citizens, are we never to be done with this? We demanded [that] our adversaries . . . surrender their arms and go to their homes. They surrendered them. We demanded that they abandon slavery, and they abandoned slavery. We demanded that they enfranchise the blacks, and the blacks were enfranchised. None but white men now stand disenfranchised on the soil of the country. . . . You cannot afford to teach a part of your country to hate you, to feel that your success, your greatness is identical with their humiliation. . . . The war is ended, let us again be fellow countrymen, and forget that we have been enemies.

So it might be suggested that Henry Watterson's description of Greeley is a description of the age: "He was a queer old man, a very medley of contradictions, shrewd and simple, credulous and penetrating;—even in his old picturesque personality whimsically attractive; a man to be reckoned with where he chose to put his power forth."

Grant was re-elected, and all that had come to be known as Grantism continued. Yet a new attitude toward it had been created, and the Democratic party had been given new status and the leadership in reform. Reconstruction had been pushed further back into the past where it belonged. All that remained was for men to recognize that fact.

IV

The realization of Reconstruction's failure came slowly but surely. It took time for Republicans to see that their program had been laid on faulty foundations. The Civil War, regardless of all the factors that had entered into its making, had ultimately been fought to preserve those democratic and Christian values to which the nation paid lip service, if nothing more—values best expressed in the Declaration of Independence.

Since the South and its slavery had assumed all the guilt that the North as a whole had felt in 1860, it was only justice that when totally defeated, the South should be remade into a land where equality, human rights, and complete justice existed. That too would remove any guilt northerners might feel for their own shortcomings.

The difficulty was that no one knew just what "equality" meant—equality of opportunity, equality before the law, or, perchance, complete political and social equality? Furthermore, the broken and beaten South, with its poverty, its racial prejudices, and its present chaos, was a poor stage for such an experiment. Racial equality of any kind would most certainly have to be forced upon the people. It would have to be sustained by a military force. How long no one could tell. Few moderate Republicans and fewer Democrats would accept an equality that held the Negro to be the white man's equal, and few would accept the invasion of local authority that would be required over an extended period. To go further and to confiscate southern lands in order to give the Negro a chance for economic independence did not appeal to property-minded Americans of any persuasion. Failure was inevitable.

This being the case, everyone knew that the real purpose behind the whole business was as much to ensure Negro votes for continuing Republican success as it was to propogate the doctrines of the Declaration of Independence. With the quick passage of the Fifteenth Amendment, the Republicans had made a last gesture toward equality for the Negro. If they wished to hold the vote in several important northern states, they could go no further.

They had built a program that might endure while passions were high, but one so out of line with their own conservative membership that it never had a chance to stand against the reactions that came with the influences of the modern business age. Americans were not yet ready for a permanent solution of the great social and moral problems that Reconstruction presented.

CHAPTER

25

THE END OF
RECONSTRUCTION

I

By the end of Grant's second term, it was quite clear
that the nation had had enough not only of corruption but
of the whole Reconstruction business. It was time to get on
with national problems. The returns from the 35 states
holding local elections in 1874 showed that 23 had gone
Democratic. Newspaper editorials revealed the same dissatisfaction. *The New York Herald* admonished the Republicans:

> Let the party trace every stream of corruption . . . to its
> source. Let the leaders begin the campaign on the violation
> of the Constitution involved in the appointment of staff of-
> ficers and not statesmen to the Cabinet. Let them show how
> the moral sense of the nation was degraded by the selection
> of worthless relatives and whiskey-drinking cronies to high
> office here and abroad.

Few dared to attack the Civil War hero personally; but, as E. L. Godkin of *The Nation* wrote:

> We see from the newspapers it was popularly supposed that General Grant would take the occasion [the Centennial Celebration] either to resign his office on the ground that he feels himself incompetent any longer to perform its duties, or else to repudiate explicitly the "third term" and announce that nothing could induce him to depart from the precedent set by Washington.[1]
>
> We are convinced that the President does not begin to know what reform means, and the proof of this is so clear and complete that we cannot expect to pay much attention to reports about his motives and intentions.[2]

Then comenting on Grant's farewell message: "The message is that of a man who is tired of public life and weary of political strife. It is a confession that his civil career has not been a success, and a plea for charitable judgments, or at least for division of blame." [3] Yet, believe it or not, some talked of a third term for Grant and pushed it hard until he himself said he would not accept "unless it was an imperative duty."

Meanwhile, a Liberal Republican group, met in New York and announced that they would vote for no man who would not carry through a thoroughgoing reform in government. Others were as ardent in their resentment of "half a nation" still under military rule. Each group was as disturbed by Grant's sending troops again into southern states.

Thus, when the Republican Convention met, the line

---

[1] *The Nation*, April 22, 1875, p. 267.

[2] *The Nation*, May 20, 1875, p. 337.

[3] "The President speaks of the fact that since 1861, he has had laid upon him a great burden of responsibility from which he should be glad to escape."—*The Nation*, March 13, 1873, p. 177. "He will at least at the end of his term obtain that retirement and freedom from responsibility for which as he quite pathetically says . . . he so much longs." "Indeed, if General Grant were not General Grant, and had not saved the Union, it would probably not be difficult to convince the people that he was entitled to anything short of impeachment for 'mal and corrupt administration.' "—*The Nation*, Dec. 3, 1874, p. 357.

was sharply drawn between the old element and the reformers. The temporizing platform drawn promised nothing. An effort to nominate James G. Blaine, regular of regulars, was blocked largely by cutting off of the lights and a quick adjournment. In the end, Republicans turned to the unknown Rutherford B. Hayes, whose qualifications were a good military record and the fact that he had recently checked and defeated the Pendelton-Allen "Ohio Idea" in his home state. It hardly looked like a move toward reform.

II

The Democrats, meeting in St. Louis, were still divided between East and West, but the chance of victory suggested compromise. The platform, therefore, aimed at success. It advocated reform and the end of Grantism. It did say that reform was necessary to establish a sound currency—a bow to the Ohio idea—but quickly checked any specific move toward soft money. It denounced the tariff as injurious, but spent most of its words on the corruption in Republican rule.

The Democratic ticket was a queer one: Samuel J. Tilden of the East and Thomas A. Hendricks of the West. Both candidates suggested reform. Tilden had been a moderate in 1860 and had supported Lincoln in 1863–1864. Some had even suggested him as the Union candidate, had Lincoln stepped aside. Tilden was a keen thinker, one of the best political scientists in the nation, and as governor of New York, after some hesitation, had stepped in to clean up the Tweed Ring and later the Canal Ring.

Yet Tilden was not a reformer at heart. He was basically a conservative. He had made his millions in railroads and land speculation. He thought of himself as superior to the masses—which, of course, he was. But you cannot lead democracy if you feel superior. In 1868, Tilden had fought Pendelton, Thurman, and Allen because he considered them against "honest money." He also had the property notion of things; he was in theory just a Democrat, not a fighting democrat like his running mate Hendricks. Furthermore, he was a half-ill man. When he was a baby, his nurse had ruined his stomach with some kind of soothing syrup, and Tilden had to spend half his time in bed—fasting and rising to meet an emergency and then going to the hospital. He had to live on a schedule.

A man who has to spend so much time taking care of himself cannot give to a democracy in danger all the time and energy it needs. So here was a reformer, half democrat but safe, running on a platform that damned Grant and was progressive only on tariff. Yet it was the first chance in modern America for Democrats and democrats.

The liberals, East and West, were thus at sea. Some broke away and nominated Peter Cooper on a greenback ticket. The Prohibitionists did likewise.

The result was the notorious disputed election. The returns indicated the election of Tilden and Hendricks with a heavy popular lead of some 250,000 votes and only one electoral vote short of certain election. Tilden had 184 certain electoral votes, Hayes 166, with most votes in dispute. Only the *New York Tribune* saw any hope for the Republicans. Whitelaw Reid, its new editor, who had spent some time in Libby Prison during the war, nevertheless proclaimed victory for Hayes by claiming all the votes that might be contested in South Carolina, Florida, and Louisiana, and perhaps one vote in Oregon. Reid telegraphed the Republican leaders in each of these states to keep order and to bring pressure. Reconstruction was thus to perform one last desperate duty—to steal a national election, if possible, for the Republican party.[4]

III

What actually happened in the disputed states of the South no one will ever know. It is futile to try to ferret out details for, after all, the facts are of no importance.

[4] Paul Leland Haworth, *The Hayes-Tilden Presidential Election of 1876* (Indianapolis, 1927), pp. 46–56.

The only thing worth noting is that conditions in these states were such that any election outcome could be managed as those in power wished. The only fact of importance is that the Republicans were in a position to turn every irregularity to their advantage and give it legality. Politicians never fished in muddier and more troubled waters. The object in it all was to make good Reid's claim that Hayes had carried these states and was elected. The method made no difference. There was no constitutional provision for such an emergency. Most certainly, Republicans would not permit the decision to be made by the Democratic House under the usual provision where no man has a majority, as had happened in 1824.

In the end, Congress appointed a committee to count votes and decide the outcome, with each party having equal representation and Associate Justice David Davis of the Supreme Court being the odd and supposedly neutral member. Illinois, however, spoiled it all by electing Davis to the Senate. As a result, a Republican was named in his place to provide an 8 to 7 majority for his party. So every question or issue was decided by that vote, and Hayes was declared elected.

Scholars who have made every effort to reach some fair conclusion have generally held that, while the votes of South Carolina and Louisiana might by some effort have been given to Hayes, the Florida vote definitely belonged to Tilden, thus legally giving him the election. Yet the committee refused to go behind such returns as their agents were able to deliver, and the party vote stood. That provided the necessary "legality," and Hayes was declared elected. At midnight on March 1, 1877, Joseph C. S. Blackburn of Kentucky arose and closed the case by observing:

> Today is Friday. On that day the Savior of the World suffered crucifixion between two thieves. On this Friday Constitutional government, justice, honesty, fair dealing, manhood and decency suffer crucifixion amid a number of thieves.

It is unnecessary to do more than note the deadlock in Congress which permitted the weeks to pass without any prospect of a peaceful agreement. The danger of the dispute erupting into violence or even civil war was not lacking, and the Democratic chairman asserted that he knew of war veterans in fifteen states organizing for military resistance to the election frauds. Paul Leland Haworth, whose pioneer study of the election of 1876 still has value, stated that more people expected a bloody outbreak at that time than in 1860.

IV

The important historical questions are: Why did violence not occur? Why did the South and the Democrats as a whole accept the election of Hayes and thus avoid the crisis? The answer has come only in recent years, largely through C. Vann Woodward's volume, *Reunion and Reaction,* in which he renames the disputed election, "The Compromise of 1877 and the End of Reconstruction." His explanation begins with the importance of the old southern Whigs and their economic or business interests in Reconstruction. He finds that these men, as "Redeemers" in the return of the southern states to "home rule," saw the future of their section in economic recovery, the development of southern resources, the railroads to link their production with markets, the improvement of southern rivers and harbors, and the acquiring of capital to perform these tasks. The Redeemers would, in other words, get the South back in step with the nation and gain their share of the matchless prosperity and wealth of the new modern day. Southerners would take their place at the table of the Great Barbecue.[5]

The difficulty was that by the time the southerners brought their hungry appetites to the feast, the extrava-

[5] C. Vann Woodward: *Reunion and Reaction: The Compromise of 1877 and the End of Reconstruction* (Boston, 1951), pp. 212–213, 233–239.

gance was over. A wave of reform had begun. Southern
politicians found that a sharp reaction had come in the
North against the lavish granting of lands and subsidies
to railroads, the huge pork-barrel appropriations to im-
prove harbors and rivers, and even the way in which the
homestead law had benefited the speculators more than
actual settlers. This reforming temper had found more
support among the Democrats, as the party out of power,
than it had among Republicans. Consequently, as the
southern representatives attempted to gain support for
their programs of economic development, they received
more assistance from the Republicans than from the party
that had sent them to Washington. When they attempted
to repeal the southern Homestead Act, which had opened
thousands of acres to settlers but temporarily excluded
ex-Confederates and all speculators, they met not only
opposition but open charges of trying to permit capitalists
to monopolize the lands. It was only with Republican
support that southern congressmen were able to repeal
the act and allow what they thought were beneficial de-
velopers to enter. It was not until later that they discovered that their timberlands had been bought by northern
mill men simply to be held and kept from competing with
their own.

Bills were now introduced by such reforming Democrats as William S. Holman of Indiana, "to forbid all
future subsidies and grants to private enterprises." These
reformers represented the disillusioned western farmers
who were beginning to feel themselves the victims of a
privileged eastern financial, industrial power that was as
much the enemy of common men as had been the "slave
power." This sharp reaction against appropriations for
public works, which the southern leaders knew their section must have for recovery, forced them to vote more
and more as a bloc with the Republicans on such issues.
In turn, Republicans who had felt safe while the South
was in reconstruction chains now saw the South, free but
neglected, as a possible ally against Democratic reform.
As Joseph Medill of the *Chicago Tribune* wrote to a

Republican friend, "We have tried for eight years to uphold Negro rule in the South officered by carpet baggers, but without exception it has resulted in failure."

The states had one by one been redeemed and lost to Republican control. The old southern Whigs were in the Democratic party only by necessity, not because of political and economic principles. They had no desire for reform measures that denied them government aid for their railroads, levies, harbors, and industry. Their votes on such issues proved the point.

V

This situation was brought to bear on the Disputed Election, and it ultimately led to what Vann Woodward calls the end of Reconstruction. It was based on "the South's hunger for Federal money."

In brief, it came about in this way. Realizing the desperate situation into which the nation had dropped, a group of newspaper men, members of the Western Associated Press, got the idea of splitting off from the Tilden forces the southern wing of the Democratic party, which was more interested in peace and Southern economic development than in a Democratic victory. If Hayes could be persuaded to promise the withdrawal of military forces from the South and to use Republican influence to further southern economic interests, these old-time southern Whigs might supply the support needed to enable Hayes to become President. Colonel A. J. Kellar of the *Memphis Avalanche* and General Henry Boynton, Washington representative of the *Cincinnati Gazette*, became the active promoters of the effort and the links between Hayes and the southern group. To supply the necessary lobby force to carry bills forward in Congress, the two men secured the powerful railroad interest of Thomas A. Scott and his plan for a Texas and Pacific Railroad. A bill for this southern line to the Pacific was introduced by Lucius Q. Lamar, Mississippi lawyer and businessman, who, for a price, brought and held the southern wing solidly behind a peaceful political settlement.

While all this was taking place and a general agreement on both sides was being reached, enough uncertainty remained to arouse violent threats if the Redeemer governments in South Carolina and Louisiana were not recognized and the army not withdrawn. Filibuster tactics still delayed the count of electoral votes, and at times it appeared that the count would not be completed in time to inaugurate a President. At this point a group of individuals led by Major E. A. Burke of Louisiana and Stanley Mathews, senator-elect from Ohio and attorney for the Texas and Pacific Railroad, met together in Washington in what became known as the Wormley Conference. Here a somewhat clearer understanding was reached regarding an agreement by both Grant and Hayes that troops would be withdrawn immediately from Louisiana and South Carolina and the Redeemer governments recognized.

With this made known, William Levy of Louisiana arose in Congress to announced satisfactory guarantees from Hayes and to ask that all filibustering end. The Wormley Conference of this second group added nothing but support to what the others had already accomplished, but that, just now, was important. The way was thus made clear to complete the count and inaugurate Hayes. His withdrawal of troops followed, with lip service to Negro rights. Reconstruction at last came to an end.

VI

What can one say of Reconstruction as a whole? In plain words, Reconstruction came to an end through a political deal between southerners willing to yield all the abstract values they had held for the sake of economic gain and northerners willing to drop their abstract values for the advancement of political and economic ends. Here the advocates of Radical Reconstruction joined hands with ex-slaveholding "rebels" in a compromise in which the Negro was forgotten, the carpetbagger repudiated, and

Republican control continued at the price demanded by ex-Confederates. After a long absence, compromise had at last returned to the American system.

In abstract terms, the outcome suggested that these compromisers

> . . . were the men who come at the end of periods of revolutionary upheaveal, when the great hopes and soaring ideals have lagged and failed, and the fervors have burned themselves out. They come to say that disorder has gone too far and the extremists must be got in hand, that order and peace must be established at any price.[6]

Reconstruction, when it turned to social revolution, had followed the normal course of revolutions and subsided in reaction. It failed because realities had been ignored in a mad plunge for perfection for which poor, stumbling, bleeding mankind was as yet unprepared. As an abstraction the Declaration of Independence was fine, but *practical* men saw it as an ideal, not as a sound program for immediate adoption.

Reconstruction failed not because perfection is not to be desired, but because it has a price. All would pay for that failure but the heaviest cost would fall on the Negro. He had, in fact, been abandoned—abandoned by the Republicans, as they themselves largely abandoned the crusading quality that from the beginning had gone along with their demands for a new economic freedom. Now the enthusiasm for more social justice gave way to an enthusiasm for big business. The interest in preserving the social and moral gains that the war justified yielded to the determination to retain the favors which the war tariffs and war finances had given. Progress required it.

This was due not only to the death and retirement of many of the chief leaders of crusading days, but to the defeat of others at the polls. The corruption and disillusionment that came with Grant also played a part, as did the failure of the Negro "utopias" set up in Canada at Wilberforce, Dawn, and Elgin. Soon E. L. Godkin was

[6] *Ibid.*, p. 215.

stating in *The Nation:* "I do not see, in short, how the negro is ever to be worked into a system of government for which you and I would have much respect." Richard Gilder, in the *Century,* went even further by insisting "that the negroes constitute a peasantry wholly untrained in, and ignorant of, the ideas of constitutional liberty and progress which are the birthright of every white voter; . . . they are gregarious and emotional rather than intelligent, and easily led in any direction by white men of energy and determination." Nathaniel Shaler, writing in the *Atlantic Monthly,* was soon doubting the wisdom of trying to impose "a race as foreign to us in every trait as the negro" on our schools and the education they provided. In trying to do so, he added, "we wrong ourselves and them." Even the *Chicago Tribune* saw the vote in the hands of the "superstitious, ignorant and brutal" Negro as "a menace to Republican institutions." Perhaps the southern attitude had been right after all! [7] At least the Supreme Court thought so. It soon accepted partial segregation, and in the end, the idea of "separate but equal."

VII

Nearly a hundred years later both the Court and the American public, with the Republican party fighting something of a rear-guard action against a dominant Democratic party, would again discover the Declaration of Independence. In the meantime a Theodore Roosevelt, a Woodrow Wilson, and a Franklin D. Roosevelt would have spent most of their energies correcting the ills that the forces generated in Reconstruction had passed on to the economic age that followed. Now a hundred years later, the Negro and the American conscience demand

---

[7] "The crisis came when an ignorant soldier, coarse in his tastes and blunt in his perceptions, fond of money and material enjoyment and of low company, was put in the Presidential chair."—*The Nation,* March 9, 1876. Nathaniel S. Slater, "An ex-Southerner on South Carolina," *Atlantic Monthly,* July, 1870, pp. 53–61; *Chicago Tribune,* Jan. 7, 1865, Aug. 14, 1872.

that we complete the unfinished work of Reconstruction. Somehow the Civil War never seems to come to an end. Perhaps it is as Lydia Child observed: "The lamentable misfortune is that emancipation was not the result of a popular *moral sentiment,* but of a miserable 'military necessity.' It was not the 'fruit of righteousness,' and therefore is not 'peace.' "

It was true, of course, that hatred of the South was often greater than love of the Negro; that cotton was often more sought after than social reform. The real trouble, however, grew out of the democratic dogma itself, where liberty and equality waged their unending struggle for supremacy. Equality for all men had been the dominant purpose behind reform in Reconstruction. There was to be no racial discrimination in the future America. On the other hand, the great economic changes wrought by the age of steam engines, electricity, and urban-industrial capitalism had shifted the emphasis heavily toward individual freedom. Hands off was to be the rule. By 1870 the tide had definitely turned. Perhaps, as *The Nation* suggested, we had done enough for the Negro.

> We owe the freedmen political rights, the means of education, and the ample protection for his person and property; but we owe him nothing else . . . we believe neither in treating him as a beast of burden nor as a spoiled child. He is a man, and must make his own way as a man; he must, now that he is launched into free life, learn its hard lessons as other poor men learn them, learn that respect comes from character, and wealth comes from industry.[8]

That was good old-fashioned democratic doctrine. It served now only to announce the end of Reconstruction and to foretell a troubled future. It was easier to go on living with a myth than to face unpleasant reality.

[8] *The Nation,* May 9, 1867, p. 376. "We ought not to have attempted the insane task of making the newly-emancipated field hands, led by barbers and barkeepers, fancy they knew as much about government, and were as capable of administering it, as the whites."—*The Nation,* Aug. 24, 1876.

SELECTED READINGS

Much of Reconstruction history lies buried away in manuscript collections, official documents, memoirs, and the proceedings of various bodies, local and national. These "primary sources" are of interest only to the specialist and are not included in a selected list of works intended to serve the needs of the average reader who may wish to widen his knowledge of this complex historical field. The classifications are purely arbitrary. Asterisks are used to show the author's preference for certain works.

GENERAL WORKS

Allen, James S., *The Battle for Democracy, 1865–1876* (New York, 1937). Reconstruction from a Marxian approach.

*Brock, W. R., *An American Crisis: Congress and Reconstruction, 1865–1877* (New York, 1967). Sharply critical of Johnson.

Burgess, John W., *Reconstruction and the Constitution, 1866–1876* (New York, 1907). An older "traditional" interpretation useful for comparison with more recent writings.

Carter, Hodding, *The Angry Scar: The Story of Reconstruction, 1865–1890* (New York, 1959). A modern southerner looks at Reconstruction.

Coulter, E. Merton, *The South During Reconstruction.*

1865–1877 (Baton Rouge, 1947). A volume in the "History of the South" series. Thought by some to be somewhat biased. The reader should form his own judgments.

De Forest, John William, *A Union Officer in the Reconstruction,* edited and with notes by James H. Croushore and David Morris Potter (New Haven, Conn., 1948).

*Donald, David, *The Politics of Reconstruction, 1863–1867* (Baton Rouge, 1965). An ingenious approach to party voting. Important.

*Du Bois, William Edward Burghardt, *Black Reconstruction* (New York, 1935). A pioneer work of great value. Revisionist and Marxian but with clear insight.

*Dunning, William A., *Reconstruction, Political and Economic, 1865–1867* (New York, 1907). A pioneer work by a master which can still be read with profit. Emphasis on race.

Fleming, Walter L. (ed.), *Documentary History of Reconstruction . . . , 1865 to the Present Time* (2 vols.; Cleveland, 1906–1907). Valuable for source material.

Franklin, John Hope, *Reconstruction After the Civil War* (Chicago, 1961). Emphasis on the Negro's part in Reconstruction.

*Kendrick, Benjamin B., *The Journal of the Joint Committee of Fifteen on Reconstruction* (New York, 1914). One of the basic studies in the field.

McPherson, Edward (ed.), *The Political History of the United States During the Period of Reconstruction* (Washington, 1875). Valuable for source material not easily available elsewhere.

Randall, James G., and Donald, David, *The Civil War and Reconstruction* (Boston, 1961). A textbook with a revisionist view of Reconstruction and an invaluable bibliography.

Rhodes, James Ford, *History of the United States from the Compromise of 1850* (7 vols.; New York, 1893–1906). Volumes 5 to 7 make interesting reading and offer a chance to compare a point of view once widely accepted, until more recent studies.

*Stampp, Kenneth M., *The Era of Reconstruction, 1865–1867* (New York, 1965). An excellent survey which at times borders on the polemic.

RECONSTRUCTION IN THE STATES

In spite of much revisionist work on certain phases of Reconstruction in the southern states, we are still forced to rely for our general information on the volumes produced by the so-called Dunning School. The two exceptions are:

Alexander, Thomas B., *Political Reconstruction in Tennessee* (Nashville, 1950).
*Simkins, Francis B., and Woody, Robert H., *South Carolina During Reconstruction* (Chapel Hill, N.C., 1932). A first-class job of revising earlier interpretations in an important state.

The older state volumes are:

Davis, William W., *The Civil War and Reconstruction in Florida* (New York, 1913).
Eckenrode, Hamilton J., *The Political History of Virginia During the Reconstruction* (Baltimore, 1904).
Ficklen, John R., *History of Reconstruction in Louisiana* (Baltimore, 1910). Goes only through 1868.
*Fleming, Walter L., *Civil War and Reconstruction in Alabama* (New York, 1905).
*Garner, James W., *Reconstruction in Mississippi* (New York, 1901). The best volume of the group. Has been added to but not revised.
Hamilton, J. G. de Rouldac, *Reconstruction in North Carolina* (New York, 1914).
Lonn, Ella, *Reconstruction in Louisiana after 1868* (New York, 1918).
Ramsdell, Charles W., *Reconstruction in Texas* (New York, 1910).

Staples, Thomas S., *Reconstruction in Arkansas* (New York, 1923).

*Thompson, C. Mildred, *Reconstruction in Georgia* (New York, 1915).

BIOGRAPHY

Bartlett, Irving, *Wendell Phillips: Brahmin Rebel* (Boston, 1961). The best biography of another puzzling figure.

*Brodie, Fawn M., *Thaddeus Stevens: Scourge of the South* (New York, 1939). A remarkable well-balanced study of a difficult man.

Current, Richard N., *Old Thad Stevens: A Story of Ambition* (Madison, Wis., 1942). Critical but scholarly.

————, *The Lincoln Nobody Knows* (New York, 1958).

Donald, David, *Charles Sumner and the Coming of the Civil War* (New York, 1960). Gives a good picture of a man who was to play a conspicuous part in Reconstruction. Realistic.

Fessenden, Francis, *Life and Public Services of William Pitt Fessenden* (2 vols.; Boston, 1907).

*Jelleson, Charles A., *Fessenden of Maine: Civil War Senator* (Syracuse, 1961). A penetrating and understanding biography.

Krug, Mark M., *Lyman Trumbull: Conservative Radical* (New York, 1965).

*McKitrick, Eric L., *Andrew Johnson and Reconstruction* (Chicago, 1960). A superior job which set the pattern for revision.

Milton, George Fort, *The Age of Hate: Andrew Johnson and the Radicals* (New York, 1930). A defense of Johnson and his administration.

Salter, William, *The Life of James W. Grimes, Governor of Iowa . . . A Senator of the United States . . .* (New York, 1876). Old and inadequate but gives needed information.

Stryker, Lloyd P., *Andrew Johnson: A Study in Courage* (New York, 1929).

Thomas, Benjamin P., and Hyman, Harold M., *Stanton: The Life and Times of Lincoln's Secretary of War* (New York, 1962). Generally favorable to Stanton.

Trafouse, Hans, *Benjamin F. Wade: Radical Republican from Ohio* (New York, 1963). A fair study, favorable but judicious.

——, *Ben Butler: The South Called Him Beast* (New York, 1957). Says all for Butler that can soundly be said.

*Winston, Robert W., *Andrew Johnson: Plebian and Patriot* (New York, 1928). Solid and favorable.

BOOKS DEALING WITH SPECIAL SUBJECTS

*Abbot, Martin, *The Freedmen's Bureau in South Carolina, 1865–1872* (Chapel Hill, N.C., 1967). An excellent study of the Bureau at state level.

Beale, Howard K., *The Critical Year: A Study of Andrew Johnson and Reconstruction* (New York, 1930). The emphasis is on economic factors and particularly on the election of 1866.

*Buck, Paul H., *The Road to Reunion* (Boston, 1937). Factors which made the rapid return to national unity possible.

Coleman, Charles H., *The Election of 1868: The Democratic Effort to Regain Control* (New York, 1933).

*Cox, LaWanda and John H., *Politics, Principle, and Prejudice, 1865–1866* (New York, 1963). An enlightening examination of early steps in Reconstruction. Critical of Johnson. Well written and well researched.

Current, Richard N., *Three Carpetbag Governors* (Baton Rouge, 1968).

De Witt, D. M., *The Impeachment and Trial of Andrew Johnson* (New York, 1903). Still the best study of impeachment.

Dorris, Jonathan T., *Pardon and Amnesty under Lincoln and Johnson* (Chapel Hill, N.C., 1953).

Duberman, Martin, *The Antislavery Vanguard* (Princeton, N.J., 1965). A superior group of essays on abolition.

Gillette, William, *The Right to Vote: Politics and the Passage of the Fifteenth Amendment* (Baltimore, 1965). An important, detached study which raises questions regarding older interpretations.

*Harris, William C., *Presidential Reconstruction in Mississippi* (Baton Rouge, 1967). The kind of study needed for every southern state.

Hesseltine, William B., *Lincoln's Plan of Reconstruction* (Tuscaloosa, Ala., 1960).

Horn, Stanley F., *The Invisible Empire: The Story of the Ku Klux Klan, 1866–1871* (Boston, 1939).

Hyman, Harold M., *Era of the Oath: Northern Loyalty Tests During the Civil War and Reconstruction* (Philadelphia, 1954). A careful, scholarly, well-balanced study of a subject that deserves more attention in Reconstruction than it has always received.

——— (ed.), *New Frontiers of the American Reconstruction* (Urbana, Ill., 1966). The essays by Alfred Kelley and C. Vann Woodward are of particular value.

James, Joseph B., *The Framing of the Fourteenth Amendment* (Urbana, Ill., 1956). The best study for this subject.

*Litwack, Leon F., *North of Slavery: The Negro in the Free States, 1790–1860* (Chicago, 1961). A work that has revised the thinking regarding the Negro in Reconstruction.

Lomask, Milton, *Andrew Johnson, President on Trial* (New York, 1960).

Morrow, Ralph, *Northern Methodism and Reconstruction.* (Lansing, Mich., 1956).

*McPherson, James M., *The Negro's Civil War* (New York, 1965). A must in the field.

*———, *The Struggle for Equality: Abolitionists and the Negro in the Civil War and Reconstruction* (Princeton, N.J., 1964).

*Rose, Willie Lee, *Rehearsal for Reconstruction: The Port*

Royal Experiment (Indianapolis, 1964). Good reading and good history.

*Sefton, James E., *The United States Army and Reconstruction, 1865–1877* (Baton Rouge, 1967). Fills an important gap.

Sharkey, Robert P., *Money, Class, and Party: An Economic Study of Civil War and Reconstruction* (Baltimore, 1959). Needs to be read with Irwin Unger's volume cited below.

Singletary, Otis A., *Negro Militia and Reconstruction* (Austin, 1957).

Swint, Henry L., *The Northern Teacher in the South* (Nashville, 1941).

Taylor, A. A., *The Negro in the Reconstruction of Virginia* (Washington, 1926).

———, *The Negro in South Carolina During Reconstruction* (Washington, 1924).

———, *The Negro in Tennessee from 1865 to 1880* (Washington, 1941). These volumes by A. A. Taylor are early revisionist studies that pioneered the study of the Negro in the Civil War and Reconstruction.

*Unger, Irwin, *The Greenback Era: A Social and Political History of American Finance, 1865–1879* (Princeton, N.J., 1964). The outstanding work in this field.

Voegeli, V. Jacque, *Free But Not Equal: The Midwest and the Negro During the Civil War* (Chicago, 1967). See footnotes for earlier study of same in Reconstruction.

Wagondt, Charles L., *The Mighty Revolution: Negro Emancipation in Maryland* (Baltimore, 1964). A good study showing what happened in the border states.

*Wharton, Vernon Lane, *The Negro in Mississippi, 1865–1890* (Chapel Hill, N.C., 1947). An outstanding work that has changed the whole approach in this field.

*Williamson, Joel R., *After Slavery: The Negro in South Carolina During Reconstruction* (Chapel Hill, N.C., 1965).

*Woodward, C. Vann, *Reunion and Reaction: The Compromise of 1877 and the End of Reconstruction* (Boston, 1951). A classic in the field.

ARTICLES

Much of the work done in "revising" the Reconstruction story has appeared in the form of articles published in local and national historical periodicals. It is impossible to list all of them, but a few of the more important can be mentioned.

William E. B. Du Bois, "Reconstruction and Its Benefits," *American Historical Review*, XV (1910), 781–799; Howard K. Beale, "On Rewriting Reconstruction History," *American Historical Review*, XLV (1940), 807–827; Francis B. Simkins, "New Viewpoints of Southern Reconstruction," *Journal of Southern History*, V (1939), 49–61; T. Harry Williams, "An Analysis of Some Reconstruction Attitudes," *Journal of Southern History*, XII (1946), 469–486; Bernard Weisberger "The Dark and Bloody Ground of Reconstruction Historiography," *Journal of Southern History*, XXV (1959), 427–447; LaWanda Cox, "The Promised Land for the Freedmen," *Mississippi Valley Historical Review*, XLV (1958), 413–440, and "General O. O. Howard and the Misrepresented Bureau," *Journal of Southern History*, XIX (1953), 427–456; Stanley Coben, "Northeastern Business and Radical Reconstruction: A Re-examination," *Mississippi Valley Historical Review*, XLVI (1959), 67–90; Everette Swenny, "Enforcing the Fifteenth Amendment, 1870–1877," *Journal of Southern History*, XXVIII (1962), 202–218; Horace M. Bond, "Social and Economic Forces in Alabama Reconstruction," *Journal of Negro History*, XXIII (1938), 290–345; David Donald, "The Scalawag in Mississippi Reconstruction," *Journal of Southern History*, X (1944), 447–460; LaWanda and John H. Cox, "Negro Suffrage and Republican Politics: The Problem of Motivation in Reconstruction Historiography," *Journal of Southern History*, XXXIII (1967), 303–330.

INDEX